High Ability and Talent Development in Latin America

Sheyla Blumen

High Ability and Talent Development in Latin America

Contexts, Challenges, and Innovations

Springer

Sheyla Blumen
Academic Department of Psychology
Pontificia Universidad Católica del Perú
Lima, Lima y Callao, Peru

ISBN 978-3-032-27467-0 ISBN 978-3-032-27468-7 (eBook)
https://doi.org/10.1007/978-3-032-27468-7

This Springer imprint is published by the registered company Springer Nature Switzerland AG
The registered company address is: Gewerbestrasse 11, 6330 Cham, Switzerland

For the children and adolescents of Latin America, whose potential shines even when it is not fully seen.
For those who care for them, believe in them, and help their paths open. To my husband, Leon, and to my children, Joshua and Shirel, who have deepened my understanding of human potential and reminded me that talent unfolds not only through accomplishment, but also through relationships, resilience, and growth. Their presence has taught me to recognize and accompany what often remains unseen.
May this book remind us to build educational systems that truly see them and help them flourish.

Preface

This book grew out of a shared conviction—and, at times, a shared frustration. Across Latin America, children and adolescents with high abilities are increasingly recognized in policies, legal frameworks, and educational discourse. Yet recognition does not always become opportunity. Policies exist, but implementation varies. Talent is acknowledged, yet too often it remains unseen in classrooms shaped by inequality, limited resources, and competing priorities.

We felt the need to pause and look closely at this reality, not with discouragement but with responsibility. This volume is the result of that reflection. It brings together perspectives from psychology, education, and public policy to understand how high-ability learners grow within contexts marked by cultural richness, social complexity, and structural inequities. Rather than adopting models uncritically, the chapters examine how talent unfolds in multilingual communities, in rural and urban schools, and in families carrying both aspiration and constraint.

Throughout the book, giftedness is not treated as a fixed label or an abstract trait. It is understood as a developmental process shaped by relationships, learning environments, institutional arrangements, and public decisions. Talent does not grow in isolation. It grows where there is recognition, guidance, intellectual challenge, and fair access to opportunity.

The chapters move across levels of analysis. After a general introductory chapter, Chap. 2 establishes the conceptual foundation and frames a central tension: formal recognition alongside uneven implementation. Subsequent chapters examine definitions, identification practices, and the cultural contexts that shape how ability is expressed and perceived. They address questions of equity, language, socioeconomic barriers, and whose forms of excellence are most likely to be valued.

The middle chapters focus on practice. Innovation is examined as efforts to align classroom differentiation, acceleration, financial support, institutional design, and governance flexibility. Clinical examples and policy analyses show how individual trajectories are intertwined with structural conditions. Fragmented systems rarely sustain talent—coordination matters.

Teacher preparation and professional development receive particular attention, recognizing that no policy can succeed without educators who are prepared, supported, and intellectually engaged. Comparative country analyses then illustrate how national systems organize governance, legal frameworks, identification processes, and services. The aim is not to rank countries, but to understand patterns and possibilities.

Chapter 11 presents the Latin American Model of Talent Development (LAMTD), an integrative framework grounded in ecological thinking. It emphasizes that individual growth, learning pathways, community contexts, and structural infrastructures are interconnected. Equity and cultural relevance must run through them all. The final chapter outlines research priorities and policy directions for a field that continues to consolidate its voice within the region and beyond.

Two commitments sustain this volume. The first is intellectual rigor: high-ability education in Latin America deserves careful theory, strong evidence, and thoughtful debate. The second is ethical clarity: supporting talent cannot be separated from confronting inequality. Excellence and justice are not competing values; they reinforce one another.

This book is written for psychologists, educators, policymakers, researchers, and graduate students who see nurturing advanced potential not as a luxury, but as part of building more reflective and innovative societies. It is also an invitation to dialogue across countries, disciplines, and perspectives.

We began this work with a simple premise: talent does not disappear when it is overlooked—it waits. It waits for recognition, for opportunity, for systems capable of seeing it. This book is offered as a contribution to building those systems so that ability, wherever it emerges, can be recognized, supported, and allowed to flourish.

Lima, Peru Sheyla Blumen

Declaration of Competing Interests

I, Sheyla Blumen, declare that there are no competing financial interests, personal relationships, institutional commitments, or funding arrangements that could have influenced the research, analysis, interpretation, or conclusions presented in this volume.

The perspectives and arguments developed in this book are solely those of the author and are grounded in independent scholarly inquiry. Institutional affiliations are indicated for purposes of academic identification only and do not constitute endorsement of the views expressed herein.

All sources of research support, where applicable, are fully acknowledged in the relevant sections of the text in accordance with academic transparency standards.

Acknowledgments

No book is written alone. Even when the writing itself is solitary, the thinking is always rel**ational.**

I am deeply grateful to **Keytha Alcantara, Arianna Benavides, and Eduardo Franco** for their invaluable support in the development of Chap. 6. Their insight, generosity, and steady intellectual companionship made that chapter stronger and more alive. Our conversations sharpened arguments, clarified evidence, and reminded me that scholarship grows best in dialogue.

My sincere thanks go to the **Pontificia Universidad Católica del Perú**, whose commitment to rigorous research and social responsibility creates a rare and vital academic environment. It was within this ecosystem—one that encourages responding thoughtfully to the problems of the country and of the broader Latin American region—that this volume was prepared. I am grateful to belong to an institution that understands research not as abstraction, but as responsibility.

I am also thankful to my colleagues from the **International Association of Applied Psychology**, the **European Council for High Abilities**, the **World Council for Gifted and Talented Children,** and the **Inter-American Society of Psychology**. The exchanges of ideas at conferences, symposia, and informal conversations have continually expanded my perspective. These international dialogues have reminded me that while contexts differ, the ethical commitment to recognizing and nurturing human potential is shared.

Finally, I want to acknowledge my Latin American colleagues from **Argentina, Brazil, Colombia, Chile, Mexico, and Peru**. Their concern for reimagining better conditions for highly able children and adolescents across our region has been both inspiring and sustaining. In systems often shaped by inequality and constraint, their persistence affirms that transformation is possible. And that visibility is the first step toward justice.

To each of you, thank you for walking this intellectual and human journey with me.

Contents

1 Introduction 1
1.1 Part I: Foundations: Reframing Talent in Context 1
1.2 Part II: Systems Under Constraint: Identification, Development, and Inequality 3
1.3 Part III: Toward Coherence: A Regional Model and Future Directions 8

Part I Foundations: Reframing Talent in Context 11

2 Why Latin America Matters in Talent Development 13
2.1 From Trait to Relational Configuration 13
2.2 Structural Inequality as Developmental Condition 14
2.3 Developmental–Systems Alignment 15
2.4 Cultural Plurality and Epistemic Legitimacy 15
2.5 Institutional Architecture and Coherence 16
2.6 Innovation under Constraint 16
2.7 Interactive Dimensions 17
2.8 Structural Progression of the Book 17
2.9 Latin America as Analytical Lens 17
References 18

3 Conceptual Frameworks: Giftedness in Cross-Cultural Contexts 21
3.1 From Analytical Lens to Structural Model 21
3.2 Foundational Perspectives 22
3.2.1 Dominant Models of Giftedness and Talent Development 22
3.2.2 Convergences across Models 25
3.3 Critical and Cross-Cultural Analysis 25
3.3.1 Epistemological Assumptions in Western Conceptions 25
3.4 Limitations in Diverse Sociocultural Contexts 27
3.4.1 Under-Identification and Structural Inequality 28
3.4.2 Language, Culture, and Recognition 29
3.4.3 Tensions between Universalism and Contextualism 29

3.4.4 Toward Contextually Responsive Approaches . . . 29
3.5 Latin American Perspectives . . . 30
3.5.1 Giftedness and Social Transformation . . . 30
3.5.2 Historical and Policy Trajectories . . . 31
3.5.3 Emerging Regional Conceptualizations . . . 31
3.5.4 Toward a Regionally Grounded Understanding . . . 32
3.6 Toward a Culturally Responsive Understanding . . . 33
3.6.1 Guiding Principles for Equity-Oriented Frameworks . . . 33
3.6.2 From Principles to Frameworks . . . 35
3.7 A Culturally Responsive Model of Giftedness in Latin America . . . 36
3.7.1 Ecological Foundations: Giftedness as Relational Development . . . 37
3.7.2 The Capability Perspective: Giftedness as Freedom . . . 37
3.7.3 Decolonial Sensibility: Epistemic Pluralization . . . 37
3.7.4 Integrative Logic of the Framework . . . 39
3.7.5 Implications for Research and Practice . . . 39
3.8 Regional Knowledge Base: Latin American Contributions . . . 40
3.8.1 Historical Development and Regional Agendas . . . 40
3.8.2 Sociocultural and Systemic Perspectives . . . 40
3.8.3 Creativity, Subjectivity, and Human Development . . . 40
3.8.4 Inclusion, Diversity, and Educational Opportunity . . . 40
3.8.5 Intercultural and Critical Approaches . . . 41
3.8.6 Implications for Conceptual Frameworks . . . 41
3.9 Concluding Remarks . . . 41
References . . . 41

Part II Systems Under Constraint: Identification, Development, and Inequality 45

4 Educational Landscapes: Institutional Architectures of Recognition and Conversion in Latin America . . . 47
4.1 Mapping the Regional Recognition Regime . . . 47
4.1.1 Acceleration and Age-Based Normativity . . . 49
4.1.2 Decentralization and Territorial Variability . . . 49
4.1.3 Policy Volatility and Structural Continuity . . . 49
4.2 Anchor Systems: Divergent National Configurations . . . 50
4.2.1 Brazil: Legal Specificity and Interpretive Ambiguity . . . 50
4.2.2 Peru: Recognition Without Structural Consolidation . . . 50
4.2.3 Mexico: Inclusion Under Decentralized Governance . . . 50
4.2.4 Chile: Excellence-Oriented Institutional Strategy . . . 51
4.2.5 Colombia: Mandated Flexibility Without National Standardization . . . 51
4.3 Peru as Layered Innovation: Institutional Negotiation Under Constraint . . . 51

4.3.1 Epistemic Reframing 51
4.3.2 PAENFTS: Incremental Enrichment 52
4.3.3 COAR: Structural Redistribution. 52
4.3.4 Layered Architecture and Fragmented Coherence. 53
4.4 Institutional Practices and Program Models Across the Region . . . 53
4.4.1 Resource Rooms and Pull-Out Services 53
4.4.2 Supplementary Enrichment Clusters 54
4.4.3 Acceleration Policies as Structural Indicators 54
4.4.4 University-Linked Talent Initiatives 54
4.5 Identification Regimes and Epistemic Constraints 55
4.6 Public–Private Stratification and Differentiated Opportunity Structures 56
4.7 From Recognition to Conversion: Structural Lessons 58
References. 60

5 Who Gets to Be Gifted? Identification and Equity in Latin America 63
5.1 Introduction 63
5.2 Conceptual Foundations of Identification 64
5.2.1 From Psychometric Gatekeeping to Developmental Recognition 64
5.2.2 Achievement as Accumulated Opportunity 65
5.2.3 Teacher Nomination as Interpretive Mediation 65
5.3 Structural Patterns of Underrepresentation 67
5.3.1 Socioeconomic Stratification 67
5.3.2 Indigenous, Afro-Descendant, and Linguistic Minorities . . 68
5.3.3 Rural–Urban Territorial Inequality 68
5.3.4 Migrant and Displaced Learners 69
5.4 National Identification Frameworks: Policy and Institutional Design 70
5.4.1 Brazil 70
5.4.2 Chile. 70
5.4.3 Mexico 71
5.4.4 Colombia 71
5.4.5 Peru 71
5.5 Cross-National Comparative Analysis: A Typology of Identification Regimes 72
5.5.1 Regime Type I: Competitive Performance-Selective Systems 72
5.5.2 Regime Type II: Decentralized Nomination-Based Systems 73
5.5.3 Regime Type III: Hybrid Selective–Corrective Systems . . . 74
5.5.4 Quantitative Contextualization of Underrepresentation. . . . 74
5.5.5 Toward a Developmental–Equity Regime 75
5.6 Alignment with the Developmental and Socially Embedded Framework (Chap. 3) 77
5.6.1 Developmental Temporality: From Threshold to Trajectory 78

5.6.2 Contextual Mediation: From Performance to Ecological Interpretation ... 78
5.6.3 Structural Equity: From Selection to Opportunity Activation ... 79
5.7 System Design Implications for Equitable Identification ... 80
5.7.1 Universal and Repeated Screening as Structural Equalizer ... 80
5.7.2 Multi-Criteria and Dynamic Assessment Models ... 81
5.7.3 Culturally and Linguistically Responsive Design ... 81
5.7.4 Monitoring, Accountability, and Data Transparency ... 82
5.7.5 From Selection to Developmental Cultivation ... 82
5.8 Conclusion: Identification as Structural Lever of Developmental Justice ... 82
References ... 83

6 Innovations in Curriculum and Instruction for High-Ability Learners in Latin America ... 85
6.1 Introduction: Innovation under Constraint ... 85
6.2 Curriculum and Instruction in Latin America: A Comparative Overview ... 86
6.2.1 Chile: University–School Partnerships as Compensatory Innovation ... 87
6.2.2 Brazil: Institutionalizing Enrichment within Public Schooling ... 87
6.2.3 Colombia: Administrative Inclusion without Pedagogical Differentiation ... 88
6.2.4 The Missing Socioemotional Dimension ... 88
6.3 Acceleration as Structural Equity in South America ... 88
6.4 The Peruvian Context: Structural Dualism and Educational Invisibility ... 89
6.5 Instructional Innovation through Structural Transformation: The COAR Model ... 90
6.5.1 Origins and Expansion ... 90
6.5.2 Selection, Redistribution, and Equalization ... 90
6.5.3 Curriculum as Structural Disruption ... 91
6.5.4 Outcomes and Structural Tensions ... 91
6.6 Enrichment within Mainstream Schooling: The International Baccalaureate in Latin America ... 92
6.7 Extending the Talent Pipeline: Beca 18 as Postsecondary Equity Intervention ... 92
6.8 University-Level Talent Development: Becas LUCET at Pontificia Universidad Católica del Perú ... 93
6.8.1 Program Architecture ... 93
6.8.2 From Access to Projection ... 94
6.9 Curricular Innovation for Equity: Well-Being and Art in School ... 94
6.9.1 Program Design ... 95

6.9.2 Findings and Interpretation 95
6.9.3 Equity in Access to Culture 95
6.10 Acceleration Revisited: Implementation Implications for Latin America 95
6.11 Integrated Discussion: Multidimensional Innovation in the Global South 96
References 99

7 **Twice-Exceptional Learners and Mental Health in Latin American Educational Systems** 103
7.1 Introduction: Twice-Exceptionality in Stratified Educational Systems 103
7.2 Conceptual Foundations: Asynchrony, Masking, and the False Binary of Categories 104
7.2.1 Asynchronous Development 105
7.2.2 Masking Patterns as Institutional Phenomena 105
7.2.3 Cultural Expectations of Excellence and the Narrowing of Recognition 106
7.3 Youth Mental Health and Neurodevelopment in Latin America: Context, Risk, and Infrastructure 106
7.3.1 Neurodevelopmental Conditions in Low-Resource Contexts 106
7.3.2 Performance Pressure and Test Anxiety 107
7.3.3 Mental Health Services and the School as a Developmental Site 107
7.4 Socioemotional Development and Identity under Conditions of Inequality 108
7.4.1 Perfectionism: Adaptive Standards and Maladaptive Self-Surveillance 108
7.4.2 Identity Conflict and Internalized Contradiction 108
7.4.3 Inequality as a Metacognitive Constraint 109
7.5 Clinical Trajectories in Context: Narrative Cases as Analytic Instruments 109
7.5.1 Case 1: Gabriel: Executive Dysfunction behind Verbal Brilliance 109
7.5.2 Case 2: Valentina: Perfectionism, Reading Inefficiency, and High-Stakes Academic Pressure 111
7.5.3 Case 3: Luis: Creative Intelligence, Dyslexia, and Structural Marginalization 114
7.5.4 Case 4: María Fernanda: Analytical Precision, Autism Spectrum Traits, and Social Asynchrony 115
7.5.5 Case 5: Inti: Indigenous Mathematical Talent, Bilingual Context, and Linguistic Misinterpretation 117
7.6 Cross-Case Macrosynthesis: Twice-Exceptionality as a Structural Indicator 118
7.6.1 Masking as Institutional Production 119

7.6.2 Socioeconomic Stratification and Diagnostic Access 119
7.6.3 Mental Health Infrastructure and Developmental Risk 120
7.6.4 Cultural and Linguistic Mediation of Intelligence 120
7.6.5 Policy Fragmentation and Institutional Silos 120
7.7 Structural Inequality and the Identification Gap 121
7.8 Fragmented Policy Architectures across Latin America 122
7.9 Toward an Integrated Ecological Model for Twice-Exceptional Learners 123
7.10 Regional Reform Blueprint 124
7.11 Concluding Synthesis: Twice-Exceptionality and Systemic Maturity 124
References 125

8 Indigenous, Rural, and Forcibly Displaced Migrant Talent: The Challenge of Visibility 127
8.1 Introduction: Recognition, Power, and the Geography of Talent ... 127
8.2 The Ecological–Capability–Decolonial Framework Revisited 128
8.2.1 Ecological Embeddedness of High Ability 128
8.2.2 Capability Expansion and Conversion Mechanisms 128
8.2.3 Decolonial Epistemology and Epistemic Justice 128
8.3 Indigenous Talent: Knowledge Systems and Recognition Gaps ... 129
8.3.1 Cognitive Sophistication in Indigenous Contexts 129
8.3.2 Underrepresentation Patterns 129
8.3.3 Ethnographic Illustration 129
8.4 Rural Talent: Territorial Inequality and Applied Intelligence 130
8.5 Forcibly Displaced Migrant Talent: Mobility and Adaptive Capacity 130
8.5.1 Regional Displacement and Educational Disruption 130
8.5.2 Adaptive Intelligence and Underrecognized Strengths 131
8.6 Case Integration: Art-Based Enrichment in Lima 131
8.6.1 Intervention Design and Identification Framework 131
8.6.2 Emotional Outcomes: Differential Effects 132
8.6.3 Displacement Ecology and Emotional Stability 132
8.6.4 Creativity Outcomes and Structural Constraint 133
8.7 Comparative Structural Diagnosis 133
8.8 Methodological Reflection 133
8.9 Policy Architecture for Recognition Reform 135
8.9.1 Identification Reform: Expanding the Epistemic Frame ... 135
8.9.2 Territorial Redistribution: Decentralizing Opportunity 135
8.9.3 Continuity and Inclusion for Forcibly Displaced Learners . 136
8.10 Conclusion: Recognition as Educational Justice 136
References 137

9 Teacher Training and Professional Development in High-Ability Education across Latin America 139

9.1 Introduction: From Recognition to Realization—Teacher Preparation as Conversion Infrastructure 139
9.2 Conceptual and Terminological Fragmentation as a Training Challenge 140
9.3 Teachers as Capability Mediators in an Ecological System 141
9.3.1 Macrosystem: Norms, Values, Cultural Scripts 141
9.3.2 Exosystem: Policy, Regulations, Certification Systems. . . . 141
9.3.3 Mesosystem: Institutional Coordination 142
9.3.4 Microsystem: Classroom Practice 142
9.4 Regional Evidence: Recognition without Preparation 142
9.4.1 Argentina: Policy Visibility, Minimal Systematic Preparation, and Low-Leverage Classroom Responses 143
9.4.2 Brazil: Formal Policy Recognition, Persistent Teacher Ambivalence toward Acceleration, and the Centrality of Socio-Emotional Concerns 143
9.4.3 Paraguay: Receptive Teachers, Weak Specialized Preparation, and the Shifting of Instructional Burden to Families under Policy Volatility 144
9.4.4 Chile: Concentrated Enrichment Ecosystems, Limited Mainstream Diffusion, and the Utility of a Learning-Resource (Actiotope) Lens 144
9.4.5 Peru: Evidence that Teacher Retraining Improves Identification Accuracy, Plus an Institutional Model (COAR) that Embeds Professional Rigor 145
9.5 Cultural Barriers: Myth, Elitism, and Age Norms 145
9.5.1 Socio-Emotional Myths about Acceleration 146
9.5.2 Elitism Narratives 146
9.5.3 Rigid Age Norms 146
9.6 Acceleration as a Professional Competency 146
9.6.1 Whole-Grade Acceleration and Early Entrance 147
9.6.2 Subject Acceleration and Systemic Suppression 147
9.6.3 Curriculum Compacting as Entry Point 147
9.7 Multicultural Contexts and Assessment Literacy 147
9.8 Twice-Exceptionality Integration 148
9.9 Promising Models for Effective Training: From COAR to Practice-Based Modules 149
9.9.1 The COAR Model (Peru): Institutionalized Professional Rigor 149
9.9.2 Peru: Historical Advocacy and Teacher Networks 149
9.9.3 Practice-Based Modules: Embed Rather than Overhaul . . . 149
9.9.4 Specialist Presence and Coaching 150
9.10 Case Vignettes: Teachers as Capability Mediators in Regional Scenarios 150
9.10.1 Vignette 1: Argentina—From Extra Tasks to Differentiation 150

9.10.2 Vignette 2: Brazil—Acceleration Resistance Reframed through Evidence . . . 150
9.10.3 Vignette 3: Paraguay—Reducing Family Pressure through Specialist Support . . . 151
9.10.4 Vignette 4: Chile—When Enrichment Knowledge Enters the Classroom . . . 151
9.10.5 Vignette 5: Peru—COAR Professional Culture as a Template . . . 151
9.11 Comparative Ecological Synthesis: Teacher Preparation as Conversion System . . . 153
9.12 Scalable Reform Pathways . . . 154
9.13 Conclusion: Investing in Teachers to Democratize Excellence . . . 155
References . . . 155

10 Country Case Studies: Policy Enactment and Systemic Variation in Latin America . . . 157
10.1 Introduction: From Regional Synthesis to National Enactment . . . 157
10.2 Recognition and Pathway: Analytical Framework . . . 158
10.2.1 Country Case Studies . . . 159
10.3 Cross-Case Comparative Analysis . . . 161
10.3.1 From Comparative Description to Conceptual Mapping . . . 161
10.3.2 Empirical Grounding: Institutional Features across Systems . . . 163
10.3.3 Patterns of Enactment . . . 163
10.3.4 Governance and Territorial Variability . . . 166
10.3.5 Identification as Institutional Practice . . . 166
10.3.6 Capacity as the Binding Constraint . . . 166
10.4 Final Analytical Reflection . . . 166
References . . . 167

Part III Toward Coherence: A Regional Model and Future Directions 169

11 Toward a Latin American Model of Talent Development . . . 171
11.1 Introduction: Why a Regional Model Is Theoretically and Practically Necessary . . . 171
11.2 Structural Conditions Shaping Talent Development . . . 172
11.2.1 Persistent Inequality as Developmental Constraint . . . 172
11.2.2 Cultural and Linguistic Plurality . . . 173
11.2.3 Institutional Fragmentation . . . 173
11.3 Theoretical Foundations: Recalibrating Global Theory for Regional Context . . . 173

11.3.1 Developmental Systems and Ecological Embeddedness ... 174
11.3.2 Differentiated Conceptions of Giftedness ... 174
11.3.3 Capability Approach as Ethical Framework ... 174
11.3.4 Culturally Responsive Pedagogy ... 175
11.3.5 Twice Exceptionality and Socio-Emotional Integration 175
11.4 Core Principles: Operationalizing the Model ... 175
11.4.1 Equity-Centered Identification ... 175
11.4.2 Development over Labeling ... 176
11.4.3 Multi-Tiered Pathways ... 176
11.4.4 Acceleration as Evidence-Based Equity ... 176
11.4.5 Teacher Preparation as Systemic Lever ... 176
11.4.6 Rural and Indigenous Inclusion ... 177
11.4.7 Regional Collaboration ... 177
11.4.8 Policy Coherence and Sustainability ... 177
11.5 Structural Architecture: Four Interacting Ecological Levels ... 178
11.5.1 Level 1: Individual Development ... 178
11.5.2 Level 2: Educational Environment ... 178
11.5.3 Level 3: Community and Family Context ... 178
11.5.4 Level 4: Policy and Structural Supports ... 178
11.6 The Latin American Model of Talent Development (LAMTD) ... 180
11.7 Implementation Pathways across Contexts ... 180
11.7.1 Low-Resource Rural Systems ... 180
11.7.2 Urban Public Systems ... 181
11.7.3 Higher Education Transition ... 181
11.8 Research Agenda for the Next Decade ... 181
11.9 Ethical Commitments and Democratic Imperatives ... 181
11.10 Conclusion: From Visibility to Architecture ... 182
References ... 182

12 Conclusions and Future Directions ... 185
12.1 Closing the Arc: From Fragmentation to Coherence ... 185
12.2 Contributions to Psychology: Expanding the Developmental Lens 186
12.2.1 From Individual Cognition to Ecological Development 186
12.2.2 Neurodiversity and Twice-Exceptionality in Stratified Systems ... 186
12.2.3 Talent as Contextually Expressed Potential ... 187
12.3 Contributions to Education: Policy, Practice, and Preparation ... 187
12.3.1 From Legislative Recognition to Institutional Coherence ... 187
12.3.2 Acceleration, Enrichment, and Differentiated Instruction ... 188
12.4 Reframing Urgency: Inequality, Diversity, and Moral Responsibility ... 188
12.5 A Forward-Looking Research Agenda ... 188

12.5.1 Longitudinal Developmental Inquiry 189
12.5.2 Culturally Responsive Identification 189
12.5.3 Mental Health Integration 189
12.5.4 Implementation Science and Teacher Preparation 189
12.5.5 Comparative and Cross-National Scholarship 190
12.6 Policy Priorities for the Next Decade 190
12.7 Toward an Internationally Informed and Regionally Grounded Field 190
12.8 A Call to Psychologists, Educators, and Decision-Makers 190
12.9 Final Reflection: Visibility as Justice 191

Index 193

List of Figures

Fig. 10.1 Model of enactment architectures in high-ability education. The figure conceptualizes variation across Latin American systems along two primary dimensions: recognition (legal and policy visibility) and pathway solidity (degree of institutional routinization). Institutional capacity mediates movement toward sustained implementation, while governance structure shapes the territorial distribution of provision. The four quadrants represent ideal-type architectures: symbolic recognition, diffuse inclusion, program ecosystems, and selective depth 162
Fig. 11.1 The Latin American model of talent development (LAMTD) 179

List of Tables

Table 3.1 Comparative overview of dominant theories of giftedness and talent development ... 24
Table 3.2 Epistemological assumptions in dominant giftedness frameworks and cross-cultural implications ... 28
Table 3.3 Guiding principles for equity-oriented and culturally responsive frameworks ... 36
Table 3.4 Integrative dimensions of the Latin American model of talent development (LAMTD) ... 38
Table 4.1 Technical, legal, and operational frameworks for children and adolescents with high abilities in selected Latin American countries ... 48
Table 5.1 Typology of identification regimes in selected Latin American contexts ... 76
Table 6.1 Multilevel architecture of talent development innovation in Latin America ... 97
Table 8.1 Comparative visibility matrix: indigenous, rural, and migrant talent in Latin America ... 134
Table 9.1 Teacher preparation as ecological conversion infrastructure in high-ability education across Latin America (selected cases) ... 153
Table 10.1 Comparative overview of high ability policy architecture in Peru, Brazil, Mexico, Colombia, Chile, and Argentina ... 164

About the Author

Sheyla Blumen, PhD is a psychologist, researcher, and academic leader specializing in high ability, talent development, educational equity, and cross-cultural perspectives on giftedness. Her scholarship examines how social contexts, public policies, and institutional practices shape the identification and development of advanced potential, with particular attention to Latin America.Dr. Blumen is affiliated with the Academic Department of Psychology at Pontificia Universidad Católica del Perú (Peru). She has contributed extensively to research, teaching, and professional training in psychology and education, maintaining a sustained commitment to connecting theory with practice. Her scholarship emphasizes culturally responsive frameworks and the ethical dimensions of supporting talent in diverse and unequal societies. Through her work, she fosters interdisciplinary and cross-regional dialogue aimed at advancing more inclusive and equitable approaches to talent development.

Chapter 1
Introduction

This book is organized into three thematic parts that move from conceptual foundations to systemic analysis and finally to model building and future directions. Together, the chapters provide a coherent examination of talent development in Latin America, integrating theoretical, empirical, and policy perspectives.

1.1 Part I: Foundations: Reframing Talent in Context

The opening section establishes the conceptual foundations of the volume. Before examining policies, programs, or institutional arrangements, a more fundamental task is required: to reconsider what is meant by talent—and from which epistemic position it is defined.

Much of the global literature on giftedness has emerged within comparatively stable and resourced educational systems. Latin America presents a different developmental terrain—marked by structural inequality, cultural plurality, linguistic diversity, and institutional discontinuity. These conditions do not simply complicate the application of existing models; they expose their limits and invite theoretical recalibration.

The chapters in this section revisit dominant frameworks and place them in dialogue with regional realities. The aim is neither rejection nor replication but refinement. Talent is reframed as relational, developmental, and ecologically embedded—situated within systems that enable or constrain its expression.

This reframing is foundational. Without it, subsequent discussions of identification and policy would rest on inherited assumptions. With it, the analytical lens shifts—from classification toward cultivation, from trait toward trajectory.

Chapter 2 establishes the conceptual stage from which the rest of the book is constructed. Rather than merely focusing on a singular region, it reinterprets the theoretical premises of talent development through Latin America as a lens for

S. Blumen, *High Ability and Talent Development in Latin America*,
https://doi.org/10.1007/978-3-032-27468-7_1

analysis. The structural shortcomings of traditional trait-based models of giftedness can be evidenced in settings characterized by entrenched inequality, cultural plurality, and institutional variability. The chapter thus promotes a relational premise: excellence does not occur independently but within integrated systems of opportunity, recognition, and governance.

Rather than positioning Latin America as the periphery that fits within top Global North frameworks, it asserts that the region clarifies the structure under which talent can flourish—or not. Inequality becomes developmental architecture. Cultural diversity challenges epistemic legitimacy. Institutional fragmentation becomes a measure of scalability and coherence. In such conditions, we render visible the systemic alignment necessary for excellence to be sustainable.

The chapter presents four mutually regulating dimensions (equity–capability, developmental–systems, cultural–decolonial, and policy–institutional architecture) that, combined, are the conceptual grammar of the book. These dimensions are not additive but interconnected structures that work together. Their interrelation defines whether talent is structurally enabled or contingently realized. The chapters that follow gradually formalize, operationalize, and empirically explore this schema.

Chapter 3 provides the theoretical foundation of this volume. If Chap. 2 positioned Latin America as an analytical lens through which the structural conditions of talent development become visible, this chapter formalizes the conceptual architecture required to interpret those conditions with precision.

The field of gifted education has moved decisively beyond psychometric reductionism. Foundational frameworks—Renzulli's interactional model, Gagné's developmental differentiation between gifts and talents, Sternberg's contextual and integrative theories, and Ziegler's actiotopic systems perspective—have expanded the construct to include multidimensionality, developmental dynamism, and environmental mediation. These models have shaped global scholarship and informed research and practice throughout Latin America.

Yet their application within contexts marked by structural inequality, linguistic diversity, and plural epistemologies reveals unresolved tensions. Educational systems in Latin America operate within historical patterns of stratification and uneven institutional capacity. Under such conditions, definitions of excellence, identification practices, and access to opportunity cannot be treated as culturally neutral or socially independent.

This chapter therefore proceeds in three movements. First, it revisits dominant theoretical models, situating their contributions and identifying their implicit normative assumptions. Second, it undertakes a critical cross-cultural analysis, engaging capability theory, decolonial scholarship, and sociocultural perspectives to examine how individualism, standardization, and achievement-centered definitions of giftedness may reproduce structural inequities. Third, it advances an integrative framework—the Latin American Model of Talent Development (LAMTD)—which synthesizes developmental–ecological, equity–capability, epistemic–decolonial, and institutional dimensions.

The framework is organized around three guiding questions: How does talent develop? Who has a genuine opportunity to develop it? According to whose criteria is it recognized? By addressing these questions simultaneously, the chapter reframes giftedness as relational, opportunity-dependent, and culturally situated.

The objective is not to regionalize theory for its own sake but to deepen the field's conceptual foundations by integrating developmental science with commitments to justice and epistemic plurality. In doing so, the chapter positions gifted education as both a field of excellence and a project of democratic inclusion.

Chapter 3 thus establishes the intellectual infrastructure of the volume. The analyses of identification, curriculum, acceleration, teacher preparation, policy, and national case studies that follow are grounded in the integrative logic articulated here.

1.2 Part II: Systems Under Constraint: Identification, Development, and Inequality

If Part I clarifies how talent should be understood, Part II examines how it is recognized and developed within real educational systems.

Across Latin America, recognition coexists with fragmentation. Legal acknowledgment does not guarantee coherent implementation. Programs emerge, yet access remains stratified. Innovation appears, often locally, yet systemic alignment is uneven. This section analyzes those tensions with precision.

The chapters explore institutional architectures, identification regimes, curricular pathways, teacher preparation, mental health infrastructures, and the experiences of learners whose abilities remain partially or wholly unseen. Together, they reveal talent development as a systemic process—mediated by governance structures, cultural interpretations, and opportunity distributions.

This is the diagnostic center of the volume. It does not romanticize innovation, nor does it reduce inequality to abstraction. Instead, it examines how developmental potential is converted—or interrupted—within layered educational ecologies. The objective is structural clarity: to understand the system sufficiently to strengthen it.

The structural inequalities and territorial disparities that condition talent development across Latin America were established in Chap. 2. The ecological–capability–decolonial framework described in Chap. 3 illustrated that even when we can recognize someone as high ability, we cannot guarantee fair opportunity in a context without institutional conditions consistent with such recognition. **Chapter 4** builds on this discussion by moving the argument from conceptual architecture to policy design, studying how national education systems institutionalize, or avoid institutionalizing, this recognition.

High ability is now present in the legislative discourse of most Latin American countries. However, legal inclusion has not led to a predictable application. Regulatory clarity, acceleration mechanisms, identification standards, teacher preparation, funding commitments, and accountability systems vary widely. In numerous settings, high-ability education is still part of inclusive education paradigms, which lack separate operational mandates that lead to a fragmented and uneven provision. Therefore, the matter is not formal recognition so much as institutional alignment.

This chapter locates the region with a comparative view on five anchor systems, i.e., Brazil, Peru, Mexico, Chile, and Colombia, in a broader legislative cartography. It scrutinizes how policy is codified, how identification regimes function, and how public–private and territorial inequalities affect access to advanced educational pathways. Innovation in enrichment initiatives, university partnerships, and residential academies is shown to be effective but scaling and systemic coordination are limited.

In contrast, the chapter states that high-ability education in Latin America is unevenly institutionalized rather than missing altogether. Progress in the field demands a departure from symbolic inclusion toward a coherent, funded, and responsible policy environment in which the distributed talent can be equitably translated into meaningful access to continuous educational opportunity. The subsequent chapter considers how these institutional arrangements condition a particular way in which lived developmental paths are constructed.

Chapter 5 turns to the decisive mechanism through which recognition occurs. It argues that identification is not a neutral assessment procedure but a structural lever in talent development. Across Brazil, Chile, Mexico, Colombia, and Peru, identification practices reflect both conceptual commitments and systemic constraints. Psychometric thresholds, achievement filters, and nomination processes operate within stratified educational ecologies. When designed without contextual correction, they risk reinforcing accumulated advantage. When aligned with developmental and equity-oriented principles, they can widen the aperture of recognition and activate distributed potential.

Chapter 5 advances a comparative typology of identification regimes and proposes a developmental–equity realignment consistent with the model articulated in Chap. 3. The transformation of identification—from selective gatekeeping to opportunity activation—is foundational to building a regionally grounded model of talent development in Latin America.

Chapter 6 advances the volume's central proposition that talent development in Latin America must be understood as a problem of structural alignment, not simply of individual potential. If earlier chapters establish how high ability is identified, named, and differentially recognized across unequal systems, this chapter turns to what recognition must enable: curriculum, instruction, institutional design, and redistribution capable of sustaining development across key educational transitions.

Rather than treating "innovation" as a discretionary enhancement imported from well-resourced contexts, this chapter situates innovation in Latin America within constraint—high inequality, uneven teacher preparation, bureaucratic rigidity, and persistent implementation gaps between legal recognition and classroom reality. In such conditions, the chapter argues, innovation becomes a form of educational necessity: the construction of mechanisms that restore fit between learner readiness and institutional opportunity, and that expand real freedoms for students whose potential would otherwise remain underdeveloped or invisible.

To do so, the chapter integrates three complementary lenses that recur across the book: an ecological view of development as system–learner fit, a capability approach emphasizing substantive freedoms and conversion conditions, and a decolonial critique attentive to inherited institutional norms—especially rigid age-grading and uniform pacing—that may be treated as neutral but function as exclusionary technologies. These lenses allow the chapter to move beyond familiar debates that isolate enrichment from acceleration, or cognitive differentiation from socioemotional support, and instead examine how multiple mechanisms must work together to produce durable developmental pathways.

Empirically, the chapter pairs a comparative regional overview with a focused analysis of Peru as an instructive case of multilevel architecture. It examines COAR as institutional redesign, the International Baccalaureate as curricular deepening whose equity effects depend on access, *Beca 18* as redistribution at the tertiary threshold, *Becas LUCET* as university-level scaffolding for excellence and projection, and an arts-based wellbeing initiative illustrating both the promise and limits of socioemotional enrichment when differentiation is absent. Across these cases, the chapter's throughline is explicit: equity and excellence are not competing goals in unequal systems; they are structurally interdependent. Without redistribution, excellence reproduces stratification. Without differentiation, equity collapses into invisibility. Sustainable innovation therefore requires coordinated alignment across the classroom, school, institutional, and policy levels—so that high potential can be converted into sustained capability and contribution.

Chapter 7 extends the argument that recognition is never neutral by focusing on twice-exceptional learners—students who combine high intellectual or creative potential with neurodevelopmental differences, learning disabilities, or significant mental health vulnerabilities. Their profiles challenge the categorical binaries that still organize many educational systems: excellence versus deficit, enrichment versus remediation, cognition versus well-being. When these domains remain institutionally separated, complexity becomes difficult to interpret and therefore difficult to support.

Situated within the ecological–developmental framework articulated earlier in this volume, this chapter argues that twice-exceptionality is not a marginal phenomenon but a structural test case. In contexts marked by inequality and fragmented service delivery, masking becomes institutional, and recognizability becomes stratified. Through regionally grounded clinical trajectories and policy analysis across Brazil, Chile, Mexico, Colombia, and Peru, the chapter demonstrates how neurodevelopmental diversity intersects with systemic design.

If equitable talent development requires coherence across identification, inclusion, and mental health, then twice-exceptionality becomes a measure of systemic maturity. The issue is not the existence of these learners; it is whether educational systems are architecturally prepared to recognize them.

Chapter 8 deepens the argument that talent development in Latin America cannot be understood apart from the structural, territorial, and epistemological conditions that govern recognition. It does so by examining patterned invisibility among three populations whose competencies develop within historically marginalized ecologies: Indigenous learners, rural learners, and forcibly displaced migrant learners. While earlier chapters interrogated systemic structures broadly, this chapter focuses on concrete sites where recognition breakdown becomes most visible. The question is not whether talent exists in these contexts. It is whether institutional frameworks are structured to perceive it.

Indigenous invisibility arises from epistemic marginalization. When academic legitimacy is defined through monolingual, urban, and individualistic standards, community-based knowledge systems are rendered peripheral rather than foundational. Rural invisibility reflects territorial inequity. Applied intelligence, ecological reasoning, and multigrade autonomy often lack the infrastructural pathways necessary for conversion into advanced educational opportunity. Invisibility among forcibly displaced migrant learners emerges from institutional discontinuity. Interrupted schooling, documentation barriers, and psychosocial stress fracture capability trajectories frequently redirect high potential into remediation rather than enrichment.

Although these justice deficits differ—epistemic, redistributive, and continuity-based—they converge structurally. In each case, competence fails to become institutionally legible. The ecological–capability–decolonial framework clarifies that under-identification is not a deficit of learners but a failure of conversion within stratified opportunity structures.

Empirically, the chapter integrates comparative policy analysis, ethnographic illustration, and findings from a Lima-based art enrichment intervention involving host-community and forcibly displaced learners. The intervention demonstrates both possibility and limitation. Enrichment can create affective openings, yet without structural continuity and redistributive support, short-term gains cannot compensate for systemic misalignment. Capability expansion requires more than programmatic inclusion; it requires architectural coherence.

This insight anticipates the argument developed in Chap. 11. If recognition remains embedded in colonial epistemologies, territorially uneven infrastructures, and discontinuous mobility regimes, expanding programs alone will not resolve invisibility. Structural justice demands redesign. It requires epistemic plurality in identification, territorial redistribution of opportunity structures, and sustained developmental continuity for learners whose trajectories traverse displacement and precarity.

By centering Indigenous, rural, and forcibly displaced learners, Chap. 8 exposes the geographic and cultural limits of existing recognition regimes. It asks whether a system calibrated to dominant norms can ever fully recognize excellence that emerges at its margins. The volume's concluding chapter returns to this question at a regional scale, proposing that talent development in Latin America must be reconceptualized not as selective advancement but as systemic capability expansion.

In this way, Chap. 8 functions as a hinge within the volume's broader arc. It demonstrates that invisibility is neither accidental nor inevitable; it is structurally produced—and therefore structurally transformable. Recognition, when understood as an instrument of educational justice, becomes not a technical procedure but an architectural commitment.

Chapter 9 addresses the structural pivot of the entire regional model: teacher preparation as conversion infrastructure. Across Argentina, Brazil, Paraguay, Chile, and Peru, legislative language acknowledging *altas capacidades* or *altas habilidades/superdotação* has expanded. Yet the recurring regional pattern is not the absence of discourse; it is the fragility of implementation. Teachers frequently encounter advanced learners without having been systematically prepared to identify, differentiate, accelerate, or scaffold them. Under such conditions, predictable outcomes emerge: add-on assignments replace deepened learning; acceleration remains constrained by fear narratives; multicultural learners are under-identified; twice-exceptional students become doubly invisible; and enrichment remains concentrated in specialized nodes rather than diffused into everyday classrooms.

This chapter argues that these are not isolated failures. They are systemic expressions of a missing conversion layer.

From the ecological perspective, teachers operate at the intersection of macrosystem beliefs (elitism narratives, age norms), exosystem regulations (policy, standards), mesosystem coordination (university–school linkages, specialist networks), and microsystem practice (daily instruction, socio-emotional climate). When teacher preparation is thin, each layer reinforces caution, rigidity, and under-recognition. When preparation is robust, those same layers can align to expand capability sets—even in constrained systems.

The chapter integrates empirical evidence from national contexts with research on acceleration, multicultural assessment, and twice-exceptionality. It also foregrounds case vignettes not as illustrations but as analytic micro-cases demonstrating how professional learning alters conversion trajectories. The analysis reveals a consistent structural insight: modest but coherent professional preparation—legal literacy, readiness assessment protocols, curriculum compacting expertise, socio-emotional monitoring frameworks—can generate disproportionate gains in capability realization.

Promising regional models underscore this claim. Peru's *Colegios de Alto Rendimiento* (COAR) demonstrates how institutionalized professional culture sustains high-conversion environments. Chile's enrichment ecosystem reveals both the strength of specialized nodes and the cost of limited diffusion. Brazil's empirical work clarifies the precise domains—particularly socio-emotional risk perception—where teacher learning must intervene. Paraguay's experience shows how insufficient preparation shifts responsibility toward families, thereby reproducing inequity. Argentina's case illustrates how low-leverage responses emerge not from unwillingness but from structural under-preparation.

The broader argument of the volume converges here: excellence cannot be democratized without professional capacity. Recognition without preparation produces symbolic inclusion. Preparation without ecological alignment produces isolated excellence. Only when teacher learning is embedded as structural infrastructure does high-ability education shift from contingent privilege to public good.

If talent development in Latin America is to become coherent, equitable, and scalable, the region must invest not only in identifying students—but in preparing the adults who mediate their trajectories. Teacher preparation is not peripheral reform. It is the mechanism through which capability becomes reality.

Chapter 10 provides an overview of how the application of high-ability and talent development policies has been implemented within six nation-states in Latin America, namely Argentina, Brazil, Colombia, Chile, Mexico, and Peru. Relying on the theoretical background and thematic discussions that have taken place in the chapter before, it moves towards institutional implementation as the analytical emphasis, rather than on regional synthesis.

The chapter thus sets out to explore how legal acknowledgment of high-ability learners manifests in certain educational pathways. Structurally, by looking at governance frameworks, legislation, institutional systems, identification instruments, and programmatic responses, it offers a framework for explaining why these vary at the level of policy practice in different nations. However, rather than suggesting a single regional model, the analysis presents a diverse spectrum of institutional configurations that come from governance, administrative capacity, and programmatic architecture. By highlighting high-ability education as a perspective, the chapter contributes to contextualizing more general dynamics of policy action and system coherence.

1.3 Part III: Toward Coherence: A Regional Model and Future Directions

The final section turns from analysis to synthesis. Having examined theory and system, the question becomes one of alignment: What would coherence look like across levels of talent development in Latin America?

Part III introduces the Latin American Model of Talent Development (LAMTD) as an integrative framework. The model does not prescribe uniform solutions; rather, it articulates interacting ecological levels through which talent can be cultivated under conditions of inequality and diversity. It synthesizes the theoretical recalibrations and structural analyses developed throughout the volume.

The concluding chapter extends this synthesis, outlining contributions to psychology and education and identifying priorities for research and policy in the coming decade. The emphasis is forward-looking but disciplined: systemic maturity requires sustained alignment across identification, instruction, teacher preparation, and governance.

The arc of the volume thus returns to its central premise: talent is not a fixed trait residing within individuals but a developmental configuration that emerges through structured relationships between persons, institutions, and society.

Chapter 11 completes the analytical trajectory initiated at the opening of the volume. Chapter 2 positioned Latin America not merely as a geographic region but as a structural lens—one through which the entanglement of excellence with inequality, culture, and institutional design becomes unmistakable. Across the chapters that followed, legislative recognition expanded, policy architectures were examined, and pedagogical tensions were made visible. Yet a central paradox persisted: formal acknowledgment of high ability has not consistently translated into coherent developmental pathways or equitable access.

Chapter 11 responds to that paradox through design rather than diagnosis. It advances a Latin American Model of Talent Development (LAMTD) that integrates developmental systems theory, differentiated conceptions of giftedness, the capability approach, culturally responsive pedagogy, and research on socio-emotional development and twice exceptionality. Rather than transplanting external models, it recalibrates established theory within contexts marked by inequality, linguistic plurality, territorial disparity, and institutional fragmentation.

The LAMTD is articulated as a multilevel ecological architecture linking individual growth, educational environments, community capital, and policy infrastructures within a coherent developmental system. Its core commitments—equity-centered identification, responsible acceleration, teacher preparation as systemic leverage, rural and Indigenous inclusion, and regional collaboration—reframe talent development as capability expansion and educational justice rather than selective differentiation.

In this sense, the chapter brings the volume's arc to structural completion. What began as visibility becomes architecture. What began as a diagnosis becomes alignment. Latin America emerges not at the margins of talent theory but at its clarifying edge—where excellence is not merely identified but institutionally enabled; not contingently achieved but developmentally sustained.

Chapter 12, the concluding chapter, represents both an intellectual synthesis and an ethical invitation. The central premise of this book is clear: in Latin America, high ability cannot be understood without explaining the structural conditions influencing recognition and opportunity. Talent is widely distributed across the region, but access to sustained development pathways is variable. This is certainly the case for many educational systems characterized by inequality, territorial disparity, and institutional fragility: the educational systems fail to produce what we might put into action. The price of that discontinuity is paid not only by individuals but also by societies.

This final chapter consolidates the volume's theoretical contributions and practical implications. How a framework of ecological–developmental thinking also reframes this topic of gifted education into a matter of inclusive excellence, not selective privilege. It situates the Latin American Model of Talent Development within broader international discourse, emphasizing the need for conceptual innovation emerging from the Global South. And it lays out a forward-looking research and policy agenda aimed at sustaining institutional continuity, preparing teachers, acknowledging the presence of cultural differences, and integrating mental health care.

Instead of a conclusion, this chapter aims to be an invitation: to psychologists to expand assessment paradigms, to educators to embrace differentiation with intellectual courage, to researchers to pursue rigorous and collaborative inquiry, and to decision-makers to enact sustained, equity-oriented policy. The visibility, voice, and value of high-potential youth in Latin America depend upon collective commitment.

Part I
Foundations: Reframing Talent in Context

Chapter 2
Why Latin America Matters in Talent Development

2.1 From Trait to Relational Configuration

Gifted education has progressed from trait identification toward systemic explanation. Early psychometric traditions, exemplified by Terman (1925), treated giftedness as a stable individual property measurable through standardized assessment. Identification constituted the field's central task.

Subsequent theoretical expansions broadened the construct without fully abandoning individual primacy. Renzulli (1978) reconceptualized giftedness as the interaction of ability, creativity, and task commitment. Gagné (2004) distinguished between natural abilities and developed talents, emphasizing environmental catalysts. Gardner (1983) pluralized domains of excellence. Yet the learner remained the principal analytic unit; context functioned as a modifier rather than a structural condition.

Systemic and ecological perspectives introduced a structural reorientation. Ziegler's Actiotope Model reconceptualized development as occurring within a dynamic person–environment system composed of actions, feedback, learning capital, and environmental affordances (Ziegler, 2005). Bronfenbrenner situated development within nested ecological layers. Contemporary developmental science emphasized reciprocal causation and longitudinal trajectories (Subotnik et al., 2011). Talent thus emerged not as possession but as enacted alignment within opportunity structures.

However, systemic description alone is insufficient. Development unfolds within distributive orders. Sen's capability approach introduces a normative criterion: justice requires expansion of substantive freedoms (Sen, 1999). Applied to talent development, the central question becomes whether opportunity systems enable or constrain the realization of potential.

S. Blumen, *High Ability and Talent Development in Latin America*,
https://doi.org/10.1007/978-3-032-27468-7_2

These traditions converge in a relational premise: giftedness is not an attribute to be detected but a configuration emerging within structured environments of opportunity, recognition, and justice.

Latin America renders this premise unavoidable. Persistent inequality (CEPAL, 2022), strong socioeconomic achievement gradients (OECD, 2019), and ethnolinguistic diversity expose the limits of trait-based and culturally narrow models. In such contexts, identification, programming, acceleration, and teacher preparation are not discrete interventions; they are interdependent elements of systemic architecture.

This chapter therefore advances a foundational claim: in unequal and culturally plural societies such as Latin America, giftedness must be conceptualized relationally—developed from within coordinated systems rather than merely identified within them. Chapter 3 formalizes this claim through four mutually regulating dimensions:

- **Equity–capability** (normative horizon)
- **Developmental–systems** (mechanism of emergence)
- **Cultural–decolonial** (epistemic legitimacy)
- **Policy–institutional architecture** (structural sustainability)

These dimensions do not operate sequentially; they operate simultaneously.

2.2 Structural Inequality as Developmental Condition

In Latin America, inequality is not a background context; it is developmental architecture.

CEPAL (2022) documents sustained income disparity across the region. OECD (2019) data confirm that socioeconomic status strongly predicts academic performance in Chile, Colombia, Mexico, Brazil, and Peru. Expanded enrollment has not eliminated structural differentiation in quality, access, and opportunity.

Where socioeconomic gradients remain steep, measured achievement reflects accumulated opportunity. Identification systems relying primarily on standardized performance or teacher nomination risk confusing privilege with potential. Under-resourced schools provide fewer advanced learning experiences, fewer trained nominators, and fewer differentiated pathways. Families with greater cultural capital navigate evaluation processes more effectively. Recognition thus becomes stratified.

From a capability perspective, this is ethically consequential. Justice requires that high-potential students from marginalized backgrounds possess real opportunities to develop their capabilities. Talent development becomes distributive design rather than selective enhancement.

Inequality in Latin America is spatially patterned. Indigenous students are disproportionately located in rural or peri-urban regions characterized by multigrade classrooms, teacher shortages, and limited curricular breadth. Public–private segmentation further differentiates opportunity structures. In Chile, Brazil, Colombia, and Peru, private institutions often offer enriched curricula, language immersion, and advanced coursework, while many public schools operate under scarcity. Migration—cross-border and internal—introduces additional discontinuity.

These structural arrangements shape developmental trajectories. Early enrichment stabilizes self-concept and aspiration; sustained under-challenge produces attrition. Talent loss is patterned, not random.

Thus, equity is not peripheral to excellence. It defines its structural possibility.

2.3 Developmental–Systems Alignment

Empirical research across the region reinforces systemic logic. Pollitt (2007) demonstrates how poverty and nutrition affect attention and memory. Blumen (2002) shows that teacher training in creativity and differentiated pedagogy alters learning outcomes. Brazilian scholarship (Alencar & Fleith, 2007) highlights classroom climate and socio-emotional support as catalysts of talent.

These findings confirm that giftedness emerges through interaction among predispositions, environmental catalysts, and institutional supports. Variability in teacher preparation, infrastructure, and curricular flexibility becomes developmentally decisive.

The implication is architectural: talent development requires ecosystem construction.

This systemic principle extends across the volume's interventions. Acceleration (Chap. 7) demands relational fit within institutional and developmental contexts. Twice-exceptionality (Chap. 8) requires coordinated environments capable of mitigating constraint while amplifying strength. Rural high achievers require expanded relational networks beyond geographically limited settings.

Across these domains, the mechanism is consistent: sustained alignment between individual potential and evolving opportunity systems.

2.4 Cultural Plurality and Epistemic Legitimacy

Latin America's cultural diversity challenges universalized definitions of giftedness. Indigenous epistemologies emphasize collective knowledge, relational identity, and ecological stewardship. Intercultural scholarship (Tubino, 2005; Walsh, 2009) underscores that educational justice requires recognition of these epistemic frameworks.

Blumen (2021) documents how linguistically incongruent identification practices have historically underserved Indigenous high achievers in Peru. Parallel findings among Māori and Aboriginal students demonstrate broader relevance (Garvis et al., 2021; Webber, 2018).

The Cultural–Decolonial dimension therefore addresses recognition at the level of epistemic legitimacy. It requires:

- Acknowledgment of culturally embedded excellence,
- Linguistically responsive assessment,
- Interrogation of postcolonial hierarchies shaping legitimacy, and.
- Integration of community-based knowledge systems.

Misrecognition is not incidental; it is structurally produced through language policy, assessment design, teacher expectations, and gatekeeping mechanisms. A decolonial orientation entails institutional recalibration, not symbolic inclusion.

2.5 Institutional Architecture and Coherence

Recognition without coherence produces fragmentation.

Brazil's national policy formally recognizes students with high abilities (Brasil, 2008), yet teacher preparation remains uneven (Pérez & Freitas, 2014). Chile combines differentiated instruction policies with accountability systems that restrict flexibility (Bellei, 2015). Argentina and Colombia demonstrate expanding research interest but limited coordination (Castellanos & Díaz, 2016).

Absent vertical alignment, professional pipelines, and sustained funding, talent initiatives become isolated "islands of excellence." Fragmentation intensifies inequity by tying access to geography and institutional affiliation. Scaling reforms in segmented systems risks amplifying inequality unless distributive safeguards are embedded.

Policy–Institutional Architecture therefore functions as structural guarantor. It determines whether innovation becomes systemic or episodic.

2.6 Innovation under Constraint

Peru's COAR initiative (Blumen, 2021) illustrates coordinated alignment under constraint. Public residential academies integrate academic rigor, socio-emotional support, regional representation, and national coordination. The model simultaneously engages capability expansion, developmental support, cultural inclusion, and institutional coherence.

COAR does not eliminate structural inequality. It demonstrates that systemic integration is feasible. Within heterogeneous regional contexts, such cases serve as proof of architectural possibility.

2.7 Interactive Dimensions

The four dimensions introduced here are mutually regulating:

- Equity–capability defines normative orientation.
- Developmental–systems clarifies the mechanism.
- Cultural–decolonial secures epistemic legitimacy.
- Policy–institutional architecture ensures durability.

Weakening any dimension produces distortion: stratification, misrecognition, fragility, or reductionism.

Chapter 3 formalizes their relational integration.

2.8 Structural Progression of the Book

The book progresses architecturally.

Chapter 3 formalizes the integrative model.

Chapter 4 analyzes regional policy coherence.

Chapter 5 examines identification systems.

Chapter 6 addresses curriculum and enrichment.

Chapter 7 analyzes twice-exceptionality and mental health.

Chapter 8 reframes acceleration.

Chapter 9 focuses on teacher preparation.

Chapter 10 provides national and comparative analyses as empirical tests of systemic alignment.

The progression moves from theory to architecture, from recognition to intervention, and from national context to comparative synthesis—culminating in the regional model articulated in Chap. 11.

2.9 Latin America as Analytical Lens

Latin America does not occupy the periphery of talent development theory; it clarifies its structural conditions.

In contexts where socioeconomic gradients remain pronounced, excellence cannot be abstracted from distributive justice. In systems marked by cultural and linguistic plurality, recognition cannot rely on singular epistemic norms. Where institutional capacity is uneven, innovation does not automatically scale. These conditions render visible what more resource-stable contexts can obscure: talent development is inseparable from opportunity architecture.

The region therefore functions as an analytical lens rather than an illustrative case. Its inequalities expose the mechanisms through which systems distribute learning capital. Its cultural plurality reveals the epistemic boundaries of dominant identification models. Its institutional fragmentation underscores the necessity of coherence. Its policy experiments and public initiatives demonstrate that systemic integration is possible, even under constraint.

Across Brazil, Chile, Colombia, Argentina, Peru, and other national contexts examined in this volume, a consistent pattern emerges: talent flourishes where ethical commitment, developmental ecosystems, cultural legitimacy, and institutional architecture converge. Where these elements remain misaligned, potential dissipates.

Latin America thus sharpens a broader theoretical proposition. Giftedness is not an attribute awaiting detection but a relational configuration sustained through coordinated systems. Excellence, in unequal societies, is neither accidental nor purely individual; it is structurally enabled.

The task that follows in Chap. 3 is not descriptive but architectural. The integrative model formalized there consolidates the four dimensions introduced in this chapter into a coherent regional framework. The argument of this book is cumulative: Latin America does not merely challenge existing paradigms of talent development. It compels their systemic reconfiguration.

In doing so, it clarifies the stakes of the field itself.

References

Alencar, E. M. L. S., & Fleith, D. S. (2007). *Desenvolvimento de talentos e altas habilidades*. Artmed.

Bellei, C. (2015). The private–public school controversy in Chile. *Journal of Educational Policy, 30*(4), 493–512.

Blumen, S. (2002). Effects of a teacher training workshop on creativity, cognition, and school achievement. *High Ability Studies, 13*(1), 47–58.

Blumen, S. (2021). Innovative practices to support high-achieving deprived young scholars in an ethnic-linguistic diverse Latin American country. In S. R. Smith (Ed.), *Handbook of giftedness and talent development in the Asia-Pacific* (pp. 223–238). Springer.

Brasil. (2008). *Política nacional de educação especial na perspectiva da educação inclusiva*. Ministério da Educação.

Castellanos, J., & Díaz, M. (2016). Percepciones docentes sobre estudiantes con altas capacidades en Colombia. *Revista Colombiana de Educación, 70*, 147–168.

CEPAL. (2022). *Panorama social de América Latina 2021*. Naciones Unidas.

Gagné, F. (2004). Transforming gifts into talents. *High Ability Studies, 15*(2), 119–147.

Gardner, H. (1983). *Frames of mind*. Basic Books.

Garvis, S., Windsor, S., & Pendergast, D. (2021). Gifted and talented aboriginal students in Australia. In S. R. Smith (Ed.), *Handbook of giftedness and talent development in the Asia-Pacific*. Springer.

OECD. (2019). *PISA 2018 results* (Vol. II). OECD.

Pérez, S. G. P. B., & Freitas, S. N. (2014). Políticas públicas para as altas habilidades/superdotação: Incluir ainda é preciso. *Revista Educação Especial, 27*(50), 627–640. https://doi.org/10.5902/1984686X14274

Pollitt, E. (2007). *Desnutrición, pobreza e inteligencia*. Universidad Ricardo Palma.

Renzulli, J. S. (1978). What makes giftedness? *Phi Delta Kappan, 60*(3), 180–184.

Sen, A. (1999). *Development as freedom*. Knopf.

Subotnik, R. F., Olszewski-Kubilius, P., & Worrell, F. C. (2011). Rethinking giftedness and gifted education. *Psychological Science in the Public Interest, 12*(1), 3–54.

Terman, L. M. (1925). *Genetic studies of genius: Vol. 1. Mental and physical traits of a thousand gifted children*. Stanford University Press.

Tubino, F. (2005). *Interculturalidad y educación*. Fondo Editorial PUCP.

Walsh, C. (2009). Interculturalidad crítica y educación intercultural. *Revista Educación y Pedagogía, 21*(55), 25–35.

Webber, M. (2018). The transformative role of tribal knowledge and genealogy in indigenous student success. In L. Smith & E. McKinley (Eds.), *Indigenous handbook of education*. Springer.

Ziegler, A. (2005). The actiotope model of giftedness. In R. J. Sternberg & J. E. Davidson (Eds.), *Conceptions of giftedness* (2nd ed., pp. 411–434). Cambridge University Press.

Chapter 3
Conceptual Frameworks: Giftedness in Cross-Cultural Contexts

3.1 From Analytical Lens to Structural Model

Chapter 2 positioned Latin America as an analytical lens through which the structural conditions of talent development become visible. This chapter formalizes the corresponding conceptual architecture. The problem is not whether giftedness is relational, but how relational emergence can be systematically apprehended and maintained in unequal and culturally plural societies.

Talent does not develop in a vacuum. It stabilizes where developmental ecosystems and distributive justice meet with epistemic legitimacy, along with institutional coherence. Where these dimensions have not aligned, this can fragment. The problem is structural rather than procedural, then. What is needed is not an incremental refinement of the program, but rather an integrated framework that can align development, equity, culture, and governance.

The Latin American Model of Talent Development (LAMTD) is proposed as such a framework. It does not replace existing theories. Rather, it reorganizes them within a relational architecture responsive to inequality, diversity, and institutional variability. Drawing from ecological systems theory, actiotopic perspectives, the capability approach, and decolonial scholarship, the model consolidates four interdependent dimensions:

- Developmental–ecological
- Equity–capability
- Epistemic–decolonial
- Policy–institutional architecture

These dimensions operate as a coherent system. Each constrains and stabilizes the others. Together, they define the structural conditions under which excellence becomes developmentally possible and socially legitimate.

S. Blumen, *High Ability and Talent Development in Latin America*,
https://doi.org/10.1007/978-3-032-27468-7_3

3.2 Foundational Perspectives

The field of gifted education has evolved from psychometric reductionism has shifted from psychometric reductionism to constructions of high ability that are multidimensional and developmental. Early models associated giftedness with high IQ tests and depended on standardized forms of measurement. Although such approaches produced methodological rigor, the theory provided little description of human potential. Subsequent theoretical developments expanded the construct to include cognitive, motivational, creative, and contextual dimensions. Among the most influential frameworks are Renzulli's Three-Ring Conception, Gagné's Differentiated Model of Giftedness and Talent (DMGT), Sternberg's contextual and integrative theories, and Ziegler's Actiotope Model. Collectively, these models mark a paradigm shift: giftedness is increasingly conceptualized as a dynamic configuration of abilities and possibilities unfolding over time rather than as a fixed individual attribute (Alencar & Fleith, 2016; Blumen, 2022; García-Cedillo & Romero-Contreras, 2014).

In Latin America, the reception of these theories has involved not only adoption but reinterpretation. Scholars and practitioners across the region have questioned such models, framing them for contextualization within the context of inequity, cultural diversity, and institutional differences. This translation and critique are part of a broader regional work that seeks to situate talent development within larger debates on equity, cultural diversity, and access to quality education.

3.2.1 Dominant Models of Giftedness and Talent Development

Renzulli's Three-Ring Conception

Renzulli's Three-Ring Conception (Renzulli, 1978, 2012) represents one of the most influential reconceptualizations of giftedness in the late twentieth century. By defining giftedness as the intersection of above-average ability, creativity, and task commitment, Renzulli expanded the construct beyond strictly cognitive definitions of intelligence, emphasizing motivational and creative engagement. This interactional perspective shifted attention from isolated traits to developmental potential.

Renzulli's model has had an important impact on enrichment-oriented practices and inclusive conceptualizations of high ability in Latin America. It has guided research and intervention programs in several countries (Alencar & Fleith, 2001; Blumen, 2013, 2016; García-Cepero, 2009; Virgolim, 2007), especially with creativity and engagement promoted as signs of potential. It has also influenced teacher training and leadership development around gifted education.

The Schoolwide Enrichment Model (SEM) (Renzulli & Reis, 2014) has been cited as a flexible framework for differentiated, interest-led learning in a variety of educational systems in Latin America (Arce-Saavedra & Blumen, 2022; Bendelman & Barrera, 2016; Wechsler et al., 2018). When standardized testing is limited in capturing different modes of ability, Renzulli's focus on creativity and engagement provides an alternative to those based solely on testing.

Gagné's Differentiated Model of Giftedness and Talent

Gagné's DMGT (Gagné, 2004) introduced a critical distinction between natural abilities ("gifts") and systematically developed competencies ("talents"). The model highlights developmental catalysts, both intrapersonal and environmental, that have the power to develop potential into performance. High achievement is thus seen as the outcome of a more complicated interplay between individual factors and situational settings.

The DMGT has also been appropriated in Latin American research to examine how socioeconomic inequities influence developmental trajectories (Blumen, 2021; Bendelman & Barrera, 2016; García-Cedillo & Romero-Contreras, 2014). Its concentration on environmental catalysts indicates the salience of opportunity structures in potential realization and can inform more textured identification practices, distinguishing between latent ability and observable performance.

Sternberg's Contextual and Integrative Perspectives

Sternberg's Triarchic Theory of Intelligence (Sternberg, 1985, 2005) extended the notion of intelligence to analytical, creative, and practical dimensions. Subsequent extensions with wisdom and socially responsible creativity added ethical and contextual competence to the giftedness construct (Sternberg, 2007).

These concepts resonate strongly with sociocultural traditions of the Latin American region. Scholars situated within cultural-historical frames stressed the relational, contextual dimension of intelligence and creativity (Mitjáns Martínez, 2008; Gonzáles Rey, 2011). Sternberg's emphasis on contextual adaptation thus aligns with regional perspectives that view high ability as culturally mediated and socially situated.

Ziegler's Actiotope Model

Ziegler's Actiotope Model (Ziegler, 2005; Ziegler & Baker, 2013) sees talent development as an adaptive optimization for behavior in a dynamic educational ecosystem. The model is based on developmental trajectories, resource coordination, and systemic adaptation over time rather than a focus on innate traits (Ziegler et al., 2017).

In the context of Latin America, this systemic orientation fits well with ongoing concerns over equity, institutional supports, and opportunity structures. The Actiotope Model has guided debates in Argentina, Brazil, and Chile about optimizing learning environments, as opposed to classifying gifted people as fixed cohorts. Its priority on resource coordination and long-term development provides an underpinning for developing paradigms of programming at the regional level.

Overall, the above overview indicates that although the predominant giftedness models focus on different dimensions, each contributes unique, relevant theoretical aspects to the development of giftedness—multidimensionality, developmental metamorphosis, contextualization, and systemic optimization.

To illustrate where they converge and diverge, Table 3.1 presents a comparative overview of the main frameworks presented, defining giftedness, developmental assumptions, the role of environmental conditions, and relevance in the context of Latin American contexts.

As shown in Table 3.1, these models, in combination, constitute a definitive move from static, psychometric typologies of high ability to developmental and contextualized accounts. Simultaneously, the conceptual origins of this framework, grounded in the traditions of the Global North, inform the need to interrogate how these assumptions manifest in various sociocultural contexts. This comparative overview becomes the basis of the critical cross-cultural analysis that I will subsequently conduct.

Table 3.1 Comparative overview of dominant theories of giftedness

Theoretical model	Core definition of giftedness	Developmental emphasis	View of environment	Relevance in Latin American contexts
Renzulli's Three-Ring Conception of Giftedness (Renzulli, 1978, 2012)	Intersection of above-average ability, creativity, and task commitment	Emphasizes interaction among traits; highlights developmental potential	Context enables expression of creativity and engagement	Influential in enrichment models (SEM); supports broader identification beyond IQ; widely adopted in Brazil, Peru, Colombia
Gagné's DMGT (Gagné, 2004)	Distinction between natural abilities ("gifts") and systematically developed competencies ("talents")	Strong developmental transformation focus	Environmental and intrapersonal catalysts transform potential into performance	Useful for analyzing inequality in opportunity structures; distinguishes potential from achievement in unequal systems
Sternberg's Triarchic and Integrative theories (Sternberg, 1985, 2005, 2007)	Analytical, creative, and practical intelligence; later integrates wisdom	Intelligence as adaptive and context-sensitive	Context shapes adaptive intelligence and socially responsible competence	Resonates with sociocultural traditions emphasizing relational and community-based competence
Ziegler's Actiotope Model (Ziegler, 2005; Ziegler & Baker, 2013)	Talent as adaptive optimization within learning ecosystems	Emphasis on developmental trajectories over time	Continuous interaction between individual and systemic learning resources	Aligns with systemic reform approaches; shifts focus from identification to ecosystem optimization

3.2.2 *Convergences across Models*

Despite theoretical differences, these paradigms converge on several key principles:

1. Giftedness is multidimensional, incorporating cognitive, creative, and motivational components (Alencar & Fleith, 2016; Blumen, 2021).
2. The realization of potential depends on environmental support and access to opportunities (Arancibia & Betancourt, 2010).
3. Identification should move beyond reliance on a single score toward more holistic assessment frameworks.

These convergences provide conceptual space for context-sensitive interpretations. Yet their diffusion into Latin American contexts reveals tensions based on epistemological assumptions that need to be critically addressed.

3.3 Critical and Cross-Cultural Analysis

While the major theories on giftedness have substantially enriched the field's conceptual repertoire, they are nevertheless attached to existing historical and cultural traditions. Most dominant concepts of intelligence, talent, and achievement were developed largely within Western educational systems reflecting industrialization, meritocratic norms, and psychometric paradigms (Subotnik et al., 2011; Sternberg & Ambrose, 2021). Thus, they embody normative definitions about what is considered excellence, how it should be evaluated, and what is intended for educational systems to promote.

The persistence of these hierarchies can be examined through Quijano's (2007) concept of the *coloniality of power*, which describes how knowledge production remains structured by Eurocentric epistemic dominance. Within gifted education, this phenomenon is evident as intelligence is perceived in relation to decontextualized psychometric standards, which tend to marginalize relational, communal, and place-based forms of cognitive processing. Recognition of this pedagogical inheritance is crucial in the recontextualization of high ability in Latin American settings.

3.3.1 *Epistemological Assumptions in Western Conceptions*

From a cross-cultural point of view, dominant models introduce tacit assumptions about what competence is, the appreciation of excellence, and the privileging of educational outcomes. These do not align with the realities of Latin American educational systems, with their social gaps, language diversity, and multiple knowledge traditions.

Regional academia, therefore, encourages a critical reflexivity toward dominant models—not to reject them, but to question how they can privilege certain knowledge and performance, and suppress others (Blumen, 2021; García-Cedillo & Romero-Contreras, 2014).

Three assumptions are particularly salient:

1. Individualism and meritocracy
2. Psychometric standardization
3. Academic achievement as a primary indicator of potential

Individualism and Meritocracy

Many influential models of giftedness have framed it as an individual trait manifest in exceptional performance and distinction (Renzulli, 1978; Gagné, 2004). It is a broader, meritocratic disposition embedded in Western schooling, where systems are structured for the identification and cultivation of high-performance individuals.

Although such strategies further solidified identification procedures and specialized programming, cross-cultural studies support the notion that notions of ability are not universally applicable. Within a variety of Latin American settings, giftedness is conceptualized as part of a continuum associated with giving back to the community and the well-being of the group and social leadership in general (Mitjáns Martínez, 2008). Competitive, individualistic educational environments risk overlooking the competencies in working with others, ethical practice, culturally grounded expertise, and competencies important in many Latin American cultures.

Measurement Paradigms and Standardization

A hallmark of Western gifted education has been focusing on psychometric testing. Standardized tests helped scientific consolidation in this domain of this area because they provided objective and comparable measures of success and failure (Pfeiffer, 2012). This reliance is epistemological in nature: complex abilities can be empirically evaluated, and normed on, across settings. But multicultural studies have repeatedly pointed out the fallibility of this contention. The development of tools in assessment is contextualized by linguistic and cultural environments. If used in different populations, they can introduce bias and distorted perception (Ford, 2013). Test scores might reflect language proficiency as significantly as cognitive ability in multilingual settings.

These worries have prompted demands for more holistic models of identification that use a range of means of obtaining evidence and culturally adapted indicators of potential (Callahan & Hertberg-Davis, 2013).

The Achievement Orientation

High academic performance is often considered evidence of high ability. In unequal systems, however, performance is an outcome of opportunity accrual. Peters et al. (2019) explain that under-identification of marginalized students often results from structural constraints rather than a lack of potential. These assumptions determine who gets identification and access and why, which situates their careful scrutiny at the forefront rather than at the margin.

Research suggests that academic performance is influenced by more than individual variables; socioeconomic status, school quality, and access to enrichment also influence students' performance (Peters et al., 2019). For Latin America, with a wide range of educational quality, performance-based identification risks systematically underestimating students from disadvantaged communities. Such findings highlight an essential shift from static evaluation metrics to developmental models that differentiate between achievement realized and latent potential.

Implications of Epistemological Assumptions

These epistemological assumptions—individualism, standardization, achievement orientation, and universalism—do not work as empirical conditions alone; they also function as structuring principles within educational systems. Their influence is more prominent in those environments characterized by social inequality and cultural plurality. Table 3.2 integrates these assumptions and describes their cross-cultural implications in the context of Latin America.

The synthesis provided in Table 3.2 explains how dominant understandings of giftedness can unwittingly replicate structural and epistemic inequities when not framed and contextualized. To understand these tensions is not to dismiss these theories, but to re-read them, considering systems oriented around distributive justice and cultural legitimacy. This awareness paves the way for an investigation into these dynamics in different sociocultural contexts in Latin America.

The following section explores how these assumptions operate within Latin American sociocultural contexts.

3.4 Limitations in Diverse Sociocultural Contexts

Empirical research in Latin America has confirmed the existing disparities in access and recognition. Research in Colombia, Chile, Mexico, Guatemala, Panama, and Peru studies patterns of under-identification which stem from the economic disparities in school and living standards (García-Cepero, 2009; Arancibia & Betancourt, 2010; Sánchez-Escobedo et al., 2021; OECD, 2023; Blumen, 2021).

Language diversity also complicates assessment practices. Within their own communities, students may show advanced skills but still find their faces invisible in standardized systems (Blumen, 2021).

These findings underscore that talent development must be analyzed within structural and cultural contexts rather than as isolated individual variance.

Table 3.2 Epistemological assumptions in dominant giftedness frameworks and cross-cultural implications

Epistemological assumption	Description in Global North traditions	Cross-cultural tension in Latin America	Structural implications
Individualism and meritocracy	Giftedness as individual distinction and exceptional performance	Ability often conceptualized relationally; emphasis on community contribution and leadership	Risk of privileging competitive, individual achievement over collaborative and culturally embedded competencies
Psychometric standardization	Intelligence measurable through norm-referenced testing	Linguistic diversity and culturally specific reasoning patterns may not align with standardized tools	Potential bias in identification; under-recognition of multilingual and indigenous learners
Achievement as proxy for potential	Academic performance equated with high ability	Educational quality varies widely; achievement reflects opportunity distribution	Under-identification of students from socioeconomically disadvantaged backgrounds
Universalism of excellence criteria	Assumes culturally neutral definitions of intelligence and creativity	Coexistence of multiple epistemologies; indigenous and community-based knowledge systems	Necessitates epistemic pluralization and culturally responsive assessment

3.4.1 Under-Identification and Structural Inequality

Under-identification of students coming from marginalized communities remains on a global level. Socioeconomic disadvantage determines early exposure to education, exposure to enrichment, and quality of education; all of which impact how visible high potential is (Callahan & Hertberg-Davis, 2013).

Research in Colombia indicates that identification tends to favor academic evidence related to access to resources. Hence, it can easily overlook students whose potential does not show up immediately on standardized assessment performance (García-Cepero, 2009). Chilean studies show that, due to early differences in school quality, later identification outcomes are affected (Arancibia & Betancourt, 2010). In Guatemala, poverty, linguistic diversity, and unequal school quality mean that high ability cannot get recognized (Cruz Grunebaum et al., 2025).

Similarly, a study in Mexico shows an excessive concentration of gifted programs in metropolises with more educational facilities than rural and Indigenous populations (Sánchez-Escobedo et al., 2021). Economic and regional disparities are key to accessing specialized education in Panama (OECD, 2023). In Peru, we find evidence that structural limitations shape the expression of creativity and ability among high performers from low-income families (Blumen, 2021).

Across contexts, identification often reflects opportunity distribution rather than ability distribution (Peters et al., 2019; Ford, 2013). Recognizing under-identification as structural rather than individual reframes the challenge and directs attention toward institutional reform.

3.4.2 Language, Culture, and Recognition

Language diversity has a large impact on identification. In multilingual contexts, assessment practices, not surprisingly, often miss out on culturally dependent reasoning and expression. In their culture, students might show impressive skills but remain invisible in the mainstream in schools (Blumen, 2021; García-Cedillo & Romero-Contreras, 2014).

Cultural values also shape definitions of excellence. Brazilian scholarship emphasizes creativity, social responsibility, and interpersonal sensitivity as key dimensions of giftedness (Alencar & Fleith, 2001; Mitjáns Martínez, 2008). In Andean communities, communal orientation and leadership may take precedence over individual academic achievement (Blumen, 2021; Arancibia & Betancourt, 2010).

These findings reinforce the need for culturally responsive frameworks capable of recognizing diverse manifestations of talent.

3.4.3 Tensions between Universalism and Contextualism

The worldwide dissemination of giftedness models creates tension between world-historical models and grounded realities relative to their settings. But while theory-filling and coherence are required, the rigor of application can obscure local identities and structural constraints.

Latin American scholarship increasingly advocates for hybrid approaches that marry international theoretical progress with notions grounded locally. Instead of dismissing universal models, scholars explore them through context-sensitive interpretations that balance theoretical and cultural.

3.4.4 Toward Contextually Responsive Approaches

The limitations identified in the preceding analysis point toward highlight the need for a context-responsive approach for gifted education. Contextualizing conceptual frameworks for teaching in homogenized and racially-biased contexts when used within a more homogeneous resource-biased system of learning should be analyzed and adapted as necessary for different contexts where language plurality and differences, inequality, and difference have their own particularities.

In Latin America, education is situated within multilayered social systems that combine poverty, regional disparities, and historical marginalization in shaping the opportunities available. Giftedness can thus not simply be viewed as a result of individual characteristics alone, and it cannot be understood as a socially ingrained phenomenon that takes place in the sites of opportunity systems and cultural meanings (Subotnik et al., 2011; Ford, 2013; García-Cedillo & Romero-Contreras, 2014; Blumen, 2021).

Contextually responsive approaches do not reject established theoretical models. Rather, they engage them dialogically. They preserve the developmental insights of frameworks such as Renzulli's interactional model, Gagné's transformational processes, Sternberg's contextual intelligence, and Ziegler's systemic adaptation, while simultaneously interrogating their implicit normative assumptions. Such approaches seek theoretical coherence alongside cultural sensitivity.

In this orientation, gifted education constitutes a locus of structural alignment: developmental processes should harmonize with distributive justice and epistemic recognition. Hence, contextual responsiveness provides a conceptual link between the diagnosis at the critical level and the design at the integrative level that lays the groundwork for the Latin American points of view presented in the next section.

3.5 Latin American Perspectives

In regional scholarship, giftedness has been conceptualized as socially embedded and culturally mediated. Usually, talent is conceptualized as a resource from the community, not just about what it is: personal distinction. Creativity, resilience, and leadership can frequently be found under situations of vulnerability (Blumen, 2021, 2022).

Intercultural scholarship emphasizes plural knowledge systems (Walsh, 2010; Bevan-Brown, 2011), enlarging definitions beyond just academic performance. These points of view are helpful for a locally informed understanding that brings excellence along with equity.

3.5.1 Giftedness and Social Transformation

From these standpoints, talent development becomes a solution for ending structural social injustice. Enrichment programs, teacher training programs, and teacher trainings suggest how the expansion of access can support social mobility.

Research in Peru has shown that giftedness varies based on cultural attitudes and adaptive skills, acquired in the context of high-performing young people's conditions of vulnerability, especially by those living in the Andes and Amazon. As these findings serve as confirmatory evidence, talent development should be equity and culturally appropriate.

3.5.2 Historical and Policy Trajectories

Early initiatives developed to train gifted Latin American children tended to replicate psychometric traditions for urban elites. But policy discourses have evolved toward an inclusion-focused conceptualization of development (Wechsler et al., 2018).

International inclusive education movements have had an impact on national policies, as their implementation is also uneven because of resource limitations and a lack of ready teacher preparedness.

3.5.3 Emerging Regional Conceptualizations

Regional scholars are progressively focused on relational conceptions of ability (Mitjáns Martínez, 2008; Alencar & Fleith, 2016). The themes of resilience under duress, culture-based creativity, and community-based capacity building recognize competence.

Further to this, indigenous and intercultural perspectives build on this construct, stressing relational intelligence, spiritual knowledge, and ecological expertise (Bevan-Brown, 2011; Walsh, 2010).

Together, these perspectives position giftedness as socially embedded and culturally mediated.

Collective and Community-Oriented Notions of Talent

Across several Latin American contexts, talent is not understood as an inherent characteristic but rather as a socially constructed quality situated in community life. Studies from sociocultural approaches suggest that high ability is often linked with leadership traits, cultural stewardship, and ethical behavior, not only with academic excellence (Mitjáns Martínez, 2008).

In settings where community life, rather than competitive edge and conformity, is the value indicator, giftedness can be acknowledged in terms of its support of collective resilience, local problem-solving, and its contribution to moral duty to collective objects. These orientations resist simple meritocratic assessments of excellence and broaden the scope of what constitutes the field.

These community-oriented notions of talent do not diminish intellectual rigor; rather, they contextualize it. They situate cognitive strengths within relational and ethical frameworks, thereby integrating personal development with social responsibility. In doing so, they illuminate how cultural values shape both the recognition and expression of high potential.

Creativity, Resilience, and Adaptive Intelligence

Regional scholarship often shows that talent appears when social and economic conditions are less favorable. As in poverty, migration, or institutional uncertainty, high potential may be conveyed through coping mechanisms in adaptive problem solving, motivational persistence, and creative ways of living in restricted surroundings, as well as creative maneuvering of constrained spaces (Blumen, 2021).

Creativity, in these settings, is not merely aesthetic production, but a mechanism of survival and transformation. Resilience emerges as a developmental outcome between individual dispositions and structural adversity. These results are in line with developmental models that view giftedness as dynamic and locally influenced (Gagné, 2004; Ziegler, 2005).

Considering resilience and adaptive intelligence as dimensions of high potential extends the evaluative lens beyond conventional academic indicators. It underscores that excellence may emerge through nonlinear pathways and that structural disadvantage does not preclude advanced capability.

Intercultural and Indigenous Perspectives

Recent academic scholarship has focused on the need to integrate cross-cultural and Indigenous epistemologies into giftedness discussions. In pluralistic cultures, there exist multiple ways of knowing, with different criteria for how to define competence and excellence (Walsh, 2010; Bevan-Brown, 2011).

Indigenous understandings of ability typically prioritize relational intelligence, ecological knowledge, spiritual insights, and practical competence based on community living. These epistemologies call into question the claim that academic achievement is the most important marker of high potential.

Engaging students from each culture's perspective requires more than the inclusion of diverse pupils in the current norms; it requires scrutiny of the norms themselves. By acknowledging epistemic plurality, gifted education can move toward broader, culturally grounded definitions of excellence that honor diverse knowledge traditions.

3.5.4 Toward a Regionally Grounded Understanding

Taken together, these strands of scholarship signal an important conceptual evolution. Giftedness in Latin America is increasingly understood as socially embedded, culturally mediated, and structurally situated. This understanding does not discard global theoretical contributions; rather, it reframes them within regional realities marked by inequality, diversity, and historical complexity.

A regionally grounded perspective integrates developmental insight with distributive justice and epistemic pluralization. It recognizes that talent development cannot be separated from educational reform efforts aimed at expanding access and improving quality.

This conceptual shift lays the groundwork for the integrative framework developed later in the chapter. By situating giftedness at the intersection of developmental processes, opportunity structures, and cultural legitimacy, the chapter moves beyond adaptation toward theoretical reorientation.

3.6 Toward a Culturally Responsive Understanding

A key understanding that emerges from attempts at culturally responsive accounts of giftedness is that high ability is not something that can be separated from the cultural, social, and historical contexts where we learn to conceptualize it. As knowledge of talent development has burgeoned internationally, frameworks that acknowledge cultural diversity and structural inequities as constitutive—not secondary—dimensions of giftedness have received attention and support (Ford, 2013; Sternberg, 2007). And it has especially accelerated in Latin America.

On the global stage, the literature on giftedness has matured, and there is an increasing number of scholarly attempts to make a distinction. Academics and educators contend that high potential is not easily pinned to standardized measures of performance. Instead, it needs to be seen as being embedded in students' abilities to become contributors to their communities, fit into new settings, adapt, and creatively understand and interact within them. This perspective is consistent with the broader movements in education, which locate inclusion as an aspect of social justice.

A culturally responsive lens, then, challenges us to think about gifted education not merely as recognizing special individuals but rather as a tool for facilitating access to enriching opportunities for students from diverse backgrounds. It provides the conceptual foundation for equity-oriented frameworks capable of addressing structural disparities while sustaining high standards of excellence.

3.6.1 Guiding Principles for Equity-Oriented Frameworks

Models based on cross-cultural research and regional literature: various themes frequently appear as guiding principles for conceptualizing giftedness within multicultural settings. Such principles are not abstract formulas but analytic supports to the theoretical and applied development.

Multidimensionality of Talent

Giftedness is intrinsically multidimensional. It comprises intellectual, creative, socio-emotional, and motivational dimensions and is not just one kind of cognitive quality (Renzulli, 1978; Sternberg, 2005). Multidimensionality is especially important in culturally diverse contexts where high potentials do not always measure up to conventional academic metrics.

Regional research on creativity, leadership, and social commitment demonstrates that broader definitions of talent better capture the complexity of human potential across sociocultural environments.

Developmental and Dynamic Perspectives

Giftedness must be understood as developmental rather than fixed. As a result of the interplay of inherent dispositions, learning experiences, and context-bound supports over time, high ability develops (Gagné, 2004; Olszewski-Kubilius & Thomson, 2015). Such developmental viewpoints move from a viewpoint where the focus is on person types to those that lead to supportive growth pathways.

Notably, in situations of less access to opportunity, this orientation is especially applicable. Potential could be dormant unless nurtured in supportive ecosystems (Blumen, 2021; Ziegler, 2005; Ziegler & Baker, 2013).

Contextual Embeddedness

Abilities are embedded in contextually interconnected cultural systems (Bronfenbrenner, 1979; Bronfenbrenner & Morris, 2006). Expectations, resources, and developmental pathways are shaped by family, school, community, and policy contexts. A study of Peruvian students studying at state-run residential academies shows that mastery-oriented and incremental approaches to intelligence predict academic resilience among adolescents from ethnic-linguistic minority backgrounds (Blumen, 2021). These findings highlight that performance is a function of the dynamic interaction of person and environment, and not individual traits in isolation. Contextual embeddedness also guards against deficit interpretations by situating underperformance within structural constraints.

Equity and Social Justice

Equity is an organizing principle in culturally responsive frameworks. Gifted education has long been criticized for replicating social inequality (Ford, 2013). It is imperative that identification and programming practices shift over the long-term to make developmental opportunities meaningful: Addressing these imbalances will require a rethinking of both methods employed in practice in order to increase access to such opportunities. This approach serves as a normative basis for this work (Sen, 1999; Nussbaum, 2011).

The capability lens reframes education as the enlargement of genuine freedoms to chase desired ends, changing the focus from placing a label on individuals to changing opportunity systems (Walker & Unterhalter, 2007). This framework emphasizes talent development as a part of broader social inclusion goals with the support of Latin American contexts (Blumen, 2021).

Recognition of Multiple Pathways to Excellence

Excellence may emerge through varied developmental routes. Students might have a lot of potential for creative production or community engagement as well as imaginative problem solving, in addition to academic performance (Sternberg, 2007). Multistep pathways disrupt hierarchical norms and value diversity in learning and contribute to an inclusive learning organization accepting all forms of contribution. Students may demonstrate high potential through creative production, community leadership, or innovative problem-solving, in addition to academic performance (Sternberg, 2007). Acknowledging multiple pathways challenges hierarchical definitions of ability and promotes inclusive educational environments that value diverse forms of contribution.

The guiding principles outlined above—multidimensionality, developmental dynamism, contextual embeddedness, equity orientation, recognition of multiple pathways, and epistemic pluralization—form the normative and analytic core of culturally responsive talent development. To consolidate these principles and clarify their theoretical roots and educational implications, Table 3.3 presents a structured synthesis.

As Table 3.3 illustrates, equity-oriented frameworks do not dilute standards of excellence but expand the conceptual boundaries within which excellence is recognized and cultivated. These principles form the basis for the integrative framework introduced in the following section, in which ecological, capability-based, and decolonial perspectives are systematically engaged in dialogue.

3.6.2 From Principles to Frameworks

Taken together, these principles serve as a scaffold for reconfiguring giftedness as multidimensional, developmental, and contextual. They also inform the integrative lens detailed in the next section in integrating ecological, capability, and decolonial perspectives into a coherent model of talent development in Latin America.

Table 3.3 Guiding principles for equity-oriented and culturally responsive frameworks

Guiding principle	Theoretical roots	Core concept	Implications for gifted education
Multidimensionality of talent	Renzulli (1978); Sternberg (2005); sociocultural psychology	Ability includes cognitive, creative, motivational, socio-emotional dimensions	Identification must move beyond single-score metrics
Developmental dynamism	Gagné (2004); Ziegler & Baker (2013); talent development research	Giftedness unfolds over time through interaction with catalysts	Focus on growth trajectories rather than fixed labels
Contextual embeddedness	Bronfenbrenner (1979); Ziegler (2005); actiotope model	Talent emerges within nested sociocultural systems	Policies must address systemic supports and barriers
Equity and capability expansion	Nussbaum (2011); Sen (1999); Walker & Unterhalter (2007)	Education expands real freedoms to develop valued capabilities	Shift from selection to opportunity expansion
Recognition of multiple pathways	Sternberg (2007); intercultural scholarship	Excellence manifests through varied developmental routes	Programs should value creative, communal, and adaptive expressions of ability
Epistemic pluralization	Mignolo (2011); Quijano (2007); Santos (2014); Walsh (2010)	Recognition of diverse knowledge systems	Critical reflection on dominant standards of excellence

3.7 A Culturally Responsive Model of Giftedness in Latin America

The framework advanced in this chapter responds to a central gap in existing literature, as no theoretical model has sufficiently integrated developmental mechanisms, distributive justice, and epistemic plurality in structural inequities contexts (Subotnik et al., 2011; García-Cedillo & Romero-Contreras, 2014).

Developmental theories highlight processes of learning but may not fully capture systemic inequities. Theories based on equity emphasize spreading opportunity, but do not fully examine cultural presuppositions about being excellent. According to sociocultural explanations, meaning is contextualized but may not have explicit normative bases for justice. The integrative model proposed here holds that giftedness is all developmental, distributive, and epistemic (Blumen, 2021; Sternberg, 2007).

3.7.1 *Ecological Foundations: Giftedness as Relational Development*

Ecological theory views giftedness development as embedded within multiple levels of interaction (Bronfenbrenner & Morris, 2006). Great talent is developed through ongoing interactions between people and their environments, such as families, schools, peer networks, and policy settings. By contrast, this approach disrupts individualistic ideas of success or failure.

It is particularly relevant in Latin American contexts that suffer from uneven school quality and access. It reframes "the other side of giftedness" as something that emerges from one person's interaction with the environment rather than a fixed trait that people inherit.

3.7.2 *The Capability Perspective: Giftedness as Freedom*

While ecological analysis clarifies developmental mechanisms, it does not independently provide normative criteria for justice. The capability approach responds to this dimension by reimagining giftedness in terms of the genuine freedom for individuals to cultivate and use their capacities (Sen, 1999; Nussbaum, 2011).

In structurally unequal societies, the achievement that is visibly marked can hardly be observed without other opportunity structures. School quality, access to enrichment, and social capital influence trajectories long before people are formally assigned one. Giftedness is not reducible to high performance under a capability lens. It is indivisible from the social conditions that make possible the turning of possibility into productive result (Walker & Unterhalter, 2007).

A prime example of this is the Peruvian COAR model. Residential academies for high-performing children from economically disadvantaged backgrounds as equalizing institutions (Blumen, 2021; Ministerio de Educación, 2014) that can open opportunities and foster democratic civic responsibilities.

In this sense, gifted education becomes an instrument of distributive justice rather than elite reproduction.

3.7.3 *Decolonial Sensibility: Epistemic Pluralization*

Ecological and capability frameworks take up the issue of development and distribution but do not thoroughly question our notions of how epistemic authority operates. Decolonial scholarship studies how dominant knowledge systems create the meanings of intelligence and how these definitions are molded (Quijano, 2007; Mignolo, 2011; Santos, 2014).

Westernized notions of giftedness privilege analytic thought and standardized performance. Despite, that said, legitimate according to specific traditions, these characteristics cannot be assumed to be universally neutral. In contexts of cultural plurality in Latin America, Indigenous and community-based epistemologies exist alongside formal schooling systems. Cultural understandings of ability may emphasise relational intelligence, ecological knowledge, and shared responsibility (Walsh, 2010; Blumen, 2021).

The integration of these perspectives brings about an enlargement of the epistemic limits of gifted education. In this chapter, the integrative model rests on the articulation of the interdependent dimensions of development, opportunity, and epistemic legitimacy. Instead of being autonomous, these dimensions are co-regulating elements of cohesive architecture.

Table 3.4 presents the main components of the Latin American Model of Talent Development (LAMTD), along with its theoretical underpinnings, guiding questions, and policy and practice implications.

The structured presentation in Table 3.4 makes explicit the integrative logic of the LAMTD framework. By aligning developmental mechanisms, distributive justice, epistemic recognition, and institutional sustainability, the model advances a reorientation of gifted education from isolated identification toward systemic cultivation. This integrative logic reframes the field around four interrelated questions: how talent develops, who has a genuine opportunity to develop it, according to whose criteria it is recognized, and how can talent development be sustained through coherent policies and institutions.

Decolonial analysis ensures that inclusion does not merely incorporate marginalized learners into pre-existing standards but critically examines those standards themselves.

Table 3.4 Integrative dimensions of the Latin American model of talent development (LAMTD)

Dimension	Theoretical foundation	Central question	Policy and practice implication
Developmental–ecological	Bronfenbrenner (1979); Ziegler & Baker (2013)	How does talent develop?	Strengthen ecosystems: Schools, families, enrichment systems
Equity–capability	Nussbaum (2011); Sen (1999)	Who has genuine opportunity to develop?	Expand access to high-quality educational resources
Epistemic–Decolonial	Mignolo (2011); Quijano (2007); Santos (2014); Walsh (2010)	According to whose criteria is talent recognized?	Incorporate plural epistemologies; culturally responsive assessment
Policy–institutional architecture	Systems theory; regional policy analysis	How can talent development be sustained structurally?	Institutional coherence and scalability (e.g., COAR model)

3.7.4 Integrative Logic of the Framework

The framework therefore consists of four interdependent dimensions:

1. **Developmental–Ecological**: Explains how talent emerges through dynamic person–environment interaction.
2. **Equity–Capability**: Addresses distributive justice and expansion of real freedoms.
3. **Epistemic–Decolonial**: Interrogates cultural authority and affirms plural knowledge systems. **4. Policy–Institutional Architecture**: Examines the governance structures, educational policies, institutional capacities, and resource systems required to sustain talent development at scale and over time.

Individually, each dimension offers only a partial understanding of giftedness. Integrated, they provide a comprehensive account of giftedness as developmental, structurally mediated, culturally situated, and institutionally sustained.

This integrative logic reframes gifted education around four foundational questions:

- How does talent develop?
- Who has a genuine opportunity to develop it?
- According to whose criteria is it recognized?
- How can talent development be sustained through coherent policies and institutions?

Addressing these questions simultaneously enables a shift from adaptation of imported models toward contextually grounded theoretical reorientation that aligns developmental excellence, social equity, cultural legitimacy, and institutional sustainability.

3.7.5 Implications for Research and Practice

Research should examine multilevel interactions rather than isolated traits. Identification practices must incorporate culturally responsive indicators and attend to developmental trajectories in addition to current performance (Olszewski-Kubilius & Thomson, 2015; García-Cedillo & Romero-Contreras, 2014).

Policy should prioritize the expansion of enriched learning environments for historically marginalized populations. Talent development must be understood as a collective responsibility involving families, schools, communities, and policymakers.

3.8 Regional Knowledge Base: Latin American Contributions

Latin American research on giftedness has expanded considerably, producing a body of scholarship that both engages international theories and articulates contextually grounded perspectives. Theme areas include sociocultural mediation, equity, creativity, subjective development, and systemic reform.

3.8.1 Historical Development and Regional Agendas

Early regional initiatives were frequently in the patterns and practices of North American psychometric methodologies. Over time, this method has been challenged by scholars in the sphere of inequality and linguistic pluralism.

Policy analyses capture enduring inequality of access and identify more inclusive identification processes that correspond to inclusive education reforms (Arancibia & Betancourt, 2010; García-Cedillo & Romero-Contreras, 2014).

3.8.2 Sociocultural and Systemic Perspectives

Regional scholarship highlights that talent development occurs within structures of the family system, educational institutions, and social inequalities (Alencar & Fleith, 2016; Virgolim, 2007). This systemic orientation mirrors wide-ranging educational equity movements.

3.8.3 Creativity, Subjectivity, and Human Development

The sociocultural psychological literature points to the relational, subjective aspects of high potential (Mitjáns Martínez, 2008; Gonzáles Rey, 2011). Creativity is seen to be woven with identity, motivation, and cultural meaning systems.

3.8.4 Inclusion, Diversity, and Educational Opportunity

Research has consistently documented under-identification of marginalized students and offers support for culturally responsive assessment approaches (Bendelman & Barrera, 2016; Wechsler et al., 2018). Talent development requires not only aptitude, but access to conditions that nurture it.

3.8.5 Intercultural and Critical Approaches

Intercultural education scholars urge redefining giftedness to have broader meanings that emphasize community-oriented competencies and collective well-being (Walsh, 2010). Such perspectives are in keeping with decolonial voices' demands for epistemic pluralization.

3.8.6 Implications for Conceptual Frameworks

Regional scholarship echoes three common themes: contextual centrality, equity as structural necessity, and multidimensional notions of ability. They deepen global arguments and provide a justification for frameworks sensitive to the cultural and socioeconomic diversity in Latin America.

3.9 Concluding Remarks

This chapter has proposed a culturally responsive reconceptualization of giftedness considering the Latin American context. By integrating ecological theory, capability ethics, and decolonial analysis, it reframes talent as developmental, opportunity-dependent, and culturally situated.

Gifted education then emerges not merely as a way of identifying those who are exceptional but as a disciplined pledge of increased freedoms, acceptance of polyvalent knowledge systems, and a dedication to quality education in the face of justice.

This integrative framework provides the theoretical foundation for subsequent chapters, enabling systematic analysis of identification, curriculum, acceleration, teacher preparation, and policy architectures within the region.

References

Alencar, E. M. L. S., & Fleith, D. S. (2001). *Superdotação: Determinantes, educação e ajustamento*. EPU.

Alencar, E. M. L. S., & Fleith, D. S. (2016). Creativity and giftedness in Brazil: A systemic perspective. *Gifted Education International, 32*(3), 207–222. https://doi.org/10.1177/0261429416640336

Arancibia, V., & Betancourt, M. (2010). High abilities in Latin America: Challenges and perspectives. *Revista Latinoamericana de Psicología, 42*(2), 251–265.

Arce-Saavedra, B. J., & Blumen, S. (2022). Pensamiento crítico, creatividad, autoeficacia y práctica pedagógica en formadores de docentes peruanos. *Revista De Psicología, 40*(1), 603–633. https://doi.org/10.18800/psico.202201.020

Bendelman, K., & Barrera, S. G. P. (2016). Altas habilidades/superdotação: O que acontece na América Latina? *Revista Educação e Políticas em Debate, 5*(2), 210–224. https://seer.ufu.br/index.php/revistaeducaopoliticas/article/view/45391

Bevan-Brown, J. (2011). Indigenous conceptions of giftedness. In W. Vialle (Ed.), *Giftedness from an indigenous perspective*. https://irp.cdn-website.com/2d95ae4a/files/uploaded/02%20Indig.pdf

Blumen, S. (2013). New trends in talent development in Peru. *Journal for the Education of the Gifted, 36*(3), 346–364.

Blumen, S. (2016). Gifted education programming: Serving the native Peruvian. In B. Wallace & D. A. White (Eds.), *Gifted children of color around the world* (pp. 1–15). Emerald.

Blumen, S. (2021). Talent development, cultural diversity, and equity: The challenge of the Andean countries. In R. J. Sternberg & D. Ambrose (Eds.), *Conceptions of giftedness and talent*. Cambridge University Press.

Blumen, S. (2022). Talent development with equity: A turning point in social change. In *The Palgrave handbook of global social change*. Palgrave Macmillan. https://doi.org/10.1007/978-3-030-87624-1_132-1

Bronfenbrenner, U. (1979). *The ecology of human development: Experiments by nature and design*. Harvard University Press.

Bronfenbrenner, U., & Morris, P. A. (2006). The bioecological model of human development. In R. M. Lerner (Ed.), *Handbook of child psychology* (Vol. 1, 6th ed., pp. 793–828). Wiley.

Callahan, C. M., & Hertberg-Davis, H. (2013). *Fundamentals of gifted education*. Routledge.

Cruz Grunebaum, A. A., Rojas Sandoval, K. R., Maldonado Bode, S. V., Gove, A., & Johnson Oliva, J. E. (2025). *Teacher researchers in Guatemala: Lessons from an action research experience to address educational gaps in the classroom*. RTI Press. https://doi.org/10.3768/rtipress.2025.op.0094.2501

de Sousa Santos, B. (2014). *Epistemologies of the South: Justice against epistemicide*. Routledge.

Ford, D. Y. (2013). *Multicultural gifted education*. Prufrock Press.

Gagné, F. (2004). Transforming gifts into talents: The DMGT as a developmental theory. *High Ability Studies, 15*(2), 119–147.

García-Cedillo, I., & Romero-Contreras, S. (2014). Gifted education in Latin America. In S. Phillipson, H. Stoeger, & A. Ziegler (Eds.), *Exceptionality in East Asia and Latin America*. Routledge.

García-Cepero, M. C. (2009). Talent development in Colombian educational contexts. *Revista Colombiana de Psicología*.

Gonzáles Rey, F. L. (2011). Lenguaje, sentido y subjetividad: yendo más allá del lenguaje y el comportamiento. *Estudos de Psicologia, 21*(3), 345–357. ISSN-e 1579-3699.

Mignolo, W. D. (2011). *The darker side of Western modernity: Global futures, decolonial options*. Duke University Press.

Ministerio de Educación del Perú. (2014). *Modelo educativo: Colegios de Alto Rendimiento (COAR)*.

Mitjáns Martínez, A. (2008). Creativity as a cultural and subjective process. *Culture & Psychology, 14*(3), 305–326.

Nussbaum, M. (2011). *Creating capabilities: The human development approach*. Harvard University Press.

OECD. (2023). *PISA 2022 results: Panama country note*. OECD.

Olszewski-Kubilius, P., & Thomson, D. (2015). Talent development as a framework for gifted education. *Gifted Child Quarterly, 59*(3), 143–154.

Peters, S. J., Gentry, M., Whiting, G. W., & McBee, M. (2019). Who gets served in gifted education? Demographic representation and a call for action. *Gifted Child Quarterly, 63*(4), 273–287.

Pfeiffer, S. (2012). *Serving the gifted: Evidence-based clinical and psycho-educational practice*. Routledge.

Quijano, A. (2007). Coloniality and modernity/rationality. *Cultural Studies, 21*(2–3), 168–178.

Renzulli, J. S. (1978). What makes giftedness? Reexamining a definition. *Phi Delta Kappan, 60*(3), 180–184.

Renzulli, J. S. (2012). Reexamining the role of gifted education and talent development for the 21st century: A four-part theoretical approach. *Gifted Child Quarterly, 56*(3), 150–159.

Renzulli, J. S., & Reis, S. M. (2014). *The Schoolwide enrichment model: A how-to guide for talent development* (3rd ed.). Prufrock Press.

Sánchez-Escobedo, P. A., Camelo-Lavadores, A. K., & Valdés-Cuervo, A. A. (2021). Gifted, talented and high-achieving students and their gifted education in Mexico. In S. R. Smith (Ed.), *Handbook of giftedness and talent development in the Asia-Pacific* (Springer International Handbooks of Education). Springer. https://doi.org/10.1007/978-981-13-3041-4_9

Sen, A. (1999). *Development as freedom*. Oxford University Press.

Sternberg, R. J. (1985). *Beyond IQ: A triarchic theory of intelligence*. Cambridge University Press.

Sternberg, R. J. (2005). The theory of successful intelligence. *Interamerican Journal of Psychology, 39*(2), 189–202.

Sternberg, R. J. (2007). Cultural concepts of giftedness. *Roeper Review, 29*(3), 160–165.

Sternberg, R. J., & Ambrose, D. (Eds.). (2021). *Conceptions of giftedness and talent*. Palgrave Macmillan.

Subotnik, R. F., Olszewski-Kubilius, P., & Worrell, F. C. (2011). Rethinking giftedness and gifted education. *Psychological Science in the Public Interest, 12*(1), 3–54.

Virgolim, A. M. R. (2007). *Altas habilidades/superdotação: Encorajando potenciais*. MEC/SEESP.

Walker, M., & Unterhalter, E. (Eds.). (2007). *Amartya Sen's capability approach and social justice in education*. Palgrave Macmillan.

Walsh, C. (2010). Interculturalidad crítica y educación intercultural. In J. Viaña, L. Tapia, & C. Walsh (Eds.), *Construyendo interculturalidad crítica* (pp. 75–96). III-CAB.

Wechsler, S., Blumen, S., & Bendelman, K. (2018). Challenges on the identification and development of giftedness in South America. In S. Pfeiffer (Ed.), *APA handbook of giftedness and talent* (pp. 97–112). American Psychological Association.

Ziegler, A. (2005). The actiotope model of giftedness. In R. J. Sternberg & J. E. Davidson (Eds.), *Conceptions of giftedness* (2nd ed.). Cambridge University Press.

Ziegler, A., & Baker, J. (2013). Talent development as adaptation: The actiotope model of giftedness. In S. Phillipson et al. (Eds.), *Exceptionality in East Asia and Latin America*. Routledge.

Ziegler, A., Chandler, K., Vialle, W., & Stoeger, H. (2017). Exogenous and endogenous learning resources in the actiotope model of giftedness and its significance for gifted education. *Journal for the Education of the Gifted, 40*, 310–333. https://doi.org/10.1177/0162353217734376

Part II
Systems Under Constraint: Identification, Development, and Inequality

Chapter 4
Educational Landscapes: Institutional Architectures of Recognition and Conversion in Latin America

4.1 Mapping the Regional Recognition Regime

High-ability education in Latin America has entered legislative discourse without achieving systemic alignment. Over the past three decades, most national systems have incorporated references to high abilities, high skills, or giftedness within legislative frameworks. This discursive shift signals that giftedness is no longer absent from public education policy. Yet, formal inclusion does not guarantee operational coherence.

Across the region, regulatory specificity, acceleration flexibility, funding mechanisms, and identification protocols vary significantly. In some systems, high ability is embedded within inclusive or special education statutes; in others, it appears in ministerial resolutions or programmatic guidelines. The result is a heterogeneous landscape in which formal acknowledgment has expanded, yet institutional alignment remains incomplete.

As Table 4.1 demonstrates, legal acknowledgment is regionally present. However, three structural dimensions differentiate national recognition regimes:

1. **Regulatory Density**. The degree to which high ability is defined with operational clarity.
2. **Acceleration Codification**. The extent to which curricular flexibility is institutionally supported rather than procedurally constrained.
3. **Implementation Architecture**. The presence or absence of standardized identification, funding commitments, teacher preparation, and monitoring mechanisms.

Where these elements align, recognition approaches conversion. Where they do not, acknowledgment remains symbolic.

Across Latin America, high-ability learners have increasingly been incorporated into national education legislation, though with varying degrees of specificity and operational clarity. Brazil explicitly embeds *altas habilidades/superdotação* within

S. Blumen, *High Ability and Talent Development in Latin America*,
https://doi.org/10.1007/978-3-032-27468-7_4

Table 4.1 Technical, legal, and operational frameworks for children and adolescents with high abilities in selected Latin American countries

Country	Technical, legal, or operational framework
Argentina	Federal Council of Education Resolution No. 155/2011; Federal Council of Education Resolution No. 114/2010; Provincial legislation (e.g., City of Buenos Aires, Córdoba); (Education Profiles, 2021a)
Brazil	Law No. 9.394/1996 (National Education Guidelines and Framework Law—LDB); Decree No. 7.611/2011; Operational Guidelines for Specialized Educational Support; (Education Profiles, 2021b)
Chile	Exempt Decree No. 67/2018; Supreme Decree No. 170/2009; Talent Development Programs of the Ministry of Education (MINEDUC); Education Profiles, 2021c)
Colombia	Decree No. 366/2009; General Education Law (Law 115 of 1994); Pedagogical Guidelines of the Ministry of National Education (MEN); (Education Profiles, 2021d)
Costa Rica	Law No. 8899/2010; Law No. 10080/2021; Executive Decree No. 38808-MEP; Ministry of Public Education (MEP) protocols. (Education Profiles, 2021e)
Ecuador	Organic Law of Intercultural Education (LOEI); General Regulation of the LOEI; Ministerial Agreements on Curricular Flexibility. (Education Profiles, 2021f)
Mexico	General Education Law (reforms of 2009 and 2019), Article 41 (reform of June 22, 2009); Articles 64 and 65 (new Law, September 23, 2019); Article 67 (2024 reforms); SEP Agreement No. 696. (Education Profiles, 2021g)
Panama	Resolution 709-MEDUCA/2016; Executive Decree No. 1/2000; Manual of the Educational Support Service (Education Profiles, 2021h)
Paraguay	Law No. 5.136/2013; Ministerial Resolution No. 376/2025; Ministry of Education and Sciences (MEC) regulations on flexible promotion. (Education Profiles, 2021i)
Peru	General Education Law No. 28044 (Ministerio de Educación del Perú, 2003); no specific national regulation on pedagogical acceleration; Education Profiles, 2021j
Suriname	Legal framework for pedagogical acceleration integrated within the inclusive education system (historically influenced by the Dutch educational structure) (Education Profiles, 2021k)
Uruguay	Evaluation Regulations (2023); Circular No. 200/2000; Act 119/2019; Circular No. 3421/2018; Personalized Work Plan (PTP); (Education Profiles, 2021l)

Note. LDB = *Lei de Diretrizes e Bases da Educação Nacional*; MINEDUC = Ministry of Education (Chile); MEN = Ministry of National Education (Colombia); MEP = Ministry of Public Education (Costa Rica); SEP = Secretariat of Public Education (Mexico); MEC = Ministry of Education and Sciences (Paraguay); LOEI = Organic Law of Intercultural Education (Ecuador); PTP = Personalized Work Plan. Legal references correspond to the most recent reforms cited in the chapter

federal special education law (Lei No. 9.394/1996; Ministério da Educação, 2008), while Mexico includes students with *aptitudes sobresalientes* in its General Education Law (Valadez & Borges, 2014; Valdés, 2017). Colombia recognizes exceptional talents in Ley 115 de 1994, and Peru's Ley 28,044 acknowledges outstanding abilities, albeit without a clearly articulated acceleration framework. Chile, by contrast, has developed excellence-oriented programs within a regulatory structure that maintains strong age-based progression norms (Villalobos & Quaresma, 2015).

Beyond these anchor systems, countries such as Argentina, Costa Rica, Ecuador, Panamá, Paraguay, Uruguay, and Suriname have issued resolutions, decrees, or ministerial guidelines referencing curricular flexibility or support for high-ability learners. Yet regulatory density and institutionalization vary substantially. In many contexts, high-ability education is subsumed under broader inclusive education frameworks without dedicated implementation mandates, resulting in a regional pattern of formal recognition that remains unevenly structured and inconsistently enacted.

4.1.1 Acceleration and Age-Based Normativity

Acceleration serves as a diagnostic indicator of system flexibility. Although most Latin American systems permit some form of curricular adaptation, age-based progression remains normatively dominant. Grade-skipping and subject acceleration are often administratively complex or socially discouraged.

From the ecological–capability perspective articulated in Chap. 3, this tension reflects competing interpretations of equity. Equality is frequently operationalized as uniformity, while developmental differentiation is treated as an exception. Recognition without flexible conversion mechanisms produces partial inclusion—students are acknowledged yet constrained within age-synchronized structures.

4.1.2 Decentralization and Territorial Variability

Federal and decentralized governance structures, particularly in Brazil, Mexico, and Argentina, distribute authority across states or provinces. While decentralization enables contextual adaptation, it also generates uneven implementation. Administrative capacity, fiscal stability, and professional preparation differ across territories.

Recognition regimes, therefore, operate not only nationally but subnationally. Conversion depends on institutional infrastructure as much as on legislative text.

4.1.3 Policy Volatility and Structural Continuity

Educational reforms across the region have shifted across political administrations. Acceleration policies and curricular guidelines are particularly susceptible to revision. Policy discontinuity weakens institutional memory and complicates long-term planning. Sustainable talent development requires structural continuity beyond electoral cycles.

Taken together, the regional landscape reveals persistent tensions:

- Recognition versus conversion
- Age-based homogeneity versus developmental differentiation
- Decentralization versus systemic coherence

These tensions materialize differently across national systems.

4.2 Anchor Systems: Divergent National Configurations

4.2.1 Brazil: Legal Specificity and Interpretive Ambiguity

Brazil offers the clearest formal recognition of high ability. The *Lei de Diretrizes e Bases da Educação Nacional* (Lei No. 9.394/1996) explicitly includes *altas habilidades/superdotação* within special education. The 2008 national policy mandates specialized educational support (*Atendimento Educacional Especializado*).

Legal specificity establishes entitlement (Alencar & Fleith, 2010). However, embedding high ability within disability-centered frameworks introduces interpretive ambiguity (Pérez & Freitas, 2014). Implementation depends on state and municipal capacity, producing uneven conversion across territories.

4.2.2 Peru: Recognition Without Structural Consolidation

Peru's Ley General de Educación (No. 28044) recognizes students with outstanding abilities (Ministerio de Educación del Perú, 2003). Yet standardized identification procedures, funding streams, and acceleration frameworks remain underdeveloped (Blumen, 2021a). Conversion mechanisms—such as institutionalized budget lines and professional training—are weakly institutionalized (Ministerio de Educación del Perú, 2014).

Peru thus exemplifies recognition without systemic consolidation.

4.2.3 Mexico: Inclusion Under Decentralized Governance

Mexico incorporates students with *aptitudes sobresalientes* within the inclusive education law. Specialized units (USAER) operate across states (Valadez & Borges, 2014; Valdés, 2017). Yet decentralization produces variability in resource allocation and identification practice.

Policy oscillates between inclusion and excellence discourse, generating hybrid institutional configurations (Secretaría de Educación Pública, 2013).

4.2.4 *Chile: Excellence-Oriented Institutional Strategy*

Chile emphasizes academic excellence through university-linked initiatives such as PENTA UC (Villalobos & Quaresma, 2015). These programs operate within an accountability-driven system. While programmatically robust, integration into inclusive education frameworks remains limited.

4.2.5 *Colombia: Mandated Flexibility Without National Standardization*

Colombia's Ley 115 de 1994 mandates curricular flexibility for exceptional talents. Implementation remains locally determined. Identification often relies on teacher nomination and psychometric testing (García-Cepero & Proestakis, 2016), and national standardization remains limited.

4.3 Peru as Layered Innovation: Institutional Negotiation Under Constraint

Peru offers a revealing microcosm of negotiated innovation. Persistent inequality and institutional fragmentation coexist with layered talent development initiatives.

4.3.1 *Epistemic Reframing*

Scholarly contributions have played a decisive role in reshaping how giftedness is conceptualized within the Peruvian context. Blumen (2021a) notes that, until the early 2000s, dominant understandings of high ability were largely derived from imported psychometric traditions equating giftedness with elevated intelligence scores and individual academic performance. In a country marked by profound ethnic, linguistic, and socioeconomic diversity, such narrow frameworks proved insufficient.

Blumen (2021b) and Blumen and Cornejo (2006) challenged universalized definitions by documenting Indigenous and community-based conceptions of talent, emphasizing collective contribution, social leadership, creativity, and communal responsibility. From a capability perspective, definitions determine visibility. Narrow operationalizations risk rendering culturally embedded competencies institutionally invisible. Peru's epistemic debate thus reflects a broader decolonial tension between standardized global frameworks and locally grounded understandings of talent.

4.3.2 PAENFTS: Incremental Enrichment

The *Programa de Atención Educativa para Niños con Facultades Talentosas Sobresalientes* (PAENFTS), established in the mid-1980s, represents one of Peru's earliest structured responses to high ability. Operating through Local Educational Management Units (UGEL), it provides state-supported after-school enrichment rather than replacing regular schooling.

As reported in *La República* (2023), students identified through psych pedagogical processes participate in multidisciplinary enrichment spanning logical-mathematical reasoning, scientific inquiry, linguistic development, creative expression, and socio-emotional learning. PAENFTS expands capability within the age-graded system without restructuring it. Yet its geographic concentration and limited scalability illustrate the fragility of innovation under resource constraint.

4.3.3 COAR: Structural Redistribution

In contrast to the incremental enrichment model represented by PAENFTS, the *Colegios de Alto Rendimiento* (COAR) constitutes a more structurally ambitious state intervention in talent development. Established by the Ministry of Education, COAR schools provide full-time, residential education for high-performing secondary students, with particular emphasis on youth from socioeconomically disadvantaged regions.

Rather than supplementing regular schooling, the COAR model reorganizes the educational environment itself: students live on campus, engage in enriched and internationally oriented curricula, and participate in academically intensive programs designed to expand postsecondary and global opportunities. In this sense, COAR represents a deliberate effort to redistribute advanced educational opportunity both territorially and socioeconomically, transforming demonstrated high achievement into structured developmental pathways.

From a capability perspective, COAR strengthens developmental translation mechanisms more directly than after-school enrichment by providing sustained academic intensity, structured mentoring, and institutional access to advanced trajectories. However, its selective admission criteria and focus on secondary education mean that it primarily captures students who have already demonstrated high performance within earlier schooling stages. Persistent challenges in early identification and regional disparities are therefore not addressed. COAR thus embodies systemic differentiation within a public framework, yet its impact depends on broader alignment between early recognition, equitable access, and sustained institutional coherence.

4.3.4 *Layered Architecture and Fragmented Coherence*

Taken together, PAENFTS and COAR illustrate a layered Peruvian architecture combining epistemic reframing, complementary enrichment, and residential acceleration. Innovation exists, yet initiatives remain only partially connected and unevenly distributed. Peru exemplifies a broader regional pattern: recognition is present and programmatic innovation occurs, but structural coherence remains incomplete.

4.4 Institutional Practices and Program Models Across the Region

Across Latin America, four recurring programmatic forms characterize institutional responses to high-ability learners: pull-out resource programs, enrichment clusters, acceleration policies, and university-linked initiatives. Although these models differ in scope, intensity, and institutional anchoring, they represent patterned attempts to translate legal recognition into pedagogical practice.

4.4.1 *Resource Rooms and Pull-Out Services*

Pull-out and resource room models are among the most widespread forms of intervention. In Brazil, *Atendimento Educacional Especializado* (AEE) resource rooms operate within the broader inclusive education framework, providing differentiated instruction and specialized support for students identified with *altas habilidades/superdotação* alongside other exceptionalities (Ministério da Educação, 2008). Similarly, Mexico's USAER units (*Unidades de Servicios de Apoyo a la Educación Regular*) offer targeted pedagogical assistance within mainstream schools (Valadez & Borges, 2014).

These models are intended to supplement regular classroom instruction, rather than substitute it, by enabling participants to do enrichment or differentiated work part-time. They can make high-ability learners more visible and provide a more structured form of support, but their effectiveness depends heavily on well-prepared teachers, flexible timetables, and strong coordination within schools. In practice, however, limited resources often reduce how frequently these interventions can occur and how deeply they can be sustained.

4.4.2 Supplementary Enrichment Clusters

Enrichment cluster models constitute a second recurring approach. These initiatives frequently operate after school or during designated enrichment periods, offering domain-specific or interdisciplinary learning experiences. Enrichment clusters tend to emphasize creative problem-solving, scientific exploration, and project-based learning. They represent incremental capability expansion within age-graded systems, allowing students to deepen engagement without formally altering grade progression. However, such programs are often locally initiated and unevenly distributed, resulting in territorially differentiated access.

4.4.3 Acceleration Policies as Structural Indicators

Acceleration policies form a third and particularly revealing dimension of institutional practice. Most countries examined in this chapter legally permit some form of grade-skipping, subject acceleration, or curricular compacting. Yet, as Pérez and Freitas (2014) note in the Brazilian context, implementation remains inconsistent. Administrative procedures, school-level discretion, parental negotiation, and cultural resistance to age-based disruption frequently constrain practical application. Acceleration thus functions as a structural indicator of systemic flexibility: where it is normalized, developmental differentiation is institutionally recognized; where it is administratively discouraged, age-based homogeneity prevails despite formal legality.

4.4.4 University-Linked Talent Initiatives

University-linked initiatives represent the most structurally consolidated pathway in several national systems. Programs such as Penta-UC, Beta-PUCV, Delta-UCN, and Proenta-UFRO in Chile provide structured enrichment through partnerships between universities and schools, offering advanced disciplinary exposure, mentorship, and access to academic resources (Villalobos & Quaresma, 2015). Similar programs in several countries link secondary students to universities, often serving as bridges to more selective higher-education pathways. These programs are academically rigorous and institutionally well established. But their concentration in major urban centers constrains territorial reach, and participation often requires prior identification in largely advantaged school settings.

Put together, these four varieties of programs suggest a terrain of both innovation and fragmentation: Institutions in the region will try new ways of working, but talent development remains taking place through an uneven series of public education pathways. Yet scaling remains uneven, coordination across levels of schooling is limited, and national monitoring mechanisms are rare. In capability terms, these models expand opportunity for some learners while leaving broader structural rigidity intact. Legal recognition has stimulated programmatic experimentation, but systemic integration—linking identification, differentiation, teacher preparation, and evaluation—remains incomplete. Institutional practice thus reflects the broader pattern identified throughout this chapter: innovation exists, yet systemic integration and equitable distribution remain ongoing challenges.

4.5 Identification Regimes and Epistemic Constraints

Identification constitutes one of the most consequential—and most uneven—dimensions of high-ability education across Latin America. Although legislation in many countries recognizes the importance of early detection, the practical guidelines are often vague, decentralized, or unevenly applied. As a result, identification practices differ not only between countries but also within them, reflecting variations in institutional capacity, professional training, and underlying conceptual approaches.

Teacher nomination continues to be one of the most common pathways into gifted education services. Classroom educators are frequently expected to identify students who demonstrate advanced academic performance, rapid learning, or exceptional classroom engagement. Although teacher observation can capture contextualized indicators of ability, reliance on nomination alone carries well-documented risks. As Alencar and Fleith (2010) note in the Brazilian context, teacher perceptions are influenced by behavioral expectations, linguistic fluency, and conformity to dominant academic norms. Students who are introverted, culturally diverse, bilingual, economically marginalized, or behaviorally nonconforming may be less likely to be nominated, even when possessing high potential. In this sense, teacher nomination can inadvertently reproduce existing social hierarchies within recognition processes.

Psychometric testing still plays a central role in formal identification processes across the region. Standardized tests of intelligence and achievement are seen as good and administratively dependable measures of giftedness (García-Cepero & Proestakis, 2016), in part because they provide clear and quantifiable thresholds through which programs enter. But an unhealthy dependence on these measures can also reduce the concept of giftedness (Sternberg, 2007). When such a high ability is perceived solely in terms of test scores, other types of high potential, such as creativity and artistic expression, leadership, and culturally rooted strengths or domain-specific talents, can be overlooked in institutions. This limitation is especially important in culturally and linguistically diverse contexts, where standardized tools may not fully reflect the range of students' cognitive profiles.

Alternative identification approaches, including dynamic assessment, performance-based evaluation, portfolio review, and multi-criteria screening, remain underdeveloped in most Latin American systems. Dynamic assessment, in particular, shifts the evaluative focus from static performance to learning potential by examining how students respond to mediated instruction. Such approaches align more closely with capability-oriented frameworks because they assess developmental responsiveness rather than fixed achievement. Yet, implementing dynamic or multi-method models requires trained personnel, sustained institutional support, and time-intensive procedures—resources that are frequently scarce in public education systems.

Territorial inequality further complicates identification. Urban schools, particularly in metropolitan centers, are more likely to have access to psychologists, testing instruments, enrichment programs, and referral networks. Rural and Indigenous communities often face structural barriers, including limited professional staffing, linguistic mismatches between assessment tools and student populations, and reduced institutional visibility (Arancibia & Rodríguez, 2018). As a result, identification becomes territorially mediated: a student's geographic location significantly influences the probability that advanced potential will be formally recognized and supported.

From a capability perspective, identification functions as the gateway to institutional enablement. It determines whose abilities enter institutional pathways and whose remain latent or unrecognized. When identification systems are narrow in definition, biased in practice, or unevenly distributed across territories, they risk reproducing rather than mitigating inequality. Expanding recognition requires not only legislative acknowledgment but plural, culturally responsive, and territorially equitable identification regimes. Without such reform, the promise of inclusive gifted education remains structurally constrained.

4.6 Public–Private Stratification and Differentiated Opportunity Structures

Public–private differentiation constitutes one of the most enduring structural cleavages shaping high-ability education across Latin America. Although national legislation may formally recognize high-ability learners as part of inclusive education frameworks, the institutional conditions under which recognition is operationalized differ markedly between private and public sectors. These differences significantly influence the probability that potential will be converted into a sustained developmental opportunity.

Elite private institutions frequently offer enriched curricula, smaller class sizes, extended instructional time, bilingual or international programs, advanced science and technology laboratories, and structured extracurricular opportunities. Such schools often possess greater autonomy in curricular pacing, assessment flexibility, and academic tracking. Subject-level acceleration, early exposure to advanced coursework, participation in international competitions, and structured mentoring are more easily implemented when institutional resources and administrative discretion are abundant. In these contexts, excellence is not merely recognized; it is structurally embedded within the school's organizational design.

By contrast, public schools—particularly those serving low-income, rural, or peri-urban communities—operate under significant material and administrative constraints (García-Cepero & Proestakis, 2016). Large-class sizes, centralized curricular mandates, limited access to specialized personnel, and high teacher workload reduce opportunities for differentiated instruction. Even when policies allow for acceleration or enrichment, putting them into practice largely depends on local institutional capacity. Even when teachers identify advanced learners, limited time, training, and support often make sustained differentiation difficult. As a result, recognition within public systems frequently depends on isolated initiatives or the personal commitment of individual educators rather than systematic policy integration.

These asymmetries produce stratified recognition pathways. In private institutions, advanced learning trajectories are often proactively cultivated and normalized. High achievement is anticipated and institutionally scaffolded through resource allocation and programmatic continuity. In many public contexts, however, access to advanced learning depends on external programs—such as university-linked enrichment initiatives, scholarship competitions, or residential academies like COAR—rather than on everyday classroom differentiation. Opportunity thus becomes episodic rather than continuous.

This stratification is not only economic but also territorial. Many private schools in the biggest cities are in bustling educational scenes, with universities, research institutes, and cultural institutions all encircling them. Public schools in rural or marginalized regions frequently lack access to comparable networks. Consequently, the ecosystem of opportunity differs substantially by geography and socioeconomic status.

From a capability perspective, these structural divides mediate opportunity realization. Legal recognition establishes entitlement in principle, but the ability to transform recognized potential into durable developmental pathways depends on institutional resources and organizational flexibility. When excellence is structurally embedded in private systems but fragmented in public ones, socioeconomic background becomes a decisive factor in the realization of high ability. Recognition may be universal in law, yet conversion remains differentially distributed.

Public-sector initiatives such as residential high-performance schools and state-funded enrichment programs represent deliberate attempts to mitigate this stratification by redistributing advanced educational opportunities. However, these initiatives tend to function as selective or complementary options rather than bringing about system-wide change. Without broader reforms addressing teacher preparation, curricular flexibility, and funding equity, structural duality persists.

High-ability education in Latin America therefore operates within a layered but unequal architecture. On one side, resource-rich institutions institutionalize excellence through abundance and autonomy; on the other, resource-constrained public systems rely on localized innovation and episodic intervention. The challenge for regional policy is not simply to expand programs but to reduce the structural distance between recognition and conversion across socioeconomic strata. Addressing this divide is central to equitable capability expansion.

4.7 From Recognition to Conversion: Structural Lessons

Across Latin America, high-ability policy occupies an intermediate institutional position—visible in statute, uneven in conversion. It occupies an intermediate and structurally ambivalent position—recognized in law, partially institutionalized in practice, yet unevenly converted into a sustainable, developmental opportunity. The regional landscape mapped in this chapter reveals that legal acknowledgment has expanded substantially over the past three decades. Most national systems now reference *altas capacidades*, *altas habilidades*, or equivalent terminology within education statutes or ministerial guidelines. Yet, the translation of recognition into coherent institutional architectures remains incomplete.

From the ecological perspective articulated in Chap. 3, development unfolds within interacting systems—family, school, community, and policy environments. The findings of this chapter demonstrate that high-ability learners encounter markedly different opportunity structures depending on how these systems align. Where regulatory density, identification procedures, teacher preparation, and curricular flexibility operate in coordination, recognition begins to approximate conversion. Where these elements are fragmented, symbolic inclusion coexists with structural rigidity.

The capability lens further clarifies this distinction. Recognition establishes entitlement: a student is acknowledged as possessing advanced potential. Conversion requires enabling conditions—material resources, institutional flexibility, professional expertise, and stable governance frameworks—that allow recognized potential to expand into meaningful educational trajectories. Across the region, conversion mechanisms remain unevenly distributed. Acceleration is legally permitted but administratively constrained; enrichment initiatives exist but are geographically concentrated; identification systems operate but are often psychometrically narrow or territorially uneven. In many contexts, the probability that high ability will be institutionally nurtured depends on socioeconomic background and geographic location.

The decolonial dimension of the framework underscores an additional structural tension. Definitions of giftedness are never neutral; they shape which abilities are recognized and which tend to be overlooked. Debates in Peru provide an example of how culturally grounded conceptions of talent can disrupt universal psychometric models. And when such systems of identification become too dependent on standardized measures, divorced from context, they stand to help maintain and legitimize existing hierarchies of knowledge. Conversion, in this way, is both material and conceptual, requiring more plural ways of apprehending aptitude across culture. In this context, the regional trends reviewed in this chapter converge around three persistent structural tensions.

Against this backdrop, the regional patterns discussed in this chapter come together around three persistent structural tensions. First, recognition frequently outpaces institutional integration; laws evolve more rapidly than systems. Second, age-based homogeneity often constrains developmental differentiation, limiting the practical application of acceleration policies. Third, stratified opportunity structures—particularly along public–private and urban–rural lines—mediate whose recognized potential becomes actionable.

Importantly, the presence of fragmentation should not be misinterpreted as the absence of innovation. Brazil's AEE resource rooms, Mexico's USAER units, Chile's university-linked enrichment programs, Peru's PAENFTS and COAR initiatives, and Colombia's curricular flexibility provisions demonstrate institutional creativity within constraint. These initiatives represent incremental expansions of capability within existing systems. Yet without systemic coordination—linking early identification, sustained differentiation, teacher preparation, funding commitments, and longitudinal monitoring—innovation remains layered rather than integrated.

The central structural lesson of this chapter is therefore not that Latin America lacks high-ability policy, but that it lacks fully coherent recognition regimes. Recognition regimes tend to strengthen when definitional clarity, identification pluralism, curricular flexibility, professional capacity, and equitable resource allocation operate as mutually reinforcing components. Where these elements are misaligned, recognition remains partial and conversion contingent.

High-ability education in the region thus stands at a crossroads. It can remain an assemblage of localized initiatives operating within broader systemic rigidity, or it can evolve toward integrated policy architectures that align recognition with equitable capability expansion. Progress in this direction will require more than legal reform; it also depends on sustained institutional support and real openness to diverse ways of knowing.

Taken together, Chaps. 2–4 demonstrate that across Latin America, high ability develops within deeply stratified educational and social structures that shape whose potential becomes visible and whose remains obscured. While national systems increasingly recognize giftedness in law, recognition alone does not ensure conversion into sustained developmental opportunity, enabling conditions—conceptual, institutional, and material—mediate that transformation. The central regional challenge is therefore not the absence of talent, but the absence of fully integrated recognition regimes capable of equitably converting distributed potential into durable educational pathways.

Chapter 5 builds upon this structural synthesis by examining how these differentiated recognition regimes shape-lived educational trajectories.

References

Alencar, E. M. L. S., & Fleith, D. S. (2010). *Superdotados: Determinantes, educação e ajustamento* (2nd ed.). EPU.

Arancibia, V., & Rodríguez, C. (2018). Talento académico en el Perú: Avances y desafíos en políticas educativas. *Revista Peruana de Investigación Educativa, 10*(12), 45–63.

Blumen, S. (2021a). Identifying and nurturing diversely gifted and talented students. In S. R. Smith (Ed.), *Handbook of giftedness and talent development in the Asia-Pacific* (pp. 457–464). Springer.

Blumen, S. (2021b). Talent development, cultural diversity, and equity. In R. J. Sternberg & D. Ambrose (Eds.), *Conceptions of giftedness and talent* (pp. 21–36). Palgrave Macmillan.

Blumen, S., & Cornejo, F. (2006). Indigenous conceptions of giftedness in Peru. *Gifted and Talented International, 21*(1), 35–46.

Brasil. (2011). *Decreto No. 7.611/2011*. Presidência da República.

Brasil. (1996). *Lei No. 9.394/1996 (Lei de Diretrizes e Bases da Educação Nacional)*. Presidência da República.

Chile. Ministerio de Educación. (2009). *Decreto Supremo No. 170/2009*. MINEDUC.

Chile. Ministerio de Educación. (2018). *Decreto Exento No. 67/2018*. MINEDUC.

Colombia. (1994). *Ley 115 de 1994 (Ley General de Educación)*. Congreso de la República.

Colombia. Ministerio de Educación Nacional. (2009). *Decreto No. 366/2009*. MEN.

Education Profiles. (2021a). *Argentina: Inclusion and education*. UNESCO Global Education Monitoring (GEM) Report/PEER country profile. https://education-profiles.org/latin-america-and-the-caribbean/argentina/~inclusion

Education Profiles. (2021b). *Brazil: Inclusion and education*. UNESCO Global Education Monitoring (GEM) Report/PEER country profile. https://education-profiles.org/latin-america-and-the-caribbean/brazil/~inclusion

Education Profiles. (2021c). *Chile: Inclusion and education*. UNESCO Global Education Monitoring (GEM) Report/PEER country profile. https://education-profiles.org/latin-america-and-the-caribbean/chile/~inclusion

Education Profiles. (2021d). *Colombia: Inclusion and education*. UNESCO Global Education Monitoring (GEM) Report/PEER country profile. https://education-profiles.org/latin-america-and-the-caribbean/colombia/~inclusion

Education Profiles. (2021e). *Costa Rica: Inclusion and education*. UNESCO Global Education Monitoring (GEM) Report/PEER country profile. https://education-profiles.org/latin-america-and-the-caribbean/costa-rica/~inclusion

Education Profiles. (2021f). *Ecuador: Inclusion and education*. UNESCO Global Education Monitoring (GEM) Report/PEER country profile. https://education-profiles.org/latin-america-and-the-caribbean/ecuador/~inclusion

Education Profiles. (2021g). *Mexico: Inclusion and education*. UNESCO Global Education Monitoring (GEM) Report/PEER country profile. https://education-profiles.org/latin-america-and-the-caribbean/mexico/~inclusion

Education Profiles. (2021h). *Panama: Inclusion and education*. UNESCO Global Education Monitoring (GEM) Report/PEER country profile. https://education-profiles.org/latin-america-and-the-caribbean/panama/~inclusion

Education Profiles. (2021i). *Paraguay: Inclusion and education*. UNESCO Global Education Monitoring (GEM) Report/PEER country profile. https://education-profiles.org/latin-america-and-the-caribbean/paraguay/~inclusion

Education Profiles. (2021j). *Peru: Inclusion and education*. UNESCO Global Education Monitoring (GEM) Report/PEER country profile. https://education-profiles.org/latin-america-and-the-caribbean/peru/~inclusion

Education Profiles. (2021k). *Suriname: Inclusion and education*. UNESCO Global Education Monitoring (GEM) Report/PEER country profile. https://education-profiles.org/latin-america-and-the-caribbean/suriname/~inclusion

Education Profiles. (2021l). *Uruguay: Inclusion and education*. UNESCO Global Education Monitoring (GEM) Report/PEER country profile. https://education-profiles.org/latin-america-and-the-caribbean/uruguay/~inclusion

García-Cepero, M. C., & Proestakis, A. (2016). Gifted education in Latin America. In S. I. Pfeiffer (Ed.), *APA handbook of giftedness and talent* (pp. 513–528). American Psychological Association.

La República. (2023, May 13). *Gifted children: How is their education at the PAENFTS in Lima?* https://larepublica.pe/sociedad/2023/05/07/como-es-la-educacion-en-el-paenfts-escuela-para-ninos-genios-en-lima-y-donde-esta-ubicado-minedu-atmp-463372

México. (2009). Ley General de Educación (Reforma al artículo 41, 22 de junio de 2009). *Diario Oficial de la Federación*.

México. (2019). Ley General de Educación (Nueva Ley, 23 de septiembre de 2019). *Diario Oficial de la Federación*.

México. (2024). Reformas al artículo 67 de la Ley General de Educación. *Diario Oficial de la Federación*.

Ministério da Educação. (2008). *Diretrizes operacionais para o atendimento educacional especializado*. MEC.

Ministerio de Educación del Perú. (2003). *Ley General de Educación No. 28044*. Congreso de la República.

Ministerio de Educación del Perú. (2014). *Colegios de Alto Rendimiento*. MINEDU

Pérez, S. G. P. B., & Freitas, S. N. (2014). Altas habilidades/superdotação. *Revista Educação Especial, 27*(49), 279–292.

Secretaría de Educación Pública. (2013). *Acuerdo No. 696*. SEP.

Sternberg, R. J. (2007). Cultural concepts of giftedness. *Roeper Review, 29*(3), 160–165.

Valadez, M. D., & Borges, Á. (2014). Atención educativa a alumnos con aptitudes sobresalientes. *Revista Electrónica de Investigación Educativa, 16*(3), 1–15.

Valdés, A. A. (2017). Educación para alumnos con aptitudes sobresalientes. *Perfiles Educativos, 39*(158), 78–93.

Villalobos, C., & Quaresma, M. L. (2015). Sistema escolar chileno y educación del talento académico. *Estudios Pedagógicos, 41*(2), 299–316.

Chapter 5
Who Gets to Be Gifted? Identification and Equity in Latin America

5.1 Introduction

In highly unequal societies, identification is not merely classificatory—it is allocative. To be recognized as gifted is to enter structured opportunity: enrichment, mentorship, accelerated learning, and institutional visibility. To remain unidentified is to be excluded from developmental pathways that convert potential into realized capacity. The question of who gets to be gifted is therefore inseparable from the question of how opportunity is distributed. In Latin America, where socioeconomic, territorial, linguistic, and racial stratification shape educational trajectories from early childhood onward, identification functions as a decisive mechanism in the allocation of future possibilities.

According to the Economic Commission for Latin America and the Caribbean (ECLAC), Latin America remains one of the most unequal regions globally in income distribution and educational access. The UNESCO Global Education Monitoring framework similarly emphasizes that equity requires targeted responses for structurally marginalized learners. Yet high-ability students from low-income, Indigenous, Afro-descendant, rural, and migrant communities rarely appear at the center of equity discourse.

This chapter advances a central claim: in Latin America, who gets to be gifted reflects how opportunity is structured. Identification systems often magnify preexisting inequality. Reforming identification is therefore foundational to a regional model of talent development.

S. Blumen, *High Ability and Talent Development in Latin America*,
https://doi.org/10.1007/978-3-032-27468-7_5

5.2 Conceptual Foundations of Identification

5.2.1 From Psychometric Gatekeeping to Developmental Recognition

Identification practices in Latin America were institutionalized within psychometric paradigms largely imported from Europe and North America. Intelligence scales, aptitude batteries, and competitive academic examinations—frequently adapted but insufficiently normed for regional diversity—became the primary mechanisms of recognition. Numerical thresholds, often framed as objective and meritocratic, established entry into gifted programming as a binary crossing of a cutoff.

This architecture rests on a fixed-ability assumption: that cognitive capacity is internally stable, measurable, independent of context, and reliably captured at a single point in time. As Sternberg (2018) and Subotnik et al. (2011) argue, such models compress complex developmental processes into static indicators. Measurement functions less as inquiry than as gatekeeping. Brazilian scholarship has consistently problematized this reductionism. Pérez and Freitas (2016) emphasize that *altas habilidades/superdotação* must be understood within sociocultural and educational ecologies rather than as isolated psychometric traits. Virgolim (2014) similarly critiques narrow intelligence-based identification, documenting how public-school students are systematically overlooked when ability is equated with test performance. Alencar and Fleith (2001) argue that creativity and contextual opportunity are indispensable dimensions of talent recognition in Brazilian settings, while Delou (2007) underscores the importance of environmental mediation in the expression of high ability.

Across Ibero-American discourse, Tourón and Santiago (2015), drawing on Gagné's Differentiated Model, reinforce the principle that environmental catalysts are constitutive—not peripheral—to talent realization. Yet despite rhetorical convergence toward multidimensionality, operational procedures across much of Latin America remain anchored in static metrics.

The result is a structural disjunction between policy language and procedural design. Documents invoke creativity, leadership, and socio-emotional strength; identification protocols privilege cognitive reasoning scores and time-bound examinations. The rhetoric expands, but the filter remains narrow. From the developmental perspective articulated in Chap. 3, this tension is foundational. If talent unfolds longitudinally and is activated through opportunity structures, then identification cannot operate as a terminal verdict. It must be iterative, growth-sensitive, and ecologically aware. The shift required is not the abandonment of assessment but its reconfiguration within a temporal and contextual frame.

5.2.2 Achievement as Accumulated Opportunity

If psychometric thresholds represent classical gatekeeping, achievement-based criteria represent structural mediation. Across Brazil, Chile, Mexico, Colombia, and Peru, high grades, standardized test scores, and competitive entrance examinations function as dominant signals of exceptional ability.

Achievement appears meritocratic. Yet in unequal systems, performance reflects accumulated opportunity. ECLAC data repeatedly demonstrate that school quality, territorial location, parental education, and income quintile significantly condition educational outcomes across Latin America. Peters et al. (2019) show in U.S. contexts that achievement-based screening disproportionately selects students from advantaged backgrounds; analogous dynamics are visible regionally.

Empirical evidence from Latin America reinforces this pattern. García-Cepero and McCoach (2009) found that Chilean talent program admissions correlated strongly with parental educational capital. Valadez and Borges (2014) report marked regional disparities in Mexican identification practices tied to infrastructural inequality. In Brazil, Ourofino and Guimarães (2007) document the under-identification of students in public schools serving low-income communities, while Fleith (2014) highlights disparities in screening implementation across municipalities.

Achievement, therefore, is not a transparent indicator of potential but an outcome sedimented through ecological conditions. It captures realized performance under unequal circumstances. When used as the primary gateway to gifted programming, it privileges students whose prior environments have aligned with institutional expectations. Those whose potential is emergent, domain-specific, or contextually suppressed may not yet display the academic markers required for entry.

The developmental framework advanced in Chap. 3 requires analytical separation between performance and capacity. Growth trajectories differ; environmental deprivation can delay but not eliminate potential expression. Renzulli and Reis (2014) emphasize that enrichment and opportunity exposure can activate high-level performance among previously overlooked students.

Without contextual correction—local norming, repeated screening, dynamic assessment—achievement-based identification risks codifying stratification. Meritocracy, in the absence of structural adjustment, becomes a mechanism of social reproduction.

5.2.3 Teacher Nomination as Interpretive Mediation

If psychometric testing formalizes gatekeeping and achievement reflects structural mediation, teacher nomination introduces interpretive mediation. In several Latin American systems, referral by classroom teachers constitutes the initial filter prior to formal assessment.

In principle, teacher observation offers ecological insight. Educators encounter students' creativity, problem-solving approaches, persistence, and socio-emotional intensity in authentic contexts. Multi-informant models (Pfeiffer, 2015) demonstrate that structured teacher input can enhance identification sensitivity.

Yet interpretive discretion carries risk. Ford (2014) demonstrates that teacher expectations significantly shape referral patterns, often disadvantaging racially and culturally diverse students. Comparable dynamics appear in Latin American contexts. García and Morales (2017) report that Colombian teachers frequently equate giftedness with excelencia académica, narrowing recognition to conventional academic performance. Brazilian research (Pérez & Freitas, 2016; Virgolim, 2014) similarly identifies misconceptions linking giftedness exclusively to high grades and early precocity.

Implicit bias operates within broader stratified systems. Expectations regarding rural learners, Indigenous students, Afro-descendant youth, or migrants may subtly depress referral rates. Linguistic fluency in Spanish or Portuguese may be misread as cognitive competence, while bilingual learners' reasoning strengths remain obscured by second-language processing demands.

Moreover, culturally embedded expressions of ability—collective leadership, ecological expertise, artistic traditions—may not align with dominant school prototypes of giftedness. When nomination depends on unstructured mental models, culturally diverse manifestations of talent are systematically underrecognized.

However, the solution is not elimination but redesign. Structured observation protocols, collaborative nomination committees, bias-awareness preparation, and explicit inclusion of creativity and leadership indicators can recalibrate teacher referral. Delou (2007) emphasizes that teacher expectations function as environmental catalysts in talent development; they can either amplify or suppress emerging potential.

Within the ecological–developmental model articulated in Chap. 3, teacher nomination represents a pivotal interface between institutional power and individual trajectories. Properly structured, it can widen the aperture of recognition. Unstructured, it becomes a silent mechanism of exclusion.

Psychometric thresholds, achievement criteria, and teacher nomination operate as layered filters within unequal systems: psychometrics assumes context–neutral measurement; achievement reflects accumulated opportunity; nomination mediates recognition through expectation. Without contextual safeguards, these layers converge to produce patterned underrepresentation. A regionally grounded developmental model, therefore, requires identification systems that are iterative, growth-sensitive, contextually calibrated, and structurally monitored.

Only through such recalibration can identification cease functioning as gatekeeping and instead operate as an instrument of opportunity expansion consistent with the regional talent development model advanced in this volume.

5.3 Structural Patterns of Underrepresentation

The identification mechanisms examined in Sect. 5.2 do not operate in a vacuum. They function within historically stratified societies characterized by income inequality, territorial asymmetry, racialized hierarchies, and uneven institutional capacity. When psychometric thresholds, achievement filters, and discretionary nomination intersect with these structures, underrepresentation emerges not as an anomaly but as a predictable outcome.

Underrepresentation must be analyzed structurally rather than descriptively, as it reflects how opportunity is distributed prior to identification.

5.3.1 Socioeconomic Stratification

Across Latin America, socioeconomic inequality remains one of the most powerful predictors of educational trajectory. According to the Economic Commission for Latin America and the Caribbean, educational attainment and learning outcomes remain strongly correlated with household income quintile, parental education, and territorial location.

In this context, identification systems that rely on academic performance inevitably intersect with unequal opportunity structures. Students from higher-income families are more likely to attend better-resourced schools, experience curricular depth and instructional continuity, access private tutoring and enrichment, and receive parental guidance in navigating competitive pathways. These accumulated advantages translate into higher standardized scores and stronger academic records—precisely the metrics often used for gifted identification.

Brazilian research consistently documents disproportionate identification of students from private and high-performing urban public schools (Fleith, 2014; Pérez & Freitas, 2016). In Chile, admissions to university-affiliated talent programs correlate with parental educational capital (García-Cepero & McCoach, 2009). Mexican scholarship similarly notes state-level disparities tied to infrastructural inequality (Valadez & Borges, 2014).

Socioeconomic stratification thus shapes not only access to schooling but also access to recognition. When achievement serves as the gateway, identification systems risk codifying advantage rather than detecting potential.

From the ecological framework of Chap. 3, socioeconomic context operates as a macro-systemic influence that conditions developmental trajectories. Without structural correction mechanisms—local norming, repeated screening, contextual interpretation—identification amplifies preexisting inequality.

5.3.2 Indigenous, Afro-Descendant, and Linguistic Minorities

Latin America is one of the most culturally and linguistically diverse regions in the world. More than 800 Indigenous peoples and hundreds of languages coexist within national systems structured primarily around Spanish or Portuguese. Afro-descendant communities, particularly in Brazil and Colombia, face longstanding patterns of racialized exclusion.

Identification systems built on dominant-language verbal reasoning measures and culturally loaded test content risk conflating linguistic fluency with cognitive ability. For bilingual or multilingual students—particularly those educated in intercultural bilingual settings—performance may reflect language processing demands rather than reasoning capacity.

Brazilian scholarship (Virgolim, 2014; Pérez & Freitas, 2016) underscores the underrepresentation of students from public schools serving marginalized communities. In Colombia, research by García and Morales (2017) indicates that Afro-Colombian and rural students are rarely referred for enrichment programs concentrated in urban centers.

A notable counterexample is Peru's Colegios de Alto Rendimiento (COAR), which incorporates multilingual accommodations in later-stage assessment. Candidates may complete components in Quechua or Aymara, and interviews are conducted in students' primary languages. This represents a significant effort to reduce linguistic distortion. However, such accommodations operate primarily at secondary selection points and do not replace the need for early-stage culturally responsive screening within mainstream schooling.

The broader regional pattern remains one of linguistic centralization. Inclusive discourse regarding intercultural education advances more rapidly than the adaptation of identification instruments.

From a developmental standpoint, cultural and linguistic context does not merely influence performance; it shapes the domains in which ability is expressed. Recognition frameworks that privilege dominant academic prototypes overlook community-based, artistic, ecological, and collective forms of expertise that may not align with conventional school metrics.

5.3.3 Rural–Urban Territorial Inequality

Territorial inequality constitutes one of the most persistent structural divides in Latin America. Rural schools frequently experience:

- Teacher shortages
- Limited advanced coursework
- Reduced access to specialized psychological assessment
- Restricted digital connectivity

Gifted programs, by contrast, cluster in metropolitan regions and university-affiliated centers. In Brazil and Mexico, screening infrastructure is concentrated in urban districts. Chile's most structured talent initiatives are linked to major universities in Santiago and other large cities. Colombia's enrichment initiatives similarly center around Bogotá and Medellín. When identification depends on centralized testing locations, specialized professionals, or digital platforms, rural students face systemic barriers before evaluation even begins. Territorial asymmetry thus operates as a pre-identification filter.

Within the ecological model, territorial context functions at the exosystem level, shaping institutional resources available to schools and families. Without decentralized screening and outreach, rural invisibility becomes institutionalized.

5.3.4 Migrant and Displaced Learners

Recent migration flows—most prominently Venezuelan displacement into Colombia, Peru, and Chile—introduce additional layers of complexity. Migrant students often experience:

- Interrupted schooling
- Credential discontinuity
- Linguistic transition
- Socio-emotional stress linked to displacement

Static identification procedures rarely account for educational disruption or transitional bilingual development. Achievement records may be incomplete or non-transferable. Standardized assessments administered without contextual adjustment risk underestimating learning potential.

The invisibility of migrant talent illustrates the interaction between mobility and institutional rigidity. When identification presumes stable schooling trajectories, displaced learners fall outside established recognition pathways.

Developmentally, migration constitutes a macro-contextual disruption that may temporarily suppress performance while leaving underlying potential intact. Identification systems attentive to growth and adaptability—rather than solely prior achievement—are better positioned to recognize such trajectories.

5.4 National Identification Frameworks: Policy and Institutional Design

While structural patterns are regionally shared, each country's identification architecture reflects distinct institutional histories. The following cases are not isolated descriptions but national instantiations of common regional tensions between inclusion discourse and procedural constraint.

5.4.1 *Brazil*

Brazil formally includes high abilities within its 2008 National Policy on Special Education. The creation of *salas de recursos* (resource rooms) institutionalized differentiated services within inclusive education structures. However, identification practices vary widely across municipalities due to decentralization.

Research indicates uneven screening procedures, limited culturally validated instruments, and insufficient teacher preparation (Fleith, 2014; Pérez & Freitas, 2016). Regional disparities are pronounced: southeastern urban centers demonstrate more structured implementation than northern rural states.

Brazil possesses one of the region's most developed academic literatures on giftedness, yet translation from scholarship to systemic practice remains incomplete. The result is conceptual recognition without universal operational consistency.

5.4.2 *Chile*

Chile's most structured identification initiatives operate through university-based talent programs such as PENTA UC. These programs combine cognitive assessment with academic performance criteria and have demonstrated strong long-term academic outcomes.

However, access remains competitive and geographically concentrated. While outreach mechanisms target low-income students, entrance examinations emphasize academic reasoning aligned with mainstream curricula. As a result, prior preparation strongly predicts selection.

Chile illustrates the tension between excellence-driven models and equity correction. Institutional sophistication does not automatically resolve structural bias.

5.4.3 Mexico

Mexico integrates giftedness within special education services but lacks a national universal screening mandate. State-level autonomy results in uneven identification rates and heterogeneous criteria.

Indigenous regions often lack formal screening infrastructure, and teacher nomination remains a dominant pathway. While Mexico's intercultural bilingual education policies formally recognize linguistic diversity, adaptation of gifted identification tools to these contexts remains limited.

The Mexican case exemplifies fragmentation: policy acknowledgment without centralized accountability mechanisms.

5.4.4 Colombia

Colombia's inclusive education framework acknowledges exceptional talents but provides limited formal identification infrastructure. Urban concentration of enrichment initiatives restricts access for rural and Afro-Colombian communities.

Teacher nomination frequently substitutes for systematic screening, reinforcing interpretive bias discussed in Sect. 5.2.3. Disaggregated national data on representation remain scarce, limiting transparency.

Colombia's case illustrates how recognition in principle does not guarantee structured pathways in practice.

5.4.5 Peru

Peru's *Colegios de Alto Rendimiento* (COAR) network represents one of the region's most visible merit-based secondary pathways. Regional quotas and multilingual accommodations aim to broaden access. Yet COAR remains a selective model operating at the secondary level. Competitive entrance examinations reflect disparities rooted in primary school quality. Without earlier universal screening and distributed enrichment, late-stage selection may reproduce preparatory inequality. Peru demonstrates both innovation and limitation: targeted equity safeguards within a fundamentally competitive structure.

Across these cases, a consistent pattern emerges: formal recognition is widespread, universal early screening remains rare, urban concentration persists, and monitoring systems are weak. National variation modifies but does not eliminate structural inequality.

From the developmental–ecological lens of Chap. 3, these patterns indicate that identification systems in the region are still primarily reactive rather than cultivation-oriented. They identify performance once manifested under favorable conditions rather than proactively detecting potential across diverse contexts. The reform question, therefore, is not whether gifted education should exist, but how identification architecture can be redesigned to function as a structural equalizer rather than a selective amplifier (Blumen, 2021).

5.5 Cross-National Comparative Analysis: A Typology of Identification Regimes

The preceding sections demonstrate that identification systems across Brazil, Chile, Mexico, Colombia, and Peru share structural features despite institutional variation. To move beyond descriptive comparison, this section proposes a typology of identification regimes based on three analytic dimensions:

1. **Degree of centralization** (national mandate vs. decentralized discretion)
2. **Primary identification filter** (psychometric, achievement-based, nomination-based, or mixed)
3. **Equity correction mechanisms** (contextual safeguards, local norming, linguistic adaptation, quotas, monitoring systems)

Across these dimensions, three regional regime types emerge.

5.5.1 Regime Type I: Competitive Performance-Selective Systems

Illustrative case: Chile and Peru

This regime type is characterized by:

- Competitive entrance examinations
- Strong academic performance criteria
- Centralized or university-affiliated administration
- Limited early-stage universal screening

Programs such as PENTA UC and Peru's *Colegios de Alto Rendimiento* (COAR) exemplify this model. These systems are institutionally structured and often demonstrate measurable academic outcomes for participants, including higher university matriculation rates. However, selection is strongly correlated with prior achievement and preparatory access. According to UNESCO regional education data (2022), students in the highest income quintile in Latin America are significantly more likely to reach advanced proficiency levels in reading and mathematics compared to those in the lowest quintile. ECLAC (2021) similarly reports persistent learning gaps between rural and urban students, with rural secondary completion rates lagging metropolitan averages in multiple countries.

In performance-selective regimes, such macro-level inequalities directly shape entry probabilities. Competitive examinations function as downstream filters that reflect upstream stratification. Equity safeguards may exist—such as regional quotas in Peru—but without universal early screening, the pipeline into competitive programs remains uneven.

Structural Risk: Meritocratic selection without contextual correction reinforces cumulative advantage.

5.5.2 *Regime Type II: Decentralized Nomination-Based Systems*

Illustrative case: Brazil, Mexico, and Colombia.

This regime type is characterized by:

- Policy recognition of giftedness within inclusive education
- Absence of mandatory national universal screening
- Strong reliance on teacher nomination
- High regional variation in implementation

Brazil's inclusion of high abilities within its National Policy on Special Education institutionalizes recognition but delegates operational responsibility to states and municipalities. Mexico and Colombia similarly integrate giftedness into broader special education frameworks without centralized identification mandates. Quantitative regional indicators underscore the implications of decentralization. According to World Bank and UNESCO statistics, disparities in per-student educational expenditure across subnational regions remain pronounced in Brazil and Mexico. Teacher preparation levels also vary significantly across rural and urban districts.

In nomination-based systems, uneven institutional capacity produces uneven identification. Municipalities with trained psychologists and professional development infrastructure identify more students; under-resourced districts identify fewer. This produces what may be termed capacity-dependent recognition. Brazilian research (Fleith, 2014; Pérez & Freitas, 2016) documents substantial intermunicipal variability in screening rates. In Colombia, García and Morales (2017) report limited formal data on national representation patterns, reflecting weak monitoring mechanisms.

Structural Risk: Recognition becomes contingent on local capacity rather than distributed potential.

5.5.3 Regime Type III: Hybrid Selective–Corrective Systems

Illustrative case: Peru partially and emerging adaptations in Brazil.

Hybrid regimes combine competitive selection with targeted equity safeguards. Peru's COAR model incorporates:

- Regional quotas
- Multilingual assessment accommodations
- State-funded residential schooling

Such measures represent explicit attempts to mitigate territorial and linguistic bias. However, these corrections occur primarily at secondary selection stages. From a quantitative standpoint, Peru has made notable progress in expanding secondary enrollment over the past decade, yet rural learning gaps persist, as documented by UNESCO regional assessments. Without systematic early identification embedded in primary schooling, hybrid models risk addressing symptoms rather than structural roots.

Structural Risk: Corrective measures at later stages cannot fully compensate for early developmental inequities.

5.5.4 Quantitative Contextualization of Underrepresentation

Regional data reinforce the structural interpretation advanced in this chapter:

- ECLAC (2021) reports that students from the highest income quintile in Latin America are multiple times more likely to complete upper secondary education than those from the lowest quintile.
- UNESCO (2022) documents persistent proficiency gaps in mathematics and reading between rural and urban students across Brazil, Mexico, and Peru.
- Digital access disparities—heightened during the COVID-19 pandemic—revealed severe infrastructural inequality affecting rural and low-income learners.

While these statistics do not directly measure gifted identification rates, they map the structural terrain within which identification operates. If high academic performance is disproportionately concentrated among socioeconomically advantaged populations, identification systems that rely on achievement proxies will reproduce that distribution.

In other words, macro-inequality predicts micro-identification disparity.

5.5.5 *Toward a Developmental–Equity Regime*

Across the three regime types, none fully operationalizes the developmental and socially embedded model articulated in Chap. 3. A fourth regime type—still largely aspirational—would integrate:

- Universal early screening
- Multi-criteria and dynamic assessment
- Local norming to correct for contextual distortion
- Mandatory teacher preparation in bias-aware identification
- Disaggregated national monitoring systems

Such a regime would treat identification not as selection among already high-performing students but as early detection within unequal opportunity landscapes. The comparative analysis thus reveals that Latin America's identification architectures remain predominantly selective rather than cultivation-oriented. Whether centralized or decentralized, competitive, or nomination-based, current regimes are insufficiently correct for structural inequality. From a regional talent development perspective, the critical shift is conceptual: identification must transition from filtering realized excellence to activating distributed potential.

To clarify cross-national variation without reducing it to isolated case descriptions, the preceding analysis can be synthesized into a comparative typology of identification regimes. Rather than categorizing countries by policy labels alone, this typology maps identification systems along analytically meaningful dimensions derived from developmental psychology and educational theory: degree of centralization, primary identification filters, developmental orientation, equity correction mechanisms, and structural vulnerabilities. These dimensions capture not just process and mechanics (or process design) but also the underlying assumptions that shape recognition practices that are predicated upon ability, context, and opportunity.

The comparative framework in Table 5.1, by framing national approaches in relation to broader regime types, provides a picture of how institutional logic intersects with structural inequality.

Table 5.1 organizes national variation into regime types defined by identification logic rather than individual policy features. The analytic dimensions—centralization, primary filters, developmental orientation, equity safeguards, and structural vulnerabilities—capture not only procedural design, but the assumptions about ability, context, and opportunity that shape the practice of recognition.

The typology reveals a consistent regional pattern: existing identification architectures remain predominantly selective rather than developmental. Whether competitive and performance-driven, decentralized and nomination-based, or hybrid with partial corrective safeguards, current regimes operate largely downstream of accumulated educational inequality. In psychological terms, they privilege realized performance over emerging capacity; in educational terms, they reward preparedness rather than detect distributed potential. The aspirational developmental–equity regime outlined above represents a conceptual reorientation consistent with the

Table 5.1 Typology of identification regimes in selected Latin American contexts

Regime type	Degree of centralization	Primary identification filters	Developmental orientation	Equity correction mechanisms	Structural vulnerabilities	Illustrative national patterns
Type I: Competitive performance-selective	Moderately centralized or university-affiliated	Competitive cognitive testing; academic achievement thresholds; entrance examinations	Low to moderate; identification often time-bound and performance-focused	Limited contextual adjustments; occasional scholarships or regional quotas	Overrepresentation of socioeconomically advantaged students; urban concentration; reliance on prior preparation	Chile (BETA PUCV, DELTA UCN, PENTA UC, PROENTA UFRO); Peru (25 COAR secondary selection)
Type II: Decentralized nomination-based	Highly decentralized; municipal or state-level discretion	Teacher nomination; inconsistent psychometric testing; school-based referral	Variable; dependent on local professional preparation	Inclusion discourse present but weak monitoring and limited universal screening	Capacity-dependent identification; regional disparities; implicit bias in referral processes	Brazil (municipal variation); Mexico; Colombia
Type III: Hybrid selective–corrective	National framework with targeted adaptations	Competitive examination combined with linguistic accommodations or quotas	Moderate; partial recognition of contextual mediation	Regional quotas; multilingual assessment; state-funded access	Corrective mechanisms occur late in developmental trajectory; early-stage inequities persist	Peru (COAR model with regional and linguistic safeguards)
Aspirational type IV: Developmental–equity oriented	Nationally coordinated with local implementation support	Universal and repeated screening; multi-criteria assessment; dynamic and learning-potential measures	High; longitudinal and growth-sensitive	Local norming; culturally responsive tools; bias-aware teacher training; disaggregated monitoring systems	Implementation complexity; resource-intensive; requires sustained policy commitment	Not yet fully institutionalized in the region

ecological model articulated in Chap. 3, one in which identification functions not as a terminal sorting mechanism but as an early and iterative process of opportunity activation.

Beyond categorizing institutional arrangements, the typology exposes the epistemological commitments that govern recognition. Competitive performance-selective systems presume that high ability is already manifest and demonstrable under standardized conditions. Decentralized nomination-based systems rely on professional judgment without systemic calibration. Hybrid models acknowledge contextual mediation but intervene primarily at later stages of selection.

What remains insufficiently institutionalized across regimes is a fully developmental understanding of talent as emergent, contextually mediated, and responsive to opportunity structures. The comparative analysis therefore points not merely to procedural variation but to conceptual misalignment between identification design and contemporary developmental theory. To move beyond typology, identification must be re-anchored within the ecological and socially embedded framework articulated in Chap. 3. If talent development is understood as the progressive interaction between individual predispositions and environmental catalysts, then identification cannot remain a threshold event; it must become structurally iterative and growth-sensitive. Section 5.6 turns to this theoretical recalibration.

5.6 Alignment with the Developmental and Socially Embedded Framework (Chap. 3)

The comparative analysis of identification regimes reveals a persistent conceptual misalignment between institutional practice and contemporary developmental theory. While national systems vary in structure—competitive, decentralized, or hybrid—they share a common operational premise: identification is treated primarily as a selective classification event rather than as a developmental process embedded within ecological systems.

Realignment requires more than procedural reform. It demands theoretical coherence with the developmental and socially embedded framework articulated in Chap. 3. Drawing on international scholarship (Subotnik et al., 2011; Sternberg, 2018; Pfeiffer, 2015; Renzulli & Reis, 2014) and Ibero-American research traditions (Pérez & Freitas, 2016; Virgolim, 2014; Tourón & Santiago, 2015; Alencar & Fleith, 2001), three interlocking recalibrations become necessary: temporality, contextual mediation, and structural equity.

5.6.1 Developmental Temporality: From Threshold to Trajectory

Classical identification models rely on threshold logic: a student either meets a predefined criterion—often a psychometric cutoff or competitive score—or does not. Such models compress development into episodic measurement, assuming that high ability is fully manifest and measurable at a single point in time.

Subotnik et al. (2011) argue that giftedness must be understood developmentally, as evolving expertise shaped by training, opportunity, and domain-specific engagement. Sternberg (2018) similarly critiques static IQ-based models for neglecting adaptive and creative dimensions of ability. Renzulli and Reis (2014), through the Schoolwide Enrichment Model, emphasize that high-level performance often emerges only after exposure to enriched learning environments.

Brazilian scholarship converges on this view. Pérez and Freitas (2016) emphasize that altas habilidades/superdotação unfold across time and cannot be reduced to early academic precocity. Virgolim (2014) documents how students in under-resourced Brazilian schools may exhibit latent high potential that remains unrecognized when identification occurs only through early psychometric screening. Alencar and Fleith (2001) further argue that creative potential frequently manifests unevenly across domains and developmental periods.

From this convergent literature, a clear implication follows: identification must shift from threshold adjudication to trajectory detection. Operationally, this entails:

- Repeated screening across developmental stages
- Flexible entry points into advanced programming
- Growth-sensitive and dynamic assessment models
- Recognition of late-emerging and domain-specific profiles

Temporality is not an administrative adjustment; it is a theoretical imperative. Talent is not a fixed state but an unfolding process.

5.6.2 Contextual Mediation: From Performance to Ecological Interpretation

Chapter 3 situated talent development within an ecological framework, drawing implicitly on Bronfenbrenner's systems theory and subsequent interactionist models. Within such a framework, observed performance reflects the interaction between individual predispositions and layered environmental catalysts.

Yet prevailing identification regimes frequently interpret test scores and academic achievement as direct indicators of internal ability. This interpretation neglects contextual mediation.

Pfeiffer (2015) emphasizes that multi-method assessment improves validity precisely because it accounts for situational influences. Ford (2014) demonstrates how culturally unresponsive identification systems disproportionately exclude minoritized students. Peters et al. (2019) provide empirical evidence that universal screening combined with local norming increases representation of low-income learners.

In Ibero-American scholarship, Tourón and Santiago (2015), discussing Gagné's Differentiated Model in Spanish contexts, highlight the decisive role of environmental catalysts in transforming giftedness into talent. Delou (2007) similarly underscores the mediating influence of teacher expectations and school climate in Brazilian settings. García-Cepero and McCoach (2009) show that Chilean talent program participation correlates with educational capital, indicating ecological mediation of performance.

Alignment with a socially embedded framework therefore requires contextual interpretation of assessment data. Mechanisms include:

- Local norming to correct for environmental variation
- Dynamic assessment of learning potential
- Culturally and linguistically responsive instruments
- Structured, bias-aware teacher nomination protocols

Ability is not merely measured; it is interpreted within its context. Without ecological calibration, identification risks conflating opportunity with aptitude.

5.6.3 Structural Equity: From Selection to Opportunity Activation

Equity in identification cannot be conceptualized solely as proportional representation after selection. It must be embedded in the architecture of recognition itself.

Competitive and decentralized regimes alike tend to identify students who have already converted environmental advantage into observable performance. In doing so, they operate downstream of inequality. ECLAC and UNESCO data demonstrate persistent gaps in learning outcomes across income quintiles and territorial regions in Latin America. When identification filters privilege high academic performance under standardized conditions, they reproduce these macro-inequalities at the micro-level of gifted programming.

Renzulli and Reis (2014) argue that enrichment opportunities should precede, not follow, high-stakes selection. Peters et al. (2019) demonstrate that universal screening increases access for historically underrepresented groups. In Brazil, Pérez and Freitas (2016) advocate broader, context-sensitive identification to counteract underrecognition in public schools. Virgolim (2014) similarly calls for systemic reform to prevent the invisibility of high-ability students in marginalized communities.

A developmental–equity alignment therefore repositions identification as an instrument of opportunity activation. Rather than ratifying realized excellence, it detects emerging potential and initiates structured support. Universal screening, multi-criteria assessment, and disaggregated monitoring systems become mechanisms of developmental justice rather than bureaucratic compliance.

Structural equity requires transparency. Without systematic data disaggregation by socioeconomic status, ethnicity, gender, rurality, and disability, inequity remains concealed within aggregate success narratives.

Across temporality, contextual mediation, and structural equity, a coherent recalibration emerges: ability develops through interaction with opportunity structures. Identification systems that ignore this interaction risk institutionalizing inequality.

Alignment with the developmental and socially embedded framework of Chap. 3 transforms the purpose of identification. The guiding question shifts from *Who qualifies under current performance conditions?* to *Where is potential emerging, and how can systems cultivate it?*

In this reconceptualization:

- Measurement becomes iterative rather than terminal.
- Assessment becomes ecological rather than context blind.
- Recognition becomes activation rather than ratification.

Only through such theoretical and structural coherence can identification systems in Latin America function not as instruments of selective reproduction but as infrastructures for distributed talent development.

5.7 System Design Implications for Equitable Identification

The preceding analysis demonstrates that identification systems across Latin America are structurally embedded within unequal educational ecologies. Psychometric thresholds, achievement filters, and discretionary nomination mechanisms intersect with socioeconomic stratification, territorial asymmetry, and cultural marginalization. Reform, therefore, cannot be limited to technical adjustments in testing instruments. It requires systemic redesign aligned with the developmental and socially embedded framework articulated in Chap. 3 and the regional structural analysis presented in Chaps. 2 and 4.

Equitable identification must be conceived as part of a broader talent development infrastructure. It is not an isolated procedural stage but an entry point into opportunity structures.

5.7.1 Universal and Repeated Screening as Structural Equalizer

As shown in Chap. 2, inequality in Latin America is cumulative and intergenerational. If identification depends solely on referral or competitive selection, it captures only those who have already benefited from favorable developmental conditions. Universal screening at multiple developmental stages—particularly in early primary years and again in early adolescence—reduces reliance on discretionary referral and increases the probability of detecting distributed potential (Peters et al., 2019).

Repeated screening is equally critical. Development is nonlinear. Students who do not initially display high performance may later demonstrate rapid growth when environmental conditions improve. A growth-sensitive identification cycle aligns with the developmental temporality discussed in Chap. 3.

Universal screening is not merely an efficiency strategy; it is a structural correction mechanism within unequal systems.

5.7.2 Multi-Criteria and Dynamic Assessment Models

Chapter 3 emphasized multidimensionality: cognitive, creative, socio-emotional, and domain-specific capacities interact over time. Identification systems that rely on a single metric compress this complexity.

Multi-criteria models—integrating cognitive measures, creativity tasks, structured teacher observations, portfolios, performance-based tasks, and student self-nomination—expand the aperture of recognition (Renzulli & Reis, 2014; Pfeiffer, 2015). Dynamic assessment approaches further evaluate learning potential under guided conditions rather than solely prior knowledge, reducing bias against students whose schooling quality has been uneven (Sternberg, 2018).

In Latin American contexts marked by linguistic diversity and rural–urban disparity, multi-method approaches are not optional enhancements; they are safeguards against systematic exclusion.

5.7.3 Culturally and Linguistically Responsive Design

As discussed in Chap. 4, regional policy discourse increasingly embraces intercultural and inclusive education frameworks. However, identification procedures often lag behind this discourse.

Culturally responsive identification requires:

- Linguistically adapted assessment tools
- Recognition of community-valued competencies
- Bias-aware teacher preparation
- Structured nomination protocols

Brazilian and Ibero-American scholarship (Pérez & Freitas, 2016; Virgolim, 2014; Tourón & Santiago, 2015) consistently emphasizes that environmental catalysts and cultural context shape talent expression. Without such responsiveness, identification systems risk privileging dominant academic prototypes while overlooking alternative forms of excellence.

5.7.4 *Monitoring, Accountability, and Data Transparency*

Chapter 4 demonstrated that policy recognition without monitoring produces symbolic inclusion rather than structural change. Identification reform must therefore include mandatory disaggregated reporting by:

- Socioeconomic status
- Ethnicity and race
- Gender
- Rural/urban location
- Disability status

Transparent monitoring systems enable ministries to detect underrepresentation patterns and recalibrate procedures. Without data visibility, inequity remains administratively invisible.

Monitoring transforms equity from aspiration to operational accountability.

5.7.5 *From Selection to Developmental Cultivation*

Perhaps the most significant shift required is conceptual. In many regional systems, identification functions as selection into scarce, high-status programs. This scarcity logic reinforces competition and concentrates on resources.

Aligned with the regional model of talent development emerging across this volume, identification should instead initiate a continuum of support. Early enrichment-for-all strategies, flexible entry and exit pathways, and distributed regional hubs reduce the zero-sum nature of recognition.

This shift parallels the argument in Chap. 2 that educational policy must move from compensatory targeting toward systemic capacity-building. Gifted education cannot operate as an enclave but as part of a broader quality-and-equity agenda. Identification becomes the first step in a developmental pathway rather than the final gate to access.

5.8 Conclusion: Identification as Structural Lever of Developmental Justice

Across Latin America, identification systems reveal a shared pattern: who is recognized depends not only on individual ability but also on how institutional structures interact with unequal opportunities. Performance-selective systems tend to favor students who have already accumulated academic advantages. Decentralized nomination processes mirror differences in professional preparation and regional capacity. Hybrid corrective models add safeguards, but they often intervene only after earlier developmental inequalities have already taken shape.

The comparative and theoretical analyses converge on a central insight: identification is not a neutral technical stage within gifted education. It is the decisive interface between potential and structured opportunity. As demonstrated throughout this chapter, psychometric thresholds, achievement filters, and interpretive nomination processes are not merely assessment tools; they are mechanisms through which stratified societies allocate developmental resources.

When aligned with the ecological and developmental framework articulated in Chap. 3, identification assumes a different function. It becomes an early mechanism of opportunity activation rather than a late-stage ratification of realized excellence. Universal and repeated screening, contextual calibration, culturally responsive interpretation, and transparent monitoring are not procedural refinements; they are structural correctives within unequal systems.

This chapter began by asking who gets to be gifted. The analysis demonstrates that the answer is not determined solely by cognitive capacity, but by how systems allocate opportunity. In unequal societies, identification functions as an allocative mechanism: it can channel enrichment, mentorship, and advanced learning toward those already advantaged, or it can widen the aperture of recognition and activate distributed potential. When designed as a single threshold event, identification ratifies stratification. When structured as a developmental, context-sensitive, and equity-embedded process, it becomes an instrument of opportunity redistribution. The question of who gets to be gifted ultimately returns to institutional design. Recognition is not neutral; it is a structural choice about whose futures are cultivated. In the regional model advanced in this volume, identification must serve not as a gate but as an opening.

References

Alencar, E. M. L. S., & Fleith, D. S. (2001). *Criatividade: Múltiplas perspectivas*. Editora Universidade de Brasília.

Blumen, S. (2021). Innovative practices to support high-achieving deprived young scholars in an ethnic-linguistic diverse Latin American country. In S. R. Smith (Ed.), *Handbook of giftedness and talent development in the Asia-Pacific* (pp. 223–238). Springer.

Delou, C. M. C. (2007). Altas habilidades/superdotação: Processos de identificação e atendimento educacional. *Revista Educação Especial, 20*(29), 113–128.

Economic Commission for Latin America and the Caribbean. (2021). *Social panorama of Latin America 2020*. United Nations.

Fleith, D. S. (2014). Gifted education in Brazil: Public policies and practices. *Gifted Education International, 30*(3), 221–230. https://doi.org/10.1177/0261429413480423

Ford, D. Y. (2014). *Recruiting and retaining culturally different students in gifted education* (2nd ed.). Prufrock Press.

García, L., & Morales, A. (2017). Identificación de estudiantes con altas capacidades en contextos colombianos. *Revista Colombiana de Educación, 72*, 155–176.

García-Cepero, M. C., & McCoach, D. B. (2009). Educating the gifted in Chile: Challenges and opportunities. *Gifted and Talented International, 24*(2), 91–101.
Ourofino, V. T. A. T., & Guimarães, T. G. (2007). Características intelectuais, emocionais e sociais do aluno com altas habilidades/superdotação. In D. S. Fleith (Ed.), *A construção de práticas educacionais para alunos com altas habilidades/superdotação: Orientação a professores* (pp. 41–52). Ministério da Educação, Secretaria de Educação Especial.
Pérez, S., & Freitas, S. N. (2016). Altas habilidades/superdotação: Identificação e atendimento no Brasil. *Revista Educação Especial, 29*(55), 343–358.
Peters, S. J., Gentry, M., Whiting, G. W., & McBee, M. T. (2019). Who gets served in gifted education? Demographic representation and a call for universal screening. *Gifted Child Quarterly, 63*(4), 273–287. https://doi.org/10.1177/0016986219833734
Pfeiffer, S. I. (2015). *Essentials of gifted assessment*. Wiley.
Renzulli, J. S., & Reis, S. M. (2014). *The schoolwide enrichment model: A comprehensive plan for the development of talents and giftedness* (3rd ed.). Creative Learning Press.
Sternberg, R. J. (2018). ACCEL: A new model for identifying the gifted. *Roeper Review, 40*(3), 152–169. https://doi.org/10.1080/02783193.2018.1468301
Subotnik, R. F., Olszewski-Kubilius, P., & Worrell, F. C. (2011). Rethinking giftedness and gifted education: A proposed direction forward. *Psychological Science in the Public Interest, 12*(1), 3–54. https://doi.org/10.1177/1529100611418056
Tourón, J., & Santiago, R. (2015). El modelo diferenciador de dotación y talento en contextos iberoamericanos. *Revista de Educación, 368*, 12–35.
UNESCO. (2022). *Education in Latin America and the Caribbean: Regional overview*. UNESCO Regional Bureau for Education in Latin America and the Caribbean.
Valadez, M., & Borges, A. (2014). La identificación de alumnos con aptitudes sobresalientes en México. *Revista Mexicana de Investigación Educativa, 19*(62), 1131–1156.
Virgolim, A. M. R. (2014). Altas habilidades/superdotação: Mitos e realidades. *Psicologia Escolar e Educacional, 18*(1), 63–72.

Chapter 6
Innovations in Curriculum and Instruction for High-Ability Learners in Latin America

6.1 Introduction: Innovation under Constraint

If Chap. 5 established identification as the allocative gateway to opportunity, this chapter focuses on what must follow recognition. Identification is necessary but insufficient: talent development depends on curriculum, instruction, institutional design, and redistributive policy capable of sustaining development across transitions. In other words, the system must supply the *conditions of conversion* through which potential becomes achievement, and achievement becomes longer-run capability.

Global gifted education has been shaped, over the last four decades, largely by theory and policy developed in North America and Western Europe. Renzulli's (2012) Schoolwide Enrichment Model and Gagné's (2009) Differentiated Model of Giftedness and Talent remain among the most widely used frameworks for conceptualizing identification, differentiation, enrichment, and acceleration. Their contribution is substantial: they frame talent as developmental rather than static, and they locate outcomes in interactions between individual assets and environmental catalysts. Yet, these models also often assume structural underpinnings that are not uniformly present across Latin America—stable funding, specialized teacher preparation, flexible curricular governance, robust identification systems, and institutional capacity to individualize instruction.

Across much of the region, gifted education has moved formally from invisibility to legal recognition. However, recognition frequently remains symbolic where it is not paired with financing, teacher training, or curricular flexibility (Navarro Guillén, 2022; García-Cepero & Iglesias-Velasco, 2020). The result is an implementation gap: macro-level policy intention without microlevel instructional transformation. International assessment patterns reflect this structural discontinuity. OECD data show that approximately 9% of students in OECD countries reach top performance levels (Levels 5–6) in PISA domains (OECD, 2023). Peru reports roughly 1% at these levels (MINEDU, 2024). Such

S. Blumen, *High Ability and Talent Development in Latin America*,
https://doi.org/10.1007/978-3-032-27468-7_6

differences do not indicate a radically different distribution of ability. Rather, they reflect opportunity structures—how systems detect, cultivate, pace, and sustain development.

This chapter advances an argument already foreshadowed in Chap. 3: in Latin American contexts marked by high inequality and institutional constraint, curricular innovation is not an optional enhancement. It is a structural recalibration. This argument is developed through three integrative lenses:

1. **Ecological fit (Bronfenbrenner):** Development depends on alignments between learner readiness and the demands, pacing, and affordances of family, school, community, and policy systems. Misfit—especially sustained curricular mismatch—produces disengagement, underachievement, and often invisibility.
2. **Capability expansion (Sen,** 1999**):** Educational justice requires expansion of *real freedoms*. Talent development is not only about maximizing scores, but about enabling learners to convert ability into valued life trajectories.
3. **Decolonial critique (Quijano,** 2000**):** Institutional norms—such as rigid age-graded progression and uniform pacing—are not neutral developmental truths. They are historically inherited arrangements that can reproduce exclusion, especially when treated as universal.

Seen from this perspective, innovation in Latin America is not merely a technical shift in pedagogy. It is the creation of mechanisms—curricular, institutional, and policy-based—that restore alignment between readiness and opportunity, and that redistribute access to high-quality pathways across the life course.

6.2 Curriculum and Instruction in Latin America: A Comparative Overview

Over the past three decades, Latin American countries have expanded the formal recognition of high-ability learners fluenced by UNESCO's Salamanca Statement (1994) and the Education 2030 Framework (UNESCO, 2016). Countries such as Costa Rica (Law 8899/2010), Ecuador (Ley Orgánica de Educación Intercultural), Argentina (Law 6614), Brazil (Diretrizes Nacionais para Educação Especial), Colombia (Decree 1421), and Peru (Law 28044) have incorporated high-ability students into legal frameworks and policy discourse.

Yet, the regional pattern is clear: recognition has outpaced instruction. The most common gap is not at the level of aspiration but of implementation—where policy exists without scalable teacher preparation, without adaptive curricular governance, or without protected time and resources for differentiated instruction. Consequently, innovation tends to appear in "structural pockets": university partnerships, specialized centers, selective schools, scholarship programs, or targeted pilots, rather than across mainstream classrooms.

6.2.1 Chile: University–School Partnerships as Compensatory Innovation

Chile offers one of the region's most consolidated enrichment models through university-based talent programs operating alongside regular schooling. Following MINEDUC reforms (e.g., Decree 230), the state funded university-led initiatives such as PENTA-UC, DeLTA-UCN, and BETA-PUCV. These programs often integrate frameworks resonant with Renzulli's enrichment principles and Gagné's DMGT (Gómez-Arizaga et al., 2024). Their signature features include curricular freedom from narrow national prescriptions, inquiry-driven pedagogy connected to research cultures, independent investigation, and scholarship models that prioritize low-income participation. Reported scale—tens of thousands of scholarships over extended periods—signals sustained public investment (DIPRES, 2021). Evaluations suggest benefits in higher-order thinking and university admissions outcomes (Barrera et al., 2013; González Adonis et al., 2017).

However, the model reveals a persistent structural tension: enrichment becomes an "add-on" (8 hours per week) alongside the dominant schooling experience (approximately 30 hours). The resulting intellectual discontinuity can amplify the rigidity of the mainstream curriculum rather than transforming it. This is a recurring theme in the region: enrichment at the margins compensates for curricular inflexibility at the center.

6.2.2 Brazil: Institutionalizing Enrichment within Public Schooling

Brazil's Atendimento Educacional Especializado (AEE) offers a different architecture: enrichment embedded within public schools via multifunctional resource rooms (Ministério da Educação, 2002, 2022). Rather than outsourcing talent development to universities, the AEE model positions enrichment as a public-school duty, often delivered during counter-shift hours and aligned with enrichment principles.

This model is structurally significant because it redefines talent development as part of inclusive service provision. Yet, implementation varies widely due to disparities in municipal budgets, teacher training pathways, and local governance capacity (Pérez Barrera & Bendelman, 2016). The result is unevenness: policy that exists nationally but materializes differentially across territories—a core equity problem in decentralized systems.

6.2.3 Colombia: Administrative Inclusion without Pedagogical Differentiation

Colombia's PIAR framework (required under Decree 1421) theoretically enables individualized curricular accommodations (MEN, 2017). Yet García-Cepero and Iglesias-Velasco (2020) show that PIAR frequently devolves into administrative documentation rather than instructional transformation. The mechanism becomes compliance-oriented rather than pedagogically generative. In such cases, inclusion is affirmed on paper while classroom practice remains uniform.

6.2.4 The Missing Socioemotional Dimension

Across the region, policies often emphasize cognitive differentiation while underspecifying socioemotional needs. Yet, empirical research increasingly emphasizes that high-ability learners in vulnerable contexts may be "doubly vulnerable": they experience advanced cognitive capacity within conditions of socioeconomic stress, institutional neglect, and heightened family expectations for upward mobility (Conejeros-Solar et al., 2025; Pinquart & Ebeling, 2020). Belonging, emotional regulation, resilience, and identity coherence become developmentally central, not optional. Consequently, Latin American innovation cannot replicate Global North debates that reduce the field to "acceleration versus enrichment." In unequal systems, innovation must include socioemotional scaffolding and transition supports as core components of talent development.

6.3 Acceleration as Structural Equity in South America

Acceleration is among the most empirically validated interventions in gifted education. Syntheses and longitudinal analyses—prominently including *A Nation Deceived* and *A Nation Empowered*—indicate that, when decisions are individualized and contextually supported, acceleration yields positive academic outcomes and neutral-to-positive socioemotional effects (Colangelo et al., 2004, 2015). Yet, evidence-based interventions are not automatically adopted: they must pass through cultural beliefs, institutional routines, and policy architectures.

Across Latin America, acceleration remains underutilized and often contested. The regional analysis by Vuyk et al. (2026) reframes acceleration as a *structural equity mechanism* in South America and documents obstacles that recur across systems: fragmented terminology; bureaucratic rigidity embedded in age-grade promotion; cultural myths about socioemotional harm; delays and discretion in authorization; and, in some jurisdictions, explicit restrictions on subject acceleration or multiple grade skips. The analysis also illustrates policy–practice conflict:

legal mandates remain inconsistently implemented; age-based integration norms constrain grade skipping; and administrative regulations limit flexibility.

The resistance to acceleration often rests on a moralized interpretation of equality: fairness is equated with uniform pacing. Yet, this is precisely where the chapter's theoretical lenses matter:

- **Ecologically,** acceleration restores alignment between readiness and instructional level. Without such alignment, learners experience chronic mismatch—boredom, disengagement, and reduced opportunities for deep learning.
- **From a capability perspective,** denial of progression constrains substantive freedoms. A student may possess ability, but without institutional permission to advance, that ability cannot be converted into expanded life choices.
- **From a decolonial perspective,** rigid age-grading can be read as an inherited institutional structure, naturalized as developmental inevitability rather than recognized as a governance technology.

Acceleration also has a paradoxical equity profile in resource-constrained contexts: it often requires *less* material infrastructure than enrichment programs. It requires administrative flexibility, training, and decision frameworks rather than extensive new funding. In that sense, acceleration is one of the least costly innovations yet one of the most resisted. This paradox makes acceleration a revealing case of how cultural and institutional factors mediate the translation of evidence into practice.

6.4 The Peruvian Context: Structural Dualism and Educational Invisibility

Before examining Peru's innovations, the structural context must be explicit. Peru's educational system is characterized by dualism: high-quality private education is concentrated among affluent families, while many public schools face overcrowding, limited resources, and uneven teacher preparation. In such settings, teachers often operate under conditions of pedagogical triage, devoting attention to students below proficiency and assuming high-ability students will succeed without support. This assumption is not merely a misconception; it is a structural response to scarcity. Yet, its developmental cost is substantial: it institutionalizes invisibility.

PISA 2022 results reinforce the magnitude of stratification. While around 9% of students in OECD contexts reach advanced levels, Peru reports approximately 1% (OECD, 2023; MINEDU, 2024). Rural–urban divides are severe: rural students disproportionately perform below basic proficiency compared with their urban peers (MINEDU, 2024). Such disparities reflect opportunity structures rather than potential distribution.

Peru's Law 28044 formally recognizes gifted students (MINEDU, 2003). Yet official identification remains extraordinarily low: ESCALE data indicate only a tiny fraction of the student population is registered as gifted (MINEDU, 2023). If prevalence estimates approximate 10% for high natural ability (Gagné, 2009), then the gap between expected prevalence and registered identification becomes staggering. In practical terms, the majority of high-potential learners remain invisible to the system. Blumen et al. (2025) attributes this to interlocking barriers: limited teacher training in identification, deficit-based service models, bureaucratic under-registration, and misconceptions that equate giftedness with compliance or consistently high grades.

Under such conditions, Peru's initial large-scale response did not begin with classroom differentiation. It created an alternative institutional architecture.

6.5 Instructional Innovation through Structural Transformation: The COAR Model

The creation of the *Colegios de Alto Rendimiento* (COAR) constitutes one of the most ambitious public-sector interventions for high-ability learners in Latin America. Rather than attempting incremental reform within under-resourced classrooms, the Peruvian state pursued institutional redesign: a strategic bypass intended to create high-quality opportunity for academically talented students emerging from disadvantaged contexts.

6.5.1 Origins and Expansion

COAR originated in 2009 with Supreme Resolution N° 034-2009-ED establishing the Colegio Mayor Secundario Presidente del Perú as a national residential school (MINEDU, 2009). The model later expanded into a nationwide network operating across 25 regions (MINEDU, 2014, 2025). Its core design combines merit-based selection, full state funding, a rigorous curriculum including international components, and a residential structure intended to neutralize socioeconomic constraints that frequently limit talent development.

6.5.2 Selection, Redistribution, and Equalization

Admission is competitive, typically drawing from high-performing students in public secondary education or national competitions (MINEDU, 2025). Selection processes incorporate cognitive measures and socio-behavioral evaluations and include a residential immersion component (*jornada vivencial*) aimed at assessing autonomy, leadership, and resilience (MINEDU, 2014). In ecological terms, selection functions not only as a cognitive filter but as an assessment of fit with a demanding developmental environment.

COAR's redistributive logic is explicit: admitted students generally come from lower-income households, with many originating from rural regions historically excluded from high-quality secondary education (Asensio & Burneo de la Rocha, 2019; MINEDU, 2025). Full funding covers housing, meals, uniforms, healthcare, and technological devices (MINEDU, 2022, 2025). From a capability perspective, COAR functions as a conversion mechanism: it increases the probability that readiness can be converted into educational opportunity and later-life options.

6.5.3 *Curriculum as Structural Disruption*

COAR's most transformative feature is the integration of the International Baccalaureate (IB) Diploma Programme during the final 2 years of secondary education (MINEDU, 2014). A preparatory year aims to reduce academic disparities among incoming students and create a leveling stage before IB intensification (Blumen, 2021). The curricular shift is epistemic rather than cosmetic: inquiry-based learning displaces rote memorization, extended research projects cultivate autonomy, community engagement is formalized, and English proficiency becomes systematically developed.

Instructional strategies such as problem-based learning and research-centered pedagogy align with contemporary talent development models that emphasize agency, productive creativity, and student-driven inquiry (Renzulli, 2012; CAF, 2021). COAR thus reshapes not only content depth but the cultural norms of learning—how knowledge is generated, evaluated, and communicated.

6.5.4 *Outcomes and Structural Tensions*

Impact evaluations report improved university admission outcomes and increased access to selective institutions (MINEDU, 2025; Hatrick & Paniagua, 2021). Decentralized campuses across 25 regions mitigate Lima-centric concentration of opportunity. Yet COAR also reveals enduring structural dilemmas. Critics argue that concentrating resources in selective schools may reinforce systemic dualism by creating "islands of excellence" within broader inequality (Alcázar & Balarin, 2016). Residential separation may produce socioemotional strain, particularly under high academic pressure. Moreover, international curricular alignment raises questions about outward migration and long-term national return on investment.

COAR therefore embodies a paradox central to talent policy in unequal contexts: it can advance equity while simultaneously exposing the fragility of mainstream provision. It is both a redistributive intervention and a diagnostic signal.

6.6 Enrichment within Mainstream Schooling: The International Baccalaureate in Latin America

If COAR represents institutional extraction from underperforming environments into redesigned settings, the International Baccalaureate (IB) also functions as an enrichment mechanism within mainstream schooling systems. IB introduces inquiry-driven pedagogy, interdisciplinary learning, and extended independent inquiry. In contexts governed by standardized national curricula and exam-driven pressure, IB can deepen epistemic rigor without relying explicitly on "gifted" labeling or age-grade acceleration.

Yet IB's equity implications are structurally contingent. In many Latin American contexts, IB remains concentrated in private schools serving socioeconomically advantaged populations. Under those conditions, IB risks functioning as a stratification amplifier: a curriculum of global capital accessible disproportionately to those already privileged. When publicly funded—such as through COAR or state-supported schools—IB can function as redistributive enrichment, democratizing access to internationally recognized credentials and learning norms.

Comparatively, patterns across Chile, Mexico, Colombia, and Brazil show that adoption trajectories reflect governance structures and inequality distributions. Where IB expansion is market-driven and urban-concentrated, rural and low-income students remain excluded. The general principle is consistent: IB democratizes excellence only when policy actively broadens access.

Thus, IB occupies an intermediate space in Latin America's talent development architecture. It deepens the curriculum without necessarily restructuring institutions. Its equity function depends less on pedagogy alone than on access design.

6.7 Extending the Talent Pipeline: Beca 18 as Postsecondary Equity Intervention

If COAR restructures secondary opportunity and IB deepens curricular rigor, the transition to higher education remains a critical bottleneck. In unequal systems, academic readiness does not reliably translate into university access without material support. Beca 18 was created to address this conversion problem precisely.

Established in 2012 and administered by Programa Nacional de Becas y Crédito Educativo (PRONABEC, 2023), Beca 18 provides comprehensive scholarships to academically high-performing youth living in poverty. It covers tuition, living expenses, materials, and often relocation costs, targeting students from rural, Indigenous, and otherwise highly vulnerable communities. The program's structural premise is direct: merit without redistribution reproduces exclusion.

From a capability perspective, higher education is a core freedom that reshapes life trajectories (Sen, 1999). By removing financial barriers, Beca 18 expands real freedoms and disrupts intergenerational poverty cycles. It also frequently functions as a continuation pathway for COAR graduates, creating a developmental continuum from selective secondary preparation to funded tertiary access.

Empirical evidence indicates increased enrollment of low-income students in competitive institutions and improved persistence among beneficiaries, though debates remain about sustainability, resource concentration, and migration. Regardless, Beca 18 addresses a distinct structural juncture: it prevents poverty from reversing gains achieved through earlier stages of preparation. In ecological terms, it modifies macrosystem opportunity structures; in capability terms, it expands developmental freedoms into adulthood.

6.8 University-Level Talent Development: Becas LUCET at Pontificia Universidad Católica del Perú

Access to higher education does not automatically produce persistence, distinction, or postgraduate projection—especially for students from socioeconomically vulnerable backgrounds. University-level talent development therefore requires institutional commitment beyond admission and tuition support.

The Becas LUCET program at Pontificia Universidad Católica del Perú (PUCP) is positioned as an integrative intervention to support high-achieving students through undergraduate and graduate trajectories. Unlike conventional aid, LUCET combines merit recognition with structured academic and vocational scaffolding: financial support, mentoring, academic planning, research integration, and pathways to internationalization and graduate preparation (Pontificia Universidad Católica del Perú, 2023a, b).

6.8.1 Program Architecture

LUCET integrates multiple facets:

- **Holistic financial support:** covering tuition and academic materials and sometimes living expenses—reducing economic pressures that otherwise compel students to reduce course loads or work excessive hours.
- **Academic mentoring:** advising and tutoring that support planning, performance, and preparation for competitive postgraduate pathways.
- **Research integration:** early incorporation into research groups, assistantships, and conferences, embedding students in scholarly communities.
- **Internationalization pathways:** exchange programs, language development, and network-building that extend academic capital.
- **Leadership and professional development:** workshops that develop civic engagement, ethical leadership, and professional skills.

The conceptual distinction is important: LUCET is not only a financial transfer but an institutional conversion mechanism. It addresses the conversion barriers that often constrain talented low-income students—limited cultural capital, restricted access to faculty networks, research isolation, and lack of postgraduate pathway knowledge (Pontificia Universidad Católica del Perú, 2025).

6.8.2 From Access to Projection

Within Peru's broader continuum, LUCET fills the gap between access and projection. Beca 18 can secure entry; LUCET increases the probability of excellence, persistence, and postgraduate advancement. Ecologically, it strengthens the mesosystem links between student, faculty, and research networks. From a capability perspective, it expands the set of realized freedoms by increasing the likelihood that high ability becomes durable academic and professional agency.

6.9 Curricular Innovation for Equity: Well-Being and Art in School

Whereas COAR and scholarship programs reflect structural redesign and redistribution, the Well-being and Art in School initiative illustrates curricular integration within mainstream public schooling, particularly in the socioemotional domain (Blumen et al., 2025). This matters because talent development in vulnerable contexts is not only cognitive: chronic poverty exposure can intensify stress and disrupt self-regulation (Bosgraaf et al., 2020; Evans & Kim, 2013), while gifted learners may simultaneously experience perfectionism and heightened sensitivity (Margot & Rinn, 2016; Stricker et al., 2019). Family pressure for upward mobility can compound stress, and school environments may lack the psychological infrastructure to support twice-exceptionality, vulnerability, or intensification.

Arts-centered education provides structured pathways for emotional processing, ambiguity tolerance, resilience, and identity expression. Reviews and policy syntheses underscore links between arts engagement and wellbeing (Fancourt & Finn, 2019), and empirical studies indicate physiological and neural correlates such as cortisol reduction following artmaking (Kaimal et al., 2016) and changes in functional connectivity associated with art production and evaluation (Bolwerk et al., 2014). In capability terms, access to arts also expands expressive and cultural freedoms—forms of human flourishing often distributed along class lines (Reeves, 2019).

6.9.1 Program Design

The pilot involved three 90-minute sessions per week with fourth- and fifth-grade students in Lima public schools. Sessions followed a structured progression: guided analysis of artworks; skill-building through drawing and painting; and a "freedom space" for autonomous creation. The design combined boundaries with autonomy (Kraehe, 2018), cultivating ambiguity tolerance—an attribute linked to creativity and adaptive functioning (Smyth et al., 2026). The program aligned with Peru's national curriculum for Arts and Culture (MINEDU, 2016, 2018), particularly the competency "creates projects through artistic languages."

6.9.2 Findings and Interpretation

Pretest–posttest results did not show significant shifts on certain measures (e.g., emotional intensity among gifted individuals; figural creativity gains), which can plausibly reflect ceiling effects: universal interventions may fail to sufficiently challenge the cognitive-emotional complexity of high-ability learners. Importantly, null results do not invalidate the intervention. They sharpen the conceptual point: inclusion without differentiation can reproduce invisibility. If gifted learners are present but not developmentally challenged—cognitively or socioemotionally—the system can claim inclusion while sustaining a mismatch.

6.9.3 Equity in Access to Culture

Highbrow cultural participation has historically functioned as a mechanism of class reproduction (Reeves, 2019). Locating arts access within public schools democratizes cultural capital and embeds expressive capability within institutional experience. Cultural engagement is associated with mental health benefits across socioeconomic strata (Fancourt & Steptoe, 2019). The program's equity contribution is therefore twofold: expanding access to cultural participation and integrating socioemotional supports within mainstream schooling.

6.10 Acceleration Revisited: Implementation Implications for Latin America

The regional evidence base suggests that acceleration can be both effective and efficient, yet it remains underused. The implementation problem is therefore not primarily technical; it is cultural and institutional. Successful acceleration in Latin America typically requires:

1. Clear national guidelines that legitimize acceleration as an evidence-based practice rather than a discretionary exception.
2. Multi-criteria decision frameworks (academic readiness, socioemotional readiness, contextual supports) that prevent arbitrary or inequitable practice.
3. Teacher training explicitly addressing myths (e.g., presumed socioemotional harm) and clarifying that well-implemented acceleration can be developmentally supportive.
4. Monitoring and follow-up to ensure that accelerated placements include appropriate supports, particularly for students from rural, Indigenous, and low-resource backgrounds.
5. Equity safeguards so acceleration does not become accessible only to families with advocacy resources.

Hybrid models—such as subject-specific acceleration combined with age-grade homeroom belonging—may reduce cultural resistance by preserving peer affiliation while enabling curricular fit. Conceptually, acceleration and enrichment are complementary: acceleration addresses *pace*, enrichment addresses *depth*, and socio-emotional programming addresses *resilience and identity coherence*.

The diversity of interventions examined in this chapter—ranging from classroom-based socioemotional enrichment to institutional redesign, financial redistribution, university-level excellence cultivation, and system-level pacing flexibility—may initially appear structurally heterogeneous. Yet their variation is precisely what reveals the underlying logic of innovation in unequal systems. Each mechanism addresses a distinct point of misalignment between learner readiness and institutional opportunity. To clarify this multilevel architecture, Table 6.1 synthesizes the primary developmental function, equity contribution, and structural tension associated with each intervention across the educational continuum.

As Table 6.1 illustrates, innovation in the Latin American context cannot be reduced to a single reform or pedagogical shift. Rather, it operates across nested levels of the system: the classroom, curriculum, institution, transition points, university structures, and governance frameworks. Each level addresses a different dimension of developmental fit—pace, depth, access, resilience, or projection. When these mechanisms function in isolation, their equity effects are partial. When aligned, they constitute an ecosystem capable of converting high potential into sustained capability. It is this alignment, rather than any individual intervention, that defines the structural horizon of talent development in the Global South.

6.11 Integrated Discussion: Multidimensional Innovation in the Global South

As the multilevel architecture summarized in Table 6.1 demonstrates, innovation in unequal systems cannot be understood as a discrete reform but must be conceptualized as systemic alignment—an intentional coordination of classroom practice,

Table 6.1 Multilevel architecture of talent development innovation in Latin America

Level of intervention	Illustrative program or mechanism	Primary developmental function	Equity contribution	Structural tension or limitation
Classroom (microlevel)	Well-being and art in school initiative	Socioemotional enrichment; development of ambiguity tolerance and expressive agency	Democratizes access to cultural capital; supports resilience in vulnerable contexts	Universal design may insufficiently differentiate for high-ability learners; ceiling effects possible
Curricular (meso-level)	International Baccalaureate (public integration)	Inquiry-based epistemic deepening; research autonomy; interdisciplinary rigor	Raises intellectual expectations within public systems when access is broadened	Stratifies when concentrated in private or urban elite schools
Institutional (school-level redesign)	COAR (Colegios de Alto Rendimiento)	Residential academic intensification; high-expectation learning culture; international curricular alignment	Redistributes high-quality secondary opportunity to high-achieving public-school students	May create selective "islands of excellence" within unequal systems; scalability constraints
Transitional (secondary–tertiary interface)	Beca 18	Financial redistribution enabling university entry	Expands substantive freedom by removing poverty barriers at tertiary threshold	Sustainability debates; potential outward migration of talent
University (advanced talent cultivation)	Becas LUCET (PUCP)	Mentorship, research integration, postgraduate projection scaffolding	Converts access into sustained excellence; reduces conversion barriers for low-income high achievers	Institutional capacity and replication limits
Governance (system-level flexibility)	Acceleration policies and subject-based advancement	Restores developmental pacing alignment; curricular fit	Low-cost mechanism to prevent underchallenge across socioeconomic groups	Cultural resistance; bureaucratic rigidity; uneven policy implementation

curricular depth, institutional design, redistribution mechanisms, and governance flexibility across the educational continuum.

At first glance, the cases examined in this chapter appear structurally heterogeneous: arts-based programming operates at the classroom level; the International Baccalaureate deepens curriculum; COAR represents institutional redesign; Beca 18 functions as financial redistribution; LUCET provides university-level scaffolding; acceleration operates through governance flexibility. Yet their diversity is precisely the point. In unequal systems, talent development is rarely secured by a single intervention. It depends upon coordinated alignment across nested levels of the educational structure.

A central structural diagnosis therefore emerges: educational fragmentation. Cognitive readiness, emotional development, financial opportunity, and institutional access frequently operate in parallel rather than in deliberate sequence. The result is discontinuity. Innovation must therefore intervene across scales to restore coherence.

- The Well-being and Art in School initiative illustrates that socioemotional resilience is not ancillary but foundational. In vulnerable contexts, increased academic challenge without emotional scaffolding may generate fragility rather than flourishing.
- The International Baccalaureate represents curricular deepening—raising epistemic expectations through inquiry, interdisciplinary study, and independent research. Yet its equity potential materializes only when public policy broadens access; otherwise, it risks amplifying stratification.
- COAR embodies institutional redesign: it constructs a new microsystem and mesosystem around academically talented public-school students, combining residential immersion, rigorous instruction, and international curricular expectations. It redistributes opportunity while simultaneously exposing the paradox of selective excellence within structurally unequal systems.
- Beca 18 secures the tertiary transition by ensuring that poverty does not nullify secondary-level gains and by reframing academic merit as a public investment rather than a private advantage.
- LUCET extends the pipeline beyond access, converting university entry into sustained excellence and projection through mentorship, research integration, and networked academic capital.
- Acceleration highlights the simplest yet most culturally resisted alignment mechanism: pacing flexibility. It restores ecological fit where curricular tempo lags behind readiness and requires institutional legitimacy more than financial expansion.

Across these cases, innovation in the Global South is best conceptualized not as a singular transformative technology but as an ecosystem of interdependent mechanisms:

1. Socioemotional scaffolding (classroom level)
2. Inquiry-based curricular deepening (IB and related models)
3. Institutional redesign (COAR)
4. Transitional redistribution (Beca 18)
5. University-level excellence cultivation and projection (LUCET)
6. Pacing flexibility through acceleration (governance level)

Ecologically, these mechanisms restore developmental fit across interacting systems. From a capability perspective, they expand substantive freedoms across the life course, strengthening the conditions under which ability can be converted into durable agency. From a decolonial perspective, they challenge inherited rigidities—particularly uniform pacing and the historical conflation of excellence with socioeconomic privilege.

The integrated lesson is not rhetorical; it is structural:

- Without differentiation, equity collapses into invisibility.
- Without redistribution, excellence reproduces stratification.
- Without socioemotional support, enrichment can increase fragility.
- Without transition scaffolding, access risks attrition and lost potential.

Excellence and equity are therefore not competing objectives but mutually reinforcing structural imperatives in unequal systems. A regionally grounded innovation agenda must coordinate curriculum, instruction, institutional design, and redistributive policy so that readiness is aligned with opportunity—and opportunity is sustained across transitions into long-term contribution.

Acknowledgments The lead author gratefully acknowledges the intellectual collaboration and sustained commitment of Eduardo Franco, Keytha Alcántara, and Arianna Benavides, members of the Research Group *Creativity, Technology, and Talent Development*, in the development of this chapter. Their contributions to the conceptual framing, empirical analysis, and critical refinement of the arguments presented here were essential to articulating the multilevel perspective on innovation in curriculum and instruction for high-ability learners in Latin America.

The authors also acknowledge the academic environment and institutional support of the Academic Department of Psychology, the Academic Social Responsibility Direction, and the Vice Rectorship of Research at Pontificia Universidad Católica del Perú. Their sustained commitment to research excellence, interdisciplinary dialogue, and social responsibility provides the intellectual foundation within which this work was conceived and developed.

References

Alcázar, L., & Balarin, M. (2016). *Informe final: Evaluación del diseño e implementación de los colegios de Alto Rendimiento (COAR)*. GRADE.

Asensio, R., & Burneo de la Rocha, M. L. (Eds.). (2019). *Estudio cualitativo: Modelo de servicio educativo para estudiantes de alto desempeño implementado a través de los colegios de Alto Rendimiento (COAR)*. Instituto de Estudios Peruanos.

Barrera, D., De La Fuente, L., Román, S., Lagos, P., Hernández, M., & Raczynski, D. (2013). Evaluación de la implementación del programa promoción de talentos académicos en liceos y escuelas municipales. *Asesorías para el Desarrollo.*

Blumen, S. (2021). Innovative practices to support high-achieving deprived young scholars in an ethnic-linguistic diverse Latin American country. In S. R. Smith (Ed.), *Handbook of giftedness and talent development in the Asia-Pacific* (pp. 223–238). Springer.

Blumen, S., Alcántara, K., Benavides, A., & Franco, E. (2025, July 29–August 2). The effects of a fine art program on feelings about school, figural creativity, and engagement in the school environment [Paper presentation]. In *2025 WCGTC World Conference, Braga, Portugal.* https://world-gifted.org/Conferences/wcgtc25/

Bolwerk, A., Mack-Andrick, J., Lang, F. R., Dörfler, A., & Maihöfner, C. (2014). How art changes your brain: Differential effects of visual art production and cognitive art evaluation on functional brain connectivity. *PLoS One, 9*(7), e101035. https://doi.org/10.1371/journal.pone.0101035

Bosgraaf, L., Spreen, M., Pattiselanno, K., & van Hooren, S. (2020). Art therapy for psychosocial problems in children and adolescents: A systematic narrative review. *Frontiers in Psychology, 11*, 584685. https://doi.org/10.3389/fpsyg.2020.584685

Colangelo, N., Assouline, S. G., & Gross, M. U. M. (2004). *A nation deceived: How schools hold back America's brightest students* (Vol. 1–2). University of Iowa.

Colangelo, N., Assouline, S. G., & Gross, M. U. M. (2015). *A nation empowered: Evidence trumps the excuses holding back America's brightest students* (Vol. 1–2). University of Iowa.

Conejeros-Solar, M. L., Gómez-Arizaga, M. P., & Sandoval Rodríguez, K. (2025). *Orientaciones para políticas de atención integral a las altas capacidades: Propuestas para políticas inclusivas*. Centro de Investigación para la Educación Inclusiva.

Corporación Andina de Fomento (CAF). (2021). *Evaluación de impacto del modelo de servicio educativo para estudiantes de alto desempeño implementado a través de los colegios de Alto Rendimiento (COAR).*

Evans, G. W., & Kim, P. (2013). Childhood poverty, chronic stress, self-regulation, and coping. *Child Development Perspectives, 7*(1), 43–48. https://doi.org/10.1111/cdep.12013

Fancourt, D., & Finn, S. (2019). *What is the evidence on the role of the arts in improving health and well-being?* WHO Regional Office for Europe.

Fancourt, D., & Steptoe, A. (2019). Cultural engagement and mental health: Does socio-economic status explain the association? *Social Science & Medicine, 236*, 112425. https://doi.org/10.1016/j.socscimed.2019.112425

Gagné, F. (2009). Building gifts into talents: Detailed overview of the DMGT 2.0. In B. MacFarlane & T. Stambaugh (Eds.), *Leading change in gifted education* (pp. 61–74). Prufrock Press.

García-Cepero, M. C., & Iglesias-Velasco, J. (2020). Hacia una comprensión de las aproximaciones institucionales a los estudiantes con capacidades y talentos excepcionales. *Revista Colombiana de Educación, 79*, 423–444. https://doi.org/10.17227/rce.num79-10040

Gómez-Arizaga, M. P., Conejeros-Solar, M. L., & Cornejo-Araya, C. (2024). Gifted education in Chile: Analyses from a learning-resource perspective. *Cogent Education, 11*(1). https://doi.org/10.1080/2331186X.2024.2397217

González Adonis, P., Arancibia Claves, V., & Boyanova, D. (2017). Talento académico, vulnerabilidad escolar y resultados en la prueba de selección universitaria. *Estudios Pedagógicos, 43*(1). https://doi.org/10.4067/S0718-07052017000100011

Hatrick, A., & Paniagua, C. (2021). *Evaluación de Impacto del Modelo de Servicio Educativo para Estudiantes de Alto Desempeño implementado a través de los Colegios de Alto Rendimiento (COAR)*. Corporación Andina de Fomento / Ministerio de Educación del Perú.

Kaimal, G., Ray, K., & Muniz, J. (2016). Reduction of cortisol levels following art making. *Art Therapy, 33*(2), 74–80. https://doi.org/10.1080/07421656.2016.1166832

Kraehe, A. M. (2018). Creative agency: Empowerment in art and design education. *Art Education, 71*(6), 4–8.

Margot, K. C., & Rinn, A. N. (2016). Perfectionism in gifted adolescents. *Journal of Advanced Academics, 27*, 190–209.

Ministério da Educação do Brasil. (2002). *Diretrizes nacionais para a educação especial na educação básica.*

Ministerio de Educación del Perú. (2003). *Ley general de educación N° 28044.*

Ministerio de Educación del Perú. (2009). *Resolución Suprema N° 034-2009-ED.*

Ministerio de Educación del Perú. (2014). *Modelo educativo: Colegios de Alto Rendimiento (COAR).*

Ministerio de Educación del Perú. (2016). *Currículo nacional de la educación básica.*

Ministerio de Educación del Perú. (2018). *Orientaciones para la enseñanza del área de arte y cultura.*

Ministerio de Educación del Perú. (2022). *Colegios de Alto Rendimiento (COAR).*

Ministerio de Educación del Perú. (2023). *Estadística de la calidad educativa (ESCALE).*

Ministerio de Educación del Perú. (2024). *El Perú en PISA 2022.*

Ministerio de Educación del Perú. (2025). *Evaluación de impacto de los colegios de Alto Rendimiento (COAR).*

Ministerio de Educación Nacional de Colombia. (2017). *Decreto 1421*.
Ministerio de Hacienda, Dirección de Presupuestos (DIPRES). (2021). *Minuta de resultados del monitoreo de la oferta programática*. Gobierno de Chile.
Navarro Guillén, M. I. (2022). Promoción del alto potencial en el marco de la atención a la diversidad. *Revista Educación, 46*(2).
OECD. (2023). *PISA 2022 results* (Vol. I). OECD.
Pérez Barrera, S. G., & Bendelman, K. (2016). *Altas habilidades/superdotación: ≃Qué, quién, cómo?* Isadora.
Pinquart, M., & Ebeling, M. (2020). Parental educational expectations and academic achievement. *Educational Psychology Review, 32*(2), 463–480.
Pontificia Universidad Católica del Perú. (2023a). *Becas LUCET: Programa integral de apoyo a estudiantes de alto rendimiento académico*. Dirección Académica de Responsabilidad Social y Apoyo al Estudiante.
Pontificia Universidad Católica del Perú. (2023b). *Informe de gestión: Becas LUCET*. Dirección Académica de Responsabilidad Social y Apoyo al Estudiante.
Pontificia Universidad Católica del Perú. (2025). *Becas LUCET*.
Programa Nacional de Becas y Crédito Educativo (PRONABEC). (2023). *Memoria anual: Beca 18*. Ministerio de Educación del Perú.
Quijano, A. (2000). Coloniality of power, Eurocentrism, and Latin America. *Nepantla: Views from South, 1*(3), 533–580.
Reeves, A. (2019). How class identities shape highbrow consumption. *Poetics, 73*, 101–114.
Renzulli, J. S. (2012). Reexamining the role of gifted education for the 21st century. *Gifted Child Quarterly, 56*(3), 150–159.
Sen, A. (1999). *Development as freedom*. Oxford University Press.
Smyth, L., Aggio-Bruce, R., Crossing, E., Lincoln, B. R., Stanojevic, V. A., Valter, K., & Webb, A. L. (2026). Embracing ambiguity and creativity. *Thinking Skills and Creativity, 60*, 102110.
Stricker, J., Buecker, S., Schneider, M., & Preckel, F. (2019). Intellectual giftedness and perfectionism. *Educational Psychology Review*.
UNESCO. (1994). *The Salamanca statement and framework for action on special needs education*.
UNESCO. (2016). *Education 2030: Incheon declaration*.
Vuyk, A., Gómez-Arízaga, M. P., & Barrios, L. A. (2026). Acceleration in South America. In J. L. Roberts & T. Clark (Eds.), *International perspectives on acceleration in gifted education* (pp. 22–37). Routledge.

Chapter 7
Twice-Exceptional Learners and Mental Health in Latin American Educational Systems

7.1 Introduction: Twice-Exceptionality in Stratified Educational Systems

Twice-exceptional (2e) learners—students who display high intellectual, creative, or domain-specific potential while also experiencing learning disabilities, neurodevelopmental differences, or clinically significant mental health challenges—occupy one of the most systematically misrecognized positions in Latin American education. International scholarship has established that 2e profiles are neither rare nor merely "complicated"; they are predictable outcomes of human neurodevelopmental diversity interacting with environments that reward particular modes of performance (Baum et al., 2014; Foley-Nicpon et al., 2012; Reis et al., 2014). In much of Latin America, however, the research base remains limited, policy recognition is uneven, and services are often fragmented across separate institutional silos: gifted education (where it exists), special and inclusive education, and school mental health or external clinical pathways.

This fragmentation is not an administrative inconvenience; it is a developmental constraint. Twice-exceptional learners expose the conceptual binaries that still organize many schooling systems: high ability versus disability; enrichment versus remediation; academic excellence versus socioemotional support. When these binaries become the implicit logic of identification and service delivery, the consequence is predictable: learners whose profiles do not conform to categorical simplicity are not seen as complex—they are seen as inconsistent, underachieving, oppositional, anxious, or "unmotivated." The system reads contradiction as a character rather than a profile.

The invisibility of 2e learners in Latin America must also be interpreted within the region's enduring structural inequality. Educational opportunity is heavily mediated by socioeconomic status, geography, and ethnicity (Economic Commission for Latin America and the Caribbean [ECLAC], 2022; United Nations Educational,

S. Blumen, *High Ability and Talent Development in Latin America*,
https://doi.org/10.1007/978-3-032-27468-7_7

Scientific and Cultural Organization [UNESCO], 2022). These macro-structures shape who has access to high-quality instruction, who is exposed to enrichment, who can receive psychoeducational assessment, and who can obtain mental health support. In contexts where specialized assessment is scarce, literacy-heavy identification tools dominate, and school psychology infrastructure is limited, the probability that a 2e learner will be recognized—rather than misread—decreases sharply. For rural, Indigenous, and low-income learners, this probability is lower still.

At the same time, adolescent mental health has become a central global and regional concern. The World Health Organization (WHO, 2021) estimates that approximately one in seven adolescents worldwide experiences a mental disorder, while the Pan American Health Organization highlights substantial treatment gaps across the Americas (PAHO, 2025). In Latin American systems where school-based mental health services are uneven or externalized, 2e learners face a particular vulnerability: the cognitive intensities often associated with advanced development may coexist with executive functioning challenges, anxiety, depression, social communication differences, or identity conflict. When high cognitive capacity is paired with high contextual stress—and when institutional supports are incoherent—the result can be a silent erosion of well-being that remains hidden behind outward competence or misbehavior.

Building on the ecological–developmental framework articulated in Chap. 3, twice-exceptionality is not treated here as a marginal anomaly but as a structural phenomenon. Recognition depends not solely on cognition, but on institutional design. Systems capable of integrating excellence, inclusion, and mental health render twice-exceptional learners visible. Systems that remain fragmented reproduce masking. Twice-exceptionality, therefore, functions as a diagnostic lens through which the coherence of educational architecture across Latin America can be evaluated.

7.2 Conceptual Foundations: Asynchrony, Masking, and the False Binary of Categories

Twice-exceptionality refers to individuals who are simultaneously gifted and have one or more disabilities. Common co-occurring conditions include specific learning disorders (e.g., dyslexia and dyscalculia), attention-deficit/hyperactivity disorder (ADHD), autism spectrum disorder (ASD), and anxiety or mood disorders (Reis et al., 2014). The conceptual challenge is not merely definitional; it is epistemic. Systems that treat giftedness and disability as mutually exclusive categories—one associated with advantage and the other with limitation—are structurally ill-equipped to recognize dual profiles.

7.2.1 Asynchronous Development

A central characteristic of 2e profiles is asynchronous development: different domains of growth—cognitive reasoning, emotional regulation, executive functioning, and social adaptation—do not develop in parallel (Silverman, 2003). A learner may show advanced abstract reasoning and creative ideation while struggling with organization, written expression, working memory, or attention regulation. In many Latin American contexts, where teachers often carry high instructional loads and where diagnostic supports are limited, asynchrony is easily misinterpreted as inconsistency or lack of effort.

Asynchrony has two further implications. First, it challenges narrow metrics of competence. A student's potential may be visible in oral reasoning, conceptual insight, and creative problem-solving, but invisible in standardized written assessments. Second, it increases the likelihood of socioemotional mismatch: the learner may think like an older student but cope like a younger one. Without contextual interpretation, this mismatch can produce chronic frustration, shame, and withdrawal.

7.2.2 Masking Patterns as Institutional Phenomena

Baum et al. (2014) identify three masking patterns among 2e learners: (a) giftedness masks disability, (b) disability masks giftedness, and (c) mutual masking. These patterns are often described as psychological dynamics, but in unequal systems, they are also institutional dynamics. Masking is not only what students do; it is what systems *produce*.

- When identification relies on high achievement, students whose disability suppresses performance are filtered out.
- When disability services assume deficit-only models, advanced potential is not sought or cultivated.
- When mental health is externalized, emotional distress becomes invisible until it becomes a crisis.

In other words, the same institutional design that claims to "identify talent" may be structurally unable to see talent when it does not appear in a preferred performance form.

7.2.3 *Cultural Expectations of Excellence and the Narrowing of Recognition*

In Latin America, conceptions of giftedness often remain closely associated with academic fluency, compliance, and visible achievement. Blumen's studies in Peru, for instance, underscore that teacher perceptions tend to privilege performance and behavior as markers of talent, which can obscure learners who are cognitively advanced but behaviorally inconsistent or emotionally distressed (Blumen, 2010, 2012). A similar tension appears in Brazilian scholarship: while *altas habilidades/superdotação* are recognized within special education policy, implementation is uneven and dual differentiation remains limited, particularly regarding learners whose disabilities suppress typical achievement markers (Fleith, 2011; Pérez & Freitas, 2014).

The conceptual consequence is critical: twice-exceptionality becomes "doubly unintelligible." Giftedness is not recognized because disability disrupts performance; disability is not recognized because giftedness can compensate until demands exceed coping capacity. The learner is then read through moralized lenses—lazy, undisciplined, anxious, and stubborn—rather than developmental ones.

7.3 Youth Mental Health and Neurodevelopment in Latin America: Context, Risk, and Infrastructure

Twice-exceptionality cannot be understood without reference to adolescent mental health and neurodevelopmental diagnosis contexts. In the Americas, mental health conditions represent a significant portion of youth disease burden, with treatment gaps that often exceed 60% (PAHO, 2025). The WHO estimates that one in seven adolescents globally experiences a mental disorder (WHO, 2021). These realities are not peripheral to education; they shape learning capacity, motivation, self-regulation, and identity formation.

7.3.1 *Neurodevelopmental Conditions in Low-Resource Contexts*

Neurodevelopmental conditions such as ADHD, learning disorders, and autism are frequently underdiagnosed or unevenly supported in low-resource systems. Even when a diagnosis occurs, services may be inconsistent or externalized, leaving schools to interpret behaviors without adequate developmental frameworks. For 2e learners, this is particularly consequential: executive dysfunction can suppress the very performance indicators used to gatekeep enrichment. A student may have advanced reasoning but limited capacity for organization, sustained attention, or task initiation. When support is absent, the student's profile is not recognized; it is punished.

The problem is not only diagnostic scarcity but diagnostic *disconnect*. Studies in Brazil, for example, have examined executive functioning in ADHD (e.g., Friedman-Nimz & Skyba, 2009), yet the integration between neurodevelopmental research and gifted education remains limited. Where psychological services do not communicate with enrichment structures, a learner may receive partial recognition—diagnosed but not challenged, challenged but not supported.

7.3.2 Performance Pressure and Test Anxiety

Organization for Economic Co-operation and Development (OECD, 2023) PISA well-being findings document substantial test anxiety among adolescents in several Latin American countries (OECD, 2023). In competitive systems, academic identity can become fused with performance outcomes, and minor deviations are experienced as existential threats. This context magnifies risk for high-ability learners who are already vulnerable to perfectionism and self-criticism—especially when perfectionism functions as a compensatory strategy for hidden learning difficulties.

Chile provides a particularly clear example of how high-stakes educational cultures can intensify pressure, as selective pathways and entrance examinations strongly shape future trajectories. Yet similar dynamics can appear in other contexts where education is perceived as the principal vehicle of mobility. When a 2e learner's self-worth is anchored to performance but performance is disrupted by disability or anxiety, the developmental risk is not simply underachievement—it is self-concept fracture.

7.3.3 Mental Health Services and the School as a Developmental Site

In many Latin American systems, mental health services are external to schools, unevenly distributed, or available primarily through private access. For 2e learners, this externalization creates a dangerous developmental gap. The school is the primary context where masking and mismatch occur; if support is absent there, the child's daily experience remains unaddressed.

From an ecological–developmental standpoint, mental health is not an "additional service" to be appended after academic concerns. It is a developmental infrastructure that shapes whether cognitive potential can be sustained. A system that accelerates without supporting well-being may intensify vulnerability. Conversely, a system that remediates without challenging ability may generate disengagement, boredom, and identity confusion. Twice-exceptionality demands both.

7.4 Socioemotional Development and Identity under Conditions of Inequality

The socioemotional dimension of twice-exceptionality is central, not supplementary. While giftedness alone does not necessarily predict psychopathology (Foley-Nicpon et al., 2013), the likelihood of distress rises when there is a chronic mismatch between the learner's cognitive needs and the environment's interpretive and instructional capacity.

7.4.1 Perfectionism: Adaptive Standards and Maladaptive Self-Surveillance

Perfectionism is often a defining dynamic in high-ability populations. Neihart et al. (2016) distinguish between adaptive perfectionism (high standards paired with self-compassion and flexibility) and maladaptive perfectionism (fear-driven performance and self-worth contingent on flawless outcomes). In Latin American contexts, where family hopes for mobility may concentrate pressure on education, maladaptive perfectionism can be reinforced through social narratives: effort is moralized; failure is stigmatized; and "discipline" is framed as character.

For many 2e learners, perfectionism functions metacognitively as compensation: if reading is slow, the student studies longer; if organization is weak, the student over-controls; if anxiety rises, the student isolates to avoid social comparison. The cost is psychological exhaustion. Over time, compensation becomes pathology.

7.4.2 Identity Conflict and Internalized Contradiction

Twice-exceptional learners often receive mixed feedback: praised for brilliance, criticized for inconsistency. The result is identity dissonance: "I am capable" and "I am failing" coexist without an interpretive bridge. In contexts where disability is stigmatized and giftedness is narrowly defined, students may also internalize shame: the disability is read as moral weakness, and the giftedness is treated as an obligation. The self becomes a site of contradiction rather than coherence.

7.4.3 *Inequality as a Metacognitive Constraint*

Structural inequality shapes not only access to resources but the formation of self-explanations. CEPAL (2022) documents persistent educational stratification by income quintile. When high-ability learners in low-income contexts are not recognized, their struggle is interpreted through deficit narratives—by teachers, by peers, and eventually by themselves. They may come to believe they are "not smart" precisely because they cannot perform in the system's preferred modality. Twice-exceptionality thus becomes a mechanism through which inequality is psychologically internalized.

This is why the ecological–developmental lens is essential. Socioemotional outcomes do not arise from individual traits alone; they are produced through the interaction between neurodevelopmental profiles and institutional responsiveness. When systems interpret asynchrony as misbehavior, they escalate distress. When they interpret asynchrony developmentally, they enable coherence.

7.5 Clinical Trajectories in Context: Narrative Cases as Analytic Instruments

The following five cases are written as *developmental ecosystems*: each narrative traces cognitive strength, neurodevelopmental vulnerability, socioemotional trajectory, and institutional response within a specific national and socioeconomic context. After each narrative, a brief **Structural Reading** translates the case into the chapter's analytic language—masking dynamics, inequality mechanisms, policy/infrastructure gaps, and implications for systemic coherence.

7.5.1 *Case 1: Gabriel: Executive Dysfunction behind Verbal Brilliance*

Urban Public-School Context (Brazil)

Gabriel was raised in a densely populated, middle-income neighborhood of São Paulo. From early childhood, his parents noticed an unusual verbal sophistication. At four, he asked questions about death, fairness, and environmental responsibility with a seriousness that unsettled adults. By seven, he read complex nonfiction independently and argued about current events at family gatherings. In conversation, he demonstrated advanced abstraction: he could compare political decisions across time, detect contradictions in adult reasoning, and generate original interpretations rather than repeating memorized information.

In primary school, teachers quickly recognized his vocabulary and oral reasoning. When engaged, Gabriel contributed insights that exceeded grade-level expectations. He could connect historical themes to contemporary politics and propose counterarguments in ways that made peers pause. His oral participation suggested advanced potential.

Yet his written work told a different story. His notebook was disorganized. Homework was frequently incomplete or missing. Written assignments were rushed and filled with errors inconsistent with his verbal ability. He often started tasks late, forgot materials, and seemed to "drift" during independent work. On timed tests, he left sections blank. Teachers described him as "brilliant but irresponsible." Some interpreted his inconsistency as arrogance; others assumed boredom. The school's identification practices for altas habilidades/superdotação emphasized teacher nomination and achievement indicators. Gabriel's grades—average in several subjects due to incomplete work—kept him outside enrichment pathways.

By age 11, the mismatch began to reshape Gabriel's self-concept. Teachers repeatedly told him he had potential but lacked discipline. At home, his parents oscillated between encouragement and frustration. They could not reconcile the child who debated philosophy at the dinner table with the child who could not submit a simple assignment on time. Gabriel began to avoid. If an assignment felt large, he delayed it until the deadline arrived, then rushed it or left it unfinished. Avoidance became protective: if he failed by not trying, he did not have to confront the possibility of failing despite trying.

The socioemotional cost became visible in subtle ways. Gabriel's confidence declined. He became reluctant to show interest in topics he cared about, as if intellectual enthusiasm had become risky. When asked why he did not submit work, he sometimes shrugged, sometimes joked, sometimes became irritated. Inside, the question had become unbearable: *If I understand so much, why can't I do what everyone else does?*

A turning point occurred when a new teacher, trained in gifted education, noticed the contradiction between Gabriel's oral sophistication and his written inconsistency. Rather than interpreting it as laziness, she read it as a profile. She recommended a full psychoeducational evaluation. The family attempted to access services through public channels but faced long delays and limited availability; eventually, at considerable financial strain, they pursued a private assessment.

The evaluation revealed a dual profile:

- Superior verbal comprehension and abstract reasoning (upper percentiles)
- Above-average processing speed
- Significant executive functioning weaknesses in planning, organization, and sustained attention
- ADHD, predominantly inattentive presentation

Gabriel's giftedness had masked his disability for years: his reasoning allowed him to compensate enough to avoid early failure. But compensation did not prevent erosion. Meanwhile, his ADHD masked his giftedness within a school system where identification depended on organized performance and completed products. The system could not "see" his thinking because it measured his output.

Following the diagnosis, a coordinated plan began to emerge. Medication was discussed cautiously and used with monitoring. Executive functioning coaching focused on task decomposition, planning routines, and external supports such as checklists. Teachers provided structured scaffolds for written assignments and extended time for tasks requiring sustained attention. Crucially, Gabriel was included in a discussion-based enrichment group where advanced reasoning was central and output demands were moderated.

Academically, improvement was visible within months. Emotionally, recovery was slower. In counseling, Gabriel voiced shame about years of misunderstanding. He described feeling "fake," as if his intelligence was a trick that could be exposed at any moment. Gradually, however, language reshaped his self-understanding: he was not "irresponsible"; he was a high-potential student with executive functioning needs.

Gabriel's trajectory demonstrates that in the absence of systemic alignment, cognitive complexity is translated into behavioral misinterpretation. Recognition was not a matter of motivation—it was a function of institutional coherence.

Structural Reading of Case 1 (Brazil)

Masking pattern: Mutual masking. High verbal giftedness compensates for ADHD-related executive dysfunction, delaying recognition; executive dysfunction suppresses performance, obscuring gifted identification.

Institutional mechanism: Performance-based selection into enrichment functions as a structural filter against 2e profiles. "Merit" is operationalized as compliance and completed output.

Equity mechanism: Access to diagnosis depends on family resources when public assessment infrastructure is limited or delayed; this reproduces stratification in recognition.

Mental health risk pathway: Chronic misinterpretation → avoidance coping → shame-based identity conflict → vulnerability to anxiety/depressive symptoms.

Coherence lesson: When enrichment, school psychology, and classroom scaffolding align, the learner becomes legible and development accelerates. Coherence—not motivation—was the turning point.

7.5.2 *Case 2: Valentina: Perfectionism, Reading Inefficiency, and High-Stakes Academic Pressure*

Selective Secondary Program Context (Chile)

Valentina grew up in Santiago in a family that embodied the aspirational promise of education. Her parents were first-generation university graduates who had experienced upward mobility through academic success. From early childhood, education was framed not merely as personal growth but as security, dignity, and responsibility. Excellence was not optional; it was ethical.

Valentina displayed exceptional quantitative reasoning from an early age. In primary school, she demonstrated rapid acquisition of mathematical concepts, unusual facility with pattern recognition, and a capacity to generalize principles beyond the scope of classroom instruction. Teachers described her as "disciplined," "precise," and "exceptionally capable." She qualified for competitive academic activities and eventually gained admission into a highly selective secondary program designed to prepare students for elite university entry.

The institutional culture of her school was clear: performance was paramount. Students were surrounded by peers who were similarly high achieving. Assessment was frequent and consequential. Small differences in score distribution were amplified in meaning. Teachers, though supportive, emphasized rigor and high expectations. Within this ecosystem, Valentina excelled outwardly. She achieved top marks in mathematics and science. She solved complex problems ahead of her classmates. She internalized the role of "the strong student."

Yet beneath this achievement, a quieter dynamic unfolded. Valentina read more slowly than her peers. She did not misread words; rather, reading required sustained effort. Timed assessments were exhausting. To maintain her grades, she compensated through extraordinary preparation. She rehearsed formulas repeatedly. She rewrote notes obsessively. She anticipated exam formats and practiced until anxiety temporarily subsided. Perfectionism functioned as an adaptive strategy.

Over time, however, the strategy intensified. The academic demands of secondary education increased both in volume and complexity. Reading-intensive assignments multiplied. University entrance examinations loomed as distant but persistent markers of future destiny. Valentina began to experience physiological symptoms of anxiety before assessments: nausea, trembling, and sleeplessness. Minor mistakes were experienced as catastrophic evidence of decline. A score slightly below her usual average triggered rumination: *I am losing my edge.*

She withdrew socially to protect study time. Leisure became suspect. Her internal narrative narrowed: if excellence ensured stability and belonging, then imperfection threatened identity itself.

The school psychologist initially met with Valentina for "stress management." What emerged in conversation was not simply stress but fear. She described reading as "climbing uphill," yet she had never considered that this effort might reflect a specific processing profile. She assumed that difficulty meant inadequacy.

A comprehensive evaluation revealed a nuanced dual profile:

- Exceptionally strong quantitative reasoning and logical–mathematical capacity
- High working memory
- Subtle specific learning disorder in reading fluency
- Elevated anxiety with perfectionistic cognitive patterns

Valentina's giftedness had masked her reading inefficiency for years. Through disciplined compensation, she maintained high grades. The disability did not produce failure; it produced overexertion. Perfectionism concealed vulnerability until the cumulative cognitive load exceeded coping capacity. Under the intensified performance culture of selective schooling, compensation became unsustainable.

Intervention required careful coordination. Extended time was provided on reading-intensive assessments to reduce processing pressure. Teachers were encouraged to differentiate between conceptual mastery and minor formal errors. Cognitive–behavioral therapy targeted catastrophic thinking and decoupled self-worth from minor performance fluctuations. Psychoeducation reframed her reading profile not as a weakness but as a domain requiring strategic support.

Gradually, Valentina's relationship to excellence shifted. She began to distinguish between striving and self-surveillance. She joined a peer mentoring initiative, discovering that vulnerability could coexist with competence. Her anxiety did not disappear, but it became intelligible. Rather than an inexplicable flaw, it was understood as the interaction between high ability, high expectation, and hidden inefficiency.

Valentina's trajectory illuminates the paradox of twice-exceptionality in high-performing environments: students may appear to thrive while internal distress intensifies. In high-stakes systems, excellence can function as camouflage. Without integrated mental health frameworks, performance stability conceals structural fragility.

Structural Reading of Case 2 (Chile)

Masking pattern: Giftedness masks disability. High quantitative ability and disciplined compensation conceal reading inefficiency; disability expresses indirectly through anxiety.

Institutional mechanism: High-stakes, performance-oriented schooling amplifies perfectionism and narrows tolerance for processing variability. Assessment formats privilege speed and volume.

Equity mechanism: Although Valentina accessed psychological services within a selective program, such infrastructure is unevenly distributed; similar profiles in nonselective or rural contexts might remain unidentified.

Mental health risk pathway: Compensation → maladaptive perfectionism → chronic anxiety → identity fusion with performance → burnout risk.

Cultural dimension: In upwardly mobile families, education is imbued with moral significance; minor academic fluctuations acquire existential meaning.

Coherence lesson: When accommodations, therapeutic intervention, and teacher awareness align, excellence and well-being need not be oppositional. Without integration, selective systems risk cultivating hidden distress among their highest achievers.

Valentina's case extends Gabriel's trajectory in a different direction. In Brazil, executive dysfunction suppressed visible achievement. In Chile, achievement concealed processing inefficiency. In both instances, the system initially interpreted performance at face value. In one, inconsistency was moralized; in the other, consistency masked vulnerability. Twice-exceptionality does not present with a single phenotype. It adapts to context.

7.5.3 *Case 3: Luis: Creative Intelligence, Dyslexia, and Structural Marginalization*

Low-Income Public-School Context (Mexico)

Luis grew up in a densely populated working-class neighborhood on the outskirts of Mexico City. His father worked intermittent construction jobs; his mother prepared food from home for supplemental income. Household stability fluctuated with the labor market. Educational aspirations were present but constrained by economic precarity.

From early childhood, Luis demonstrated remarkable visual–spatial creativity. He constructed intricate models from discarded materials—bridges, towers, irrigation systems—often with structural balance beyond what adults expected from a child his age. He drew detailed urban landscapes with perspective accuracy and complex spatial layering. Teachers noticed his imagination and frequently displayed his drawings. "He sees things differently," one remarked.

Yet literacy posed a persistent difficulty. Luis read slowly and hesitantly. He avoided reading aloud. Spelling errors were frequent and resistant to correction. Writing tasks provoked visible frustration. During literacy-heavy instruction, he became restless, sometimes disruptive. Teachers interpreted this behavior as oppositional or inattentive. In a classroom culture where standardized academic performance shaped opportunity, Luis's reading difficulties positioned him as "average" at best and "problematic" at worst.

Identification for enrichment programs in his district depended primarily on standardized academic metrics—especially literacy and mathematics achievement scores. Luis's literacy profile suppressed his composite performance. His spatial reasoning, creativity, and problem-solving were not captured by the instruments used. No teacher nomination was submitted.

By age ten, Luis had internalized a narrative of deficiency. He masked embarrassment with humor. "If I make people laugh," he later said during counseling, "they don't notice I read slow." Humor functioned as protective camouflage. Rather than confront the possibility that he might be incapable, he preempted judgment with self-directed irony.

A turning point came when a community-based nonprofit organization began offering free psychological screenings in local schools. An evaluator trained in nonverbal reasoning assessment administered tasks that minimized reading demands. Luis excelled. His performance in pattern recognition, spatial reasoning, and complex visual problem-solving was in the upper percentiles. A full evaluation confirmed:

- High nonverbal intelligence
- Exceptional visual–spatial reasoning
- Specific learning disorder with impairment in reading (dyslexia)

For the first time, Luis encountered language that described his profile coherently. He was not "bad at school"; he was a creative, high-potential student with a reading disorder. Intervention included structured literacy instruction, assistive reading software, and enrollment in an enrichment program focused on design and engineering concepts. Teachers received training in strengths-based feedback.

The transformation was gradual but tangible. Luis began participating in project-based learning with confidence. His humor shifted from defense to expression. Literacy remained challenging, but it was contextualized rather than moralized. Importantly, his family gained understanding of dyslexia, reducing stigma and frustration at home.

Luis's case demonstrates how literacy-dominant assessment systems systematically obscure nonverbal giftedness—especially in low-income contexts where enrichment resources are scarce. Luis was not overlooked because of limited ability; he was filtered out by literacy-dominant identification systems. Structural design, not cognitive absence, produced invisibility.

Structural Reading of Case 3 (Mexico)
Masking pattern: Disability masks giftedness. Dyslexia suppresses performance in literacy-based identification systems, obscuring high spatial intelligence.

Institutional mechanism: Standardized academic metrics function as gatekeepers to enrichment; creative and nonverbal domains remain under-assessed.

Equity mechanism: Access to diagnosis depended on an external nonprofit initiative; without it, recognition would likely not have occurred. Low-income status delayed identification.

Mental health risk pathway: Repeated literacy struggle → classroom misinterpretation → humor as defensive masking → internalized inadequacy.

Cultural dimension: In contexts where formal academic success is linked to social mobility, reading difficulties carry a stigma that suppresses open dialogue.

Coherence lesson: When culturally responsive assessment and structured literacy intervention align with enrichment, previously "average" students become visible as high-potential learners.

7.5.4 Case 4: María Fernanda: Analytical Precision, Autism Spectrum Traits, and Social Asynchrony

Private Urban School Context (Colombia)
María Fernanda was raised in Bogotá in an academically oriented, upper-middle-class family. Both parents were engineers and valued precision, structure, and analytical reasoning. From early childhood, María Fernanda exhibited intense interests. At three, she memorized train schedules; at four, she explained planetary systems with technical vocabulary. Her fascination with classification and systems extended beyond play—it defined her cognitive style.

In primary school, she excelled in mathematics and physics. She identified patterns quickly, solved multistep logical problems with ease, and often completed assignments ahead of schedule. Teachers used her work as exemplars. Academically, she thrived.

Socially, however, she struggled. Group work provoked anxiety. She preferred solitary activities. She interpreted figurative language literally and was confused by sarcasm. Unpredictable changes in routine caused visible distress. Classmates described her as "brilliant but strange." Teachers initially interpreted these behaviors as introversion or intellectual intensity. Because she achieved at high levels, socioemotional concerns were minimized.

During early adolescence, peer dynamics became more complex. Social cues became subtler. María Fernanda's isolation deepened. She reported sensory overwhelm in noisy classrooms and increasing anxiety before collaborative tasks. Panic episodes began emerging before presentations.

A comprehensive evaluation revealed:

- Highly advanced perceptual reasoning
- Strong working memory
- Autism spectrum disorder (Level 1 support needs)
- Elevated anxiety linked to social unpredictability

The diagnosis clarified long-standing patterns. Yet institutional gaps became evident. The school had enrichment structures and acceleration policies but no integrated pathway linking gifted programming with socioemotional supports for neurodiverse learners. María Fernanda continued in advanced mathematics seminars without coordinated social skills coaching or structured collaboration scaffolds.

Her parents advocated for accommodations: explicit group roles, predictable schedules, written transition instructions, sensory breaks, and structured social coaching. When these supports were implemented, María Fernanda began participating more comfortably in collaborative robotics competitions, where communication followed clearer rule structures.

Her autism was not a barrier to intellectual excellence; it shaped her interaction style. María Fernanda's development illustrates that acceleration without socioemotional integration is incomplete. Institutional differentiation must address neurodiversity alongside excellence.

Structural Reading of Case 4 (Colombia)

Masking pattern: Giftedness masks disability. High academic achievement delays recognition of autism spectrum traits.

Institutional mechanism: Enrichment structures operate separately from inclusive education services; acceleration lacks socioemotional scaffolding.

Equity mechanism: Private-school resources enabled diagnosis and accommodation; similar profiles in public contexts may remain unrecognized.

Mental health risk pathway: Social mismatch → peer isolation → anxiety → panic episodes.

Cultural dimension: Academic excellence can shield socioemotional concerns from scrutiny; introversion and intensity are normalized in high-performing students.

Coherence lesson: Acceleration without socioemotional integration is incomplete. Gifted education must incorporate neurodiversity frameworks to sustain development.

7.5.5 Case 5: Inti: Indigenous Mathematical Talent, Bilingual Context, and Linguistic Misinterpretation

Rural Indigenous Community Context (Peru)
Inti was born in a Quechua-speaking rural Andean community. His family practiced small-scale agriculture, and daily life required complex practical reasoning—estimating crop yields, calculating irrigation flow, and predicting seasonal variation. From early childhood, Inti demonstrated extraordinary numerical intuition. He mentally computed distances and yields with remarkable accuracy. In his community, these abilities were valued informally but not labeled as "giftedness."

Formal schooling occurred primarily in Spanish, his second language. Although Peru has intercultural bilingual education policies, implementation is uneven across regions. Standardized assessments were administered in Spanish and relied heavily on verbal comprehension.

In class, Inti appeared quiet. His limited fluency in academic Spanish constrained participation. Written assignments were grammatically inconsistent; teachers attributed errors to inattentiveness or limited ability. Standardized mathematics assessments did not capture his informal reasoning strengths, as linguistic complexity obscured quantitative insight.

At thirteen, a regional educational initiative introduced culturally responsive screening. An evaluator used dynamic, low-language problem-solving tasks. Inti excelled in pattern recognition, spatial reasoning, and nonverbal quantitative tasks. Further evaluation revealed:

- High nonverbal intelligence
- Advanced quantitative reasoning
- Dysgraphia
- Language-processing challenges within a bilingual context

Inti's invisibility had multiple layers: linguistic bias in assessment, rural marginalization, and limited psychoeducational infrastructure. Recognition introduced new dilemmas. Advanced programming was available only in urban centers, requiring travel and financial sacrifice. His family faced difficult choices between community continuity and educational opportunity.

Accommodations included bilingual instructional support, oral rather than written mathematical explanation formats, and structured writing assistance. As his confidence grew, Inti began mentoring younger students in mental arithmetic within his community.

His trajectory illustrates that giftedness can manifest in culturally embedded, nonacademic forms. Inti's case reveals that when assessment privileges dominant-language fluency, intelligence is conflated with assimilation. Equity in talent development therefore requires epistemic expansion, not merely procedural adjustment.

Structural Reading of Case 5 (Peru)
Masking pattern: Mutual masking mediated by language. Bilingual processing challenges and dysgraphia obscure advanced quantitative reasoning.

Institutional mechanism: Standardized Spanish-language assessments privilege dominant linguistic capital.

Equity mechanism: Rural location and Indigenous identity restrict access to enrichment and diagnostic infrastructure.

Mental health risk pathway: Quiet misinterpretation → internal withdrawal → suppressed participation.

Cultural dimension: Community-valued competence is not institutionally recognized; epistemic bias narrows definitions of intelligence.

Coherence lesson: Culturally responsive and bilingual assessment is not optional—it is foundational for equitable talent development.

Across Brazil, Chile, Mexico, Colombia, and Peru, five distinct developmental trajectories reveal converging structural patterns:

- Masking operates differently across contexts but is always institutionally mediated.
- Socioeconomic and geographic inequality shape diagnostic exposure.
- Mental health vulnerabilities intensify when compensation becomes chronic.
- Policy silos fragment recognition and support.
- Cultural and linguistic norms narrow definitions of excellence.

Twice-exceptionality is therefore not a marginal anomaly. It is a stress test for systemic coherence.

7.6 Cross-Case Macrosynthesis: Twice-Exceptionality as a Structural Indicator

The five cases presented—Gabriel (Brazil), Valentina (Chile), Luis (Mexico), María Fernanda (Colombia), and Inti (Peru)—are not isolated psychological portraits. When read comparatively, they reveal patterned institutional responses to neurodevelopmental diversity within stratified systems. The cases function as microlevel developmental ecosystems through which macro-level structures become visible.

Across contexts, five recurrent structural mechanisms emerge.

7.6.1 Masking as Institutional Production

Masking in twice-exceptionality is frequently described as an individual phenomenon: students compensate, overperform, or underperform. Yet the cases demonstrate that masking is co-produced by institutional design.

- In Brazil, enrichment selection relied on completed work and teacher nomination grounded in compliance.
- In Chile, a timed, performance-driven evaluation amplified compensation while concealing reading inefficiency.
- In Mexico, literacy-dominant standardized metrics excluded nonverbal strengths.
- In Colombia, academic excellence shielded socioemotional needs from scrutiny.
- In Peru, Spanish-language assessment misread bilingual processing profiles.

In each case, the identification system privileged one form of observable performance and filtered out asynchronous profiles. Masking therefore becomes structural: systems equate giftedness with uniform academic output and disability with overt failure. Students whose profiles do not produce either extreme remain illegible.

This pattern aligns with OECD findings that socioeconomic status strongly predicts achievement outcomes across Latin America (OECD, 2023). When achievement becomes the proxy for ability, learners whose disabilities suppress performance are doubly disadvantaged—by neurodevelopmental profile and by institutional logic.

7.6.2 Socioeconomic Stratification and Diagnostic Access

The cases reveal stark contrasts in access to psychoeducational assessment.

- Gabriel's family incurred financial strain to obtain private evaluation.
- Valentina accessed services within a selective school environment.
- Luis was identified only through nonprofit intervention.
- María Fernanda benefited from private–school infrastructure.
- Inti required a regional initiative to receive culturally responsive screening.

These trajectories reflect broader inequities documented by UNESCO (2022) and CEPAL (2022): educational opportunity across Latin America remains stratified by income quintile, geography, and ethnicity. Diagnostic access follows similar gradients.

From a capability perspective (Sen, 1999), high cognitive potential is insufficient without institutional conditions that convert potential into recognized functioning. Twice-exceptional learners require conversion factors—assessment, scaffolding, and mental health support. Where these are unequally distributed, recognition itself becomes stratified.

Thus, the identification gap is not merely technical; it is structural. It mirrors and reinforces social inequality.

7.6.3 Mental Health Infrastructure and Developmental Risk

Across cases, socioemotional vulnerability intensified when institutional interpretation failed.

- Gabriel developed avoidance and shame.
- Valentina experienced escalating anxiety and self-surveillance.
- Luis internalized inadequacy masked by humor.
- María Fernanda encountered social isolation and panic.
- Inti withdrew into silence within linguistically misaligned classrooms.

These trajectories reflect broader regional patterns. WHO (2021) estimates that one in seven adolescents globally experiences a mental disorder. PAHO (2025) reports substantial treatment gaps across the Americas. In systems where mental health support is peripheral or externalized, twice-exceptional learners face cumulative risk: cognitive intensity intersects with contextual stress.

Importantly, none of the cases suggest that giftedness inherently produces pathology. Rather, distress emerges at the intersection of asynchrony and institutional misfit. When recognition and support align, trajectories stabilize. When systems remain fragmented, psychological erosion accelerates.

7.6.4 Cultural and Linguistic Mediation of Intelligence

Inti's case foregrounds epistemic bias. Standardized assessments privilege dominant-language fluency and Western academic norms. Indigenous forms of reasoning, community-based mathematical practices, and bilingual processing patterns are often underrepresented in formal identification frameworks.

Research in Peru (Blumen, 2010, 2012) indicates that teacher conceptions of giftedness frequently emphasize academic fluency and behavioral conformity. This narrows recognition and amplifies "double invisibility": giftedness masked by disability and disability misinterpreted through linguistic inequity.

Cultural mediation also appears in Chile's performance ethos and Brazil's behavioral expectations. Definitions of excellence shape who becomes visible.

7.6.5 Policy Fragmentation and Institutional Silos

Perhaps the most consistent pattern across cases is institutional compartmentalization.

1. Gifted programming operates separately from inclusive education.
2. Mental health services are detached from enrichment structures.

3. Bilingual education policy is unevenly implemented and rarely integrated with talent development.

This fragmentation reflects broader policy architectures across Latin America. Although countries have made strides in inclusive education frameworks and, in some cases, formal recognition of high ability, dual differentiation remains underdeveloped. Excellence and inclusion are often positioned as parallel agendas rather than integrated ones.

Twice-exceptionality sits precisely at this intersection. When subsystems fail to communicate, complexity is lost.

Taken together, these trajectories reveal that twice-exceptionality is not a peripheral variation within talent development but a structural convergence point. It is where neurodevelopmental diversity encounters institutional design, where inequality shapes recognizability, and where policy fragmentation becomes developmentally consequential. When systems align, potential stabilizes. When systems remain siloed, masking persists. The visibility of the twice-exceptional learner thus becomes a measure of systemic coherence.

7.7 Structural Inequality and the Identification Gap

The invisibility of twice-exceptional learners cannot be separated from educational stratification.

Across Latin America, access to quality schooling varies significantly by income quintile and region (CEPAL, 2022). OECD PISA data demonstrate persistent achievement gaps correlated with socioeconomic background (OECD, 2023). These macro-patterns shape microlevel recognition processes.

Identification systems that rely on standardized achievement disproportionately exclude:

1. Students with learning disorders
2. Students with executive dysfunction
3. Bilingual and Indigenous learners
4. Students in under-resourced schools

When identification thresholds are performance-based rather than profile-based, they reproduce structural inequality under the guise of meritocracy.

Furthermore, diagnostic infrastructure is unevenly distributed. Private schools and urban centers often have access to psychologists and multidisciplinary teams; rural and low-income public schools frequently do not. This produces a paradox: the students most in need of early recognition are often those least likely to receive it.

Over time, delayed identification compounds the disadvantage:

1. Missed early intervention reduces skill acquisition.
2. Lack of enrichment narrows cognitive stimulation.
3. Untreated anxiety or executive dysfunction increases disengagement risk.

4. Internalized deficit narratives undermine self-concept.

Twice-exceptionality magnifies inequality not because of inherent vulnerability, but because institutional thresholds are calibrated narrowly. When identification depends on uniform performance, diversity is misread as deficiency. When diagnostic access is stratified, recognition follows privilege. Structural inequality therefore operates not only through access to schooling but through access to legibility. Who is seen as capable becomes a policy outcome, not a natural fact.

7.8 Fragmented Policy Architectures across Latin America

While policy contexts vary, common themes emerge across Brazil, Mexico, Chile, Colombia, and Peru.

Brazil
High abilities/superdotação are formally recognized within special education policy. However, implementation varies widely by region, and integration between gifted programming and mental health services remains inconsistent (Fleith, 2011; Pérez & Freitas, 2014).

Mexico
Programs for aptitudes sobresalientes exist but are not systematically linked with inclusive education frameworks. Identification often relies on academic metrics, and rural access is uneven.

Chile
Selective academic programs emphasize excellence but rarely articulate dual-exceptionality frameworks within policy discourse. Mental health services exist but are not structurally integrated with enrichment pathways.

Colombia
Inclusive education reforms grounded in disability rights have expanded, yet explicit integration with high-ability programming remains limited (Lombana Martínez, 2025).

Peru
Intercultural bilingual education policies exist, but implementation gaps affect equitable identification. Gifted education remains limited in scope and often centralized in urban initiatives.

Across contexts, three silos persist:

1. Gifted education → enrichment and acceleration.
2. Inclusive education → disability accommodation.
3. Mental health → externalized or fragmented support.

Fragmentation is not merely administrative; it is conceptual. When excellence, inclusion, and mental health are governed through separate logics, complexity is redistributed onto the learner. Twice-exceptional students become the site where institutional incoherence is absorbed. The reform challenge, therefore, is not additive—it is integrative.

7.9 Toward an Integrated Ecological Model for Twice-Exceptional Learners

Building on Bronfenbrenner's ecological theory and the ecological–developmental framework of this volume, a coherent response requires multilevel integration.

1. **Multidimensional and Culturally Responsive Assessment**
   Assessment must document strengths and vulnerabilities simultaneously. Dynamic assessment approaches, bilingual instruments, and nonverbal reasoning tasks are essential in linguistically diverse contexts. Static achievement scores are insufficient.
2. **Embedded School-Based Mental Health Infrastructure**
   Mental health services must be integrated within educational planning. Executive coaching, anxiety intervention, and social communication supports should be aligned with academic differentiation rather than externalized.
3. **Dual Differentiation**
   Instruction must cultivate advanced reasoning while scaffolding areas of difficulty. Acceleration without accommodation exacerbates vulnerability; remediation without challenge suppresses engagement.
4. **Family and Community Engagement**
   Outreach programs should reduce stigma and provide accessible information about neurodevelopmental diversity. Recognition cannot depend solely on family advocacy capacity.
5. **Policy Alignment and Data Monitoring**
   Formal recognition of twice-exceptionality within national frameworks is necessary. Data systems should monitor dual identification rates by socioeconomic status and region to ensure equity.

Integration does not imply bureaucratic merger but developmental alignment across ecological levels. Assessment must recognize strength and vulnerability simultaneously. Instruction must differentiate without diminishing rigor. Mental health must be embedded rather than externalized. Policy must coordinate rather than compete. When these domains operate within a shared developmental logic, twice-exceptionality becomes intelligible rather than anomalous. Coherence transforms an isolated intervention into structural capacity.

7.10 Regional Reform Blueprint

To move from conceptual integration to operational coherence, five reform priorities emerge:

1. **Formal Policy Recognition**
   Explicit inclusion of twice-exceptionality in education law and regulatory guidelines.
2. **Interdisciplinary School-Based Teams**
   Coordinated planning among teachers, psychologists, special educators, and administrators.
3. **Teacher Preparation**
   Training in:
   - Neurodevelopmental diversity.
   - Gifted education principles.
   - Socioemotional development.
   - Dual differentiation strategies.
4. **Linked Funding Streams**
   Gifted education, inclusive education, and mental health services should not compete but align within shared budgets.
5. **Regional Research Networks**
   Comparative Latin American research on 2e learners is limited. Cross-national collaboration can generate culturally responsive frameworks.

Reform, in this context, is not the creation of a new category but the maturation of an existing system. Recognizing twice-exceptional learners requires recalibrating identification, reconfiguring service delivery, and rethinking merit itself. The question is not whether these learners exist—they do—but whether systems are architecturally prepared to recognize them.

7.11 Concluding Synthesis: Twice-Exceptionality and Systemic Maturity

Twice-exceptional learners destabilize categorical simplicity. They reveal the inadequacy of dividing excellence from inclusion and cognition from mental health.

Across five national contexts, a consistent pattern emerges: invisibility is structurally produced. Masking is institutional. Inequality shapes recognizability. Policy fragmentation diffuses responsibility.

Yet the cases also demonstrate possibility. When systems align assessment, mental health support, and enrichment, development stabilizes. Coherence enables potential.

Twice-exceptional learners destabilize categorical simplicity. They reveal the insufficiency of dividing excellence from inclusion, cognition from mental health, potential from vulnerability. Their trajectories expose the limits of systems organized around binary logic.

Across five national contexts, a consistent pattern emerges: invisibility is structurally produced. Masking is institutional. Inequality shapes recognizability. Fragmentation diffuses responsibility. When complexity exceeds categorical design, the learner absorbs the consequences.

Yet the cases also demonstrate possibility. When assessment becomes multidimensional, when mental health is embedded within schooling, and when enrichment and accommodation operate in concert, development stabilizes. Coherence enables potential. Alignment reduces erosion.

Twice-exceptionality therefore functions as a diagnostic lens on systemic maturity. Educational systems capable of holding cognitive strength and vulnerability simultaneously demonstrate conceptual depth. Systems that cannot remain constrained by reductive meritocratic or deficit paradigms.

If this volume advances a regionally grounded model of equitable talent development, twice-exceptionality stands as its most revealing test case. To recognize these learners is not an auxiliary reform. It is a structural commitment to developmental integration across Latin America.

References

Baum, S. M., Schader, R. M., & Hébert, T. P. (2014). *Through a different lens: Reflecting on a strengths-based, talent-focused approach for twice-exceptional learners*. Prufrock Press.

Blumen, S. (2010). Academic talent development in Peru: Cultural and educational considerations. *High Ability Studies, 21*(1), 65–76. https://doi.org/10.1080/13598139.2010.488083

Blumen, S. (2012). Talent development and socioemotional characteristics in Peruvian students. *High Ability Studies, 23*(2), 141–156. https://doi.org/10.1080/13598139.2012.679085

Economic Commission for Latin America and the Caribbean. (2022). *Social panorama of Latin America and the Caribbean 2022: Transforming education as a basis for sustainable development.* https://www.cepal.org/en/presentations/social-panorama-latin-america-and-caribbean-2022-transforming-education-basis

Fleith, D. S. (2011). Creativity in the Brazilian culture. *Online Readings in Psychology and Culture, 4*(3).

Foley-Nicpon, M., Rickels, H., Assouline, S. G., & Richards, A. (2012). Social and emotional development of twice-exceptional students. *Gifted Child Quarterly, 56*(4), 195–206. https://doi.org/10.1177/0016986212456071

Foley-Nicpon, M., Assouline, S. G., & Colangelo, N. (2013). Twice-exceptional learners: Who needs to know what? *Gifted Child Quarterly, 57*(3), 169–180. https://doi.org/10.1177/0016986213490021

Friedman-Nimz, R., & Skyba, O. (2009). The relationship between giftedness and ADHD: A systematic literature review. *Gifted Child Quarterly, 53*(2), 79–93. https://doi.org/10.1177/0016986208330565

Lombana Martínez, O. I. (2025). *Atención educativa de la diversidad: Enfoques didácticos*. Politécnico Grancolombiano.

Neihart, M., Reis, S. M., Robinson, N. M., & Moon, S. M. (Eds.). (2016). *The social and emotional development of gifted children: What do we know?* (2nd ed.). Prufrock Press.

Organization for Economic Co-operation and Development. (2023). *PISA 2022 results (Volume I): The state of learning and equity in education*. OECD. https://doi.org/10.1787/53f23881-en

Pan American Health Organization. (2025). *A mental health crisis in the Americas: Effective solutions for social development with equity*. https://www.paho.org/en/documents/mental-health-crisis-americas-effective-solutions-social-development-equity

Pérez, S. G., & Freitas, S. N. (2014). Políticas públicas para altas habilidades/superdotação no Brasil. *Revista Educação Especial, 27*(49), 251–266. https://doi.org/10.5902/1984686X14263

Reis, S. M., Baum, S. M., & Burke, E. (2014). An operational definition of twice-exceptional learners: Implications and applications. *Gifted Child Quarterly, 58*(3), 217–230. https://doi.org/10.1177/0016986214534976

Sen, A. (1999). *Development as freedom*. Oxford University Press.

Silverman, L. K. (2003). *Counseling the gifted and talented*. Love Publishing.

United Nations Educational, Scientific and Cultural Organization. (2022). *Global education monitoring report 2022: Non-state actors in education*. UNESCO.

World Health Organization. (2021). *WHO results report 2020–2021*. Author. https://www.who.int/about/accountability/results/who-results-report-2020-2021

Chapter 8
Indigenous, Rural, and Forcibly Displaced Migrant Talent: The Challenge of Visibility

8.1 Introduction: Recognition, Power, and the Geography of Talent

Legal recognition of students with high intellectual potential has expanded across Latin America over the past two decades. Yet formal acknowledgment has not consistently translated into effective institutional practice. Indigenous, rural, and forcibly displaced migrant learners remain systematically under-identified in gifted education programs. This underrepresentation does not stem from an absence of talent but from the persistence of epistemically narrow and territorially centralized definitions of excellence.

This chapter argues that invisibility is structurally produced at the intersection of colonial knowledge hierarchies, uneven opportunity distribution, and mobility-driven educational discontinuity. Whereas Chaps. 5–7 examined systemic barriers and twice-exceptionality, the present chapter addresses the patterned invisibility of specific populations whose talents develop within marginalized ecologies.

Invisibility does not denote lack of ability. Rather, it signals misalignment between dominant epistemological standards, the territorial distribution of opportunity structures, and the lived environments in which competencies emerge. Three propositions guide the analysis:

- Talent is ecologically embedded and culturally mediated.
- Recognition systems in Latin America remain epistemically narrow and territorially centralized.
- Educational justice requires structural realignment of identification, pedagogy, and policy.

Building on the ecological–capability–decolonial framework introduced in Chap. 3, this chapter examines Indigenous, rural, and forcibly displaced migrant contexts as distinct yet interconnected sites of recognition failure.

S. Blumen, *High Ability and Talent Development in Latin America*,
https://doi.org/10.1007/978-3-032-27468-7_8

8.2 The Ecological–Capability–Decolonial Framework Revisited

8.2.1 Ecological Embeddedness of High Ability

Bronfenbrenner's (1979) ecological systems theory conceptualizes development as emerging from reciprocal interactions between individual potential and layered environmental systems. Within this framework, talent cannot be abstracted from its ecological sources: family cultural practices, community knowledge traditions, school climates, and national policy structures.

In rural Andean communities, cognitive development may be intertwined with agricultural cycles. In Indigenous Amazonian settings, classification systems and memory practices evolve through oral transmission. In forcibly displaced migrant households, executive functioning may be strengthened through multilingual negotiation and bureaucratic navigation. High ability thus manifests as context-responsive competence rather than as a detached psychometric trait.

When identification systems rely exclusively on decontextualized standardized measures, ecological misalignment occurs: the microsystem produces competence that the mesosystem fails to recognize.

8.2.2 Capability Expansion and Conversion Mechanisms

Sen's (1999) capability approach reframes justice in terms of substantive freedoms rather than formal equality. In gifted education, identification is not merely diagnostic but capability-expanding. Enrichment programs function as conversion mechanisms, translating potential into realized opportunity. Conversely, institutional barriers operate as capability constraints.

Indigenous learners may possess culturally embedded knowledge that remains unrecognized in formal schooling. Rural learners may demonstrate applied intelligence without access to advanced coursework. Forcibly displaced migrant learners may experience interrupted educational trajectories that disrupt cumulative development. In each case, invisibility reflects a failure of conversion rather than a lack of capacity.

8.2.3 Decolonial Epistemology and Epistemic Justice

Decolonial scholarship (Quijano, 2000; Walsh, 2009) critiques the persistence of colonial hierarchies in knowledge production. Within schooling systems, coloniality manifests when Western literate abstraction is privileged over oral reasoning, individual competition over collective leadership, and dominant-language fluency over multilingual competence.

López (2009) documents ongoing implementation gaps in intercultural bilingual education across Andean countries. Although Indigenous languages are formally recognized, assessment systems remain largely monolingual. Fricker's (2007) concept of epistemic injustice clarifies how individuals may be undermined in their capacity as knowers when their knowledge forms are dismissed as "traditional" rather than analytical.

The marginalization of Indigenous and rural talent must therefore be understood as both institutional and epistemic.

8.3 Indigenous Talent: Knowledge Systems and Recognition Gaps

8.3.1 Cognitive Sophistication in Indigenous Contexts

Research in Peru, Bolivia, and Mexico demonstrates that Indigenous knowledge systems involve complex reasoning structures (López, 2009; Walsh, 2009). Astronomical timing in Andean agriculture, botanical classification in Amazonian communities, and juridical mediation among Mapuche communities require multivariable inference, hierarchical categorization, and symbolic abstraction embedded in oral narrative traditions.

Yet identification protocols for high-ability education rarely incorporate these competencies. As Blumen (2021) notes, gifted education in Peru remains predominantly urban and secondary-level focused despite constitutional recognition of interculturality.

8.3.2 Underrepresentation Patterns

Across Brazil and Peru, Indigenous learners are underrepresented in formal high-ability programs (Pérez & Freitas, 2014; Blumen, 2013). Although Brazilian federal policy mandates inclusion of students with altas habilidades/superdotação, implementation varies by region (Fleith & Alencar, 2016). Structural barriers include centralized identification procedures, limited teacher preparation, linguistic bias in testing, and scarcity of culturally responsive enrichment models.

8.3.3 Ethnographic Illustration

In a Quechua-speaking school in southern Peru, a student demonstrated advanced narrative structuring during community storytelling sessions. Although his standardized reading scores were average, his oral performance displayed recursive structuring, symbolic mapping, and audience-adaptive modulation. Within community recognition systems, he was regarded as intellectually precocious. Within standardized assessment frameworks, he was not identified as high ability. This case illustrates epistemic misalignment between community-based and institutional criteria of excellence.

8.4 Rural Talent: Territorial Inequality and Applied Intelligence

Multigrade classrooms are common in rural Latin America. Although often framed as a disadvantage, research suggests they can foster peer tutoring, distributed leadership, and autonomy (Corbett, 2007). Students frequently develop applied mathematical reasoning, resource optimization skills, and practical engineering improvisation. However, structural constraints—including limited enrichment infrastructure, teacher turnover, and restricted access to advanced coursework—impede conversion of competence into formal opportunity.

OECD (2019) and ECLAC (2020) document persistent rural–urban disparities in educational achievement and digital access. Territorial inequity thus reinforces epistemic bias by privileging urban forms of excellence.

8.5 Forcibly Displaced Migrant Talent: Mobility and Adaptive Capacity

8.5.1 *Regional Displacement and Educational Disruption*

If Indigenous invisibility emerges from epistemic marginalization and rural invisibility from territorial inequity, invisibility among forcibly displaced migrant learners arises from institutional discontinuity under conditions of forced mobility.

The Venezuelan displacement crisis has significantly reshaped the educational landscape of Latin America. More than 7.7 million Venezuelans have fled their country (R4V, 2024), with approximately 6.7 million residing in Latin America and the Caribbean. Peru has become one of the principal receiving countries, hosting more than 1.5 million Venezuelan migrants (Organización Internacional para las Migraciones, 2025).

Educational systems already marked by structural inequality have absorbed rapid increases in enrollment. In Peru, the number of Venezuelan students in public education rose sharply between 2016 and 2022. Dropout rates for Venezuelan learners reached 18.1%, compared to 3.6% for Peruvian peers (Ministerio de Educación del Perú, 2023). Age–grade lag was also significantly higher among Venezuelan students. These indicators reflect not merely adaptation challenges but disruptions to developmental continuity.

From a capability perspective (Sen, 1999), forcibly displaced learners experience interrupted conversion pathways. Displacement entails loss of cumulative educational advantage, documentation barriers limiting program access, economic precarity constraining enrichment participation, and social exclusion affecting emotional functioning. The result is compounded misrecognition: prior developmental trajectories are fractured, institutional responses prioritize remediation, and psychosocial strain may obscure manifestations of high ability. In these conditions, invisibility is both structural and internalized.

8.5.2 Adaptive Intelligence and Underrecognized Strengths

Despite structural barriers, forcibly displaced migrant learners frequently demonstrate adaptive strengths. Research on migrant youth highlights multilingual flexibility, bicultural competence, contextual social reading, and strategic institutional navigation (Suárez-Orozco et al., 2010). These competencies reflect advanced executive functioning under dynamic environmental conditions.

However, traditional gifted identification frameworks rarely interpret adaptive intelligence as high ability. Language-dependent testing may underestimate reasoning during linguistic transition, and remediation-oriented practices often overshadow strengths. Thus, mobility-generated competencies remain institutionally illegible.

8.6 Case Integration: Art-Based Enrichment in Lima

To examine how these structural dynamics operate in practice, this section integrates findings from a Lima-based enrichment intervention involving host-community and forcibly displaced learners.

8.6.1 Intervention Design and Identification Framework

The study included 284 fourth- and fifth-grade students attending low-income public schools in Lima. Participants comprised Peruvian host-community students, Venezuelan forcibly displaced students, and learners identified with elevated intellectual or creative potential.

Identification followed a developmental equity-based model. Students scoring above the 50th percentile on Raven's Colored Progressive Matrices and the CREA test were included in the high-ability subgroup. This operationalization treated high ability as prospective developmental potential rather than elite performance, aligning with the capability framework.

The intervention, *Well-Being & Art in the School*, was informed by the Schoolwide Enrichment Model (Renzulli & Reis, 2014). Over three 50-minute sessions, students engaged in creative reinterpretation of major works of art, including a structured "Freedom Space" for original expression. Measures assessed emotional intensity (Modified Differential Emotions Scale) and creative performance (TCT-DP), alongside cognitive and verbal indicators.

8.6.2 Emotional Outcomes: Differential Effects

Findings revealed differentiated effects across groups. Non-gifted Peruvian students experienced statistically significant reductions in negative emotional intensity following participation. In contrast, identified high-ability students and forcibly displaced Venezuelan students showed no significant emotional change. Control groups remained stable, suggesting that reductions among non-gifted Peruvian students were attributable to the intervention.

These results challenge assumptions that enrichment universally benefits all participants. For non-gifted host-community students, artistic engagement may have constituted an ecological novelty within under-resourced schools where arts programming is limited. Expanded affective space likely contributed to emotional improvement.

The absence of measurable change among identified high-ability students suggests insufficient cognitive challenge. Research indicates that well-being in high-ability learners is linked to intellectual stimulation, mastery, and optimal difficulty (Kroesbergen et al., 2016). Enrichment that does not reach appropriate levels of cognitive activation may fail to produce emotional transformation. From a capability perspective, the intervention expanded affective opportunity but did not significantly enhance advanced intellectual conversion for this subgroup.

8.6.3 Displacement Ecology and Emotional Stability

The most instructive findings concern the forcibly displaced Venezuelan subgroup, which exhibited no meaningful emotional change despite participation. This stability must be interpreted within the broader displacement ecology: elevated dropout risk, economic insecurity, acculturative stress (Salas-Wright et al., 2022), and documented experiences of xenophobia (Amnesty International, 2023).

Trauma research underscores that improvements in emotional regulation require sustained conditions of safety, stability, and belonging (Hobfoll et al., 2021). A brief three-session intervention, however well designed, cannot offset chronic structural stressors. These findings suggest a capacity ceiling for short-term enrichment in context of displacement.

This does not diminish the value of art-based programming. Rather, it indicates that effective support for forcibly displaced high-ability learners must be sustained, trauma-informed, and embedded within broader inclusion frameworks. Recognition requires continuity.

8.6.4 Creativity Outcomes and Structural Constraint

An unexpected finding was that figural creative performance (TCT-DP) increased significantly in control groups but not in experimental groups. Possible explanations include maturation effects, implicit structuring within the intervention context, and the TCT-DP's sensitivity to autonomy and risk-taking.

Urban (2004) emphasizes that boundary-breaking, humor, and unconventional elaboration are central to figural creativity scoring. Even within designated "Freedom Space," structured sessions may convey implicit expectations that constrain expressive risk-taking. For forcibly displaced youth navigating precarious social environments, expressive risk may entail psychological cost.

Creativity enhancement therefore requires sustained autonomy-supportive climates rather than isolated enrichment exposure. Structural conditions shape not only emotional regulation but also creative expression.

8.7 Comparative Structural Diagnosis

Table 8.1 synthesizes mechanisms of invisibility across Indigenous, rural, and migrant contexts. Although justice deficits differ—epistemic for Indigenous learners, redistributive for rural learners, and continuity-based for migrant learners—all reflect failure to convert competence into recognized opportunity.

8.8 Methodological Reflection

This chapter integrates policy analysis, ethnographic illustration, and experimental evidence. Psychometric instruments remain central to identification, yet normed tools may reproduce bias if applied without contextual adaptation. Blumen's (2000) adaptation of the TCT-DP underscores the importance of local validation. Ethnographic approaches enable documentation of applied cognition and community recognition processes. Decolonial methodologies (Smith, 2012; Walsh, 2009) further emphasize participatory engagement with communities as epistemic partners.

Table 8.1 Comparative visibility matrix: indigenous, rural, and migrant talent in Latin America

Dimension	Indigenous students	Rural students	Migrant students
Primary source of invisibility	Epistemic marginalization; monolingual assessment; colonial curricular hierarchies	Territorial inequity; resource scarcity; urban-centric standards	Linguistic disruption; documentation barriers; curricular discontinuity
Dominant deficit narrative	"Language delay"; "low literacy"; knowledge framed as nonacademic	"Low aspirations"; "limited exposure"; cultural isolation	"Interrupted schooling"; "learning gaps"; remediation framing
Systemic factors	Weak implementation of intercultural bilingual education (López, 2009); centralized identification	Multigrade classrooms; teacher turnover; digital divide (ECLAC, 2020; OECD, 2019)	Policy instability; credential recognition gaps; mobility-based assessment disruption (Suárez-Orozco et al., 2010)
Underrepresentation pattern	Minimal participation in formal gifted programs; overrepresentation in compensatory tracks	Low identification rates; limited enrichment access	Under-identification due to language-based testing; nomination discontinuity
Culturally embedded forms of high ability	Ecological classification; oral narrative mastery; collective leadership	Applied mathematics in agriculture; mechanical ingenuity; resource optimization	Multilingual flexibility; intercultural negotiation; adaptive executive functioning
Relevant theoretical lens	Decoloniality (Mignolo, 2011); epistemic justice (Fricker, 2007)	Ecological systems theory (Bronfenbrenner, 1979); place-based education (Corbett, 2007)	Transnationalism (Portes & Rumbaut, 2014); bicultural competence (Suárez-Orozco et al., 2010)
Assessment limitations	Standardized tests misaligned with linguistic and cultural cognition	Narrow academic benchmarks; neglect of practical intelligence	Language-dependent instruments underestimate cognitive capacity
Alternative identification strategies	Community nomination; bilingual dynamic assessment; portfolio documentation	Performance-based tasks; project evaluation; local innovation showcases	Dynamic assessment; multilingual testing; socio-cognitive mapping
Pedagogical implications	Land-based STEM; integration of ancestral knowledge; intergenerational inquiry	Place-based problem-solving; rural innovation labs	Culturally sustaining pedagogy; translanguaging; newcomer leadership programs
Policy levers	Legal recognition of indigenous epistemologies; intercultural resource commitments	Redistributive funding commitments; decentralized enrichment hubs	Protected fiscal provisions; migrant inclusion frameworks; flexible identification windows

(continued)

Table 8.1 (continued)

Dimension	Indigenous students	Rural students	Migrant students
Equity rationale (capability lens)	Expansion of culturally grounded intellectual freedoms (Sen, 1999; Nussbaum, 2011)	Territorial equalization of opportunity structures	Protection and cultivation of adaptive capabilities under mobility
Core justice issue	Epistemic recognition	Territorial redistribution	Inclusion and continuity of opportunity

8.9 Policy Architecture for Recognition Reform

8.9.1 Identification Reform: Expanding the Epistemic Frame

Identification must not be neutral; it inscribes assumptions about intelligence and merit. In many parts of Latin America, high-ability policies rely heavily on standardized testing or teacher nomination systems that replicate dominant academic norms (Blumen, 2013; Pérez & Freitas, 2014).

Reform should involve dynamic assessment models that evaluate learning potential rather than static performance, bilingual and culturally relevant testing models that address Indigenous and forcibly displaced linguistic situations, community nomination pathways that integrate local knowledge systems, and application- and eco-competence-based portfolio recognition mechanisms.

High-ability students are legally recognized in Peru under the General Education Law (Supreme Decree No. 011-2012-ED; Ministerio de Educación del Perú, 2021). However, implementation remains concentrated in secondary-level institutions such as the Colegios de Alto Rendimiento (COAR). Early detection remains limited, especially in rural and migrant-dense areas (Blumen, 2021). In addition, age-based legislative strictures and prohibitive acceleration policies in many Latin American countries—discussed in Chap. 4—make flexible recognition of high ability among marginalized populations more difficult.

Dynamic assessment, bilingual testing models, community nomination pathways, and portfolio-based evaluation can expand epistemic frames. Expanding epistemic criteria constitutes a commitment to epistemic justice.

8.9.2 Territorial Redistribution: Decentralizing Opportunity

Invisibility in rural areas reflects the unequal distribution of educational infrastructure. As OECD (2019) and ECLAC (2020) document, persistent gaps remain between rural and metropolitan areas in access to advanced coursework, digital resources, and specialized staff.

Policy levers must include redistributive resource commitments for rural high-ability development, decentralized enrichment hubs, remote and hybrid enrichment platforms, and teacher education on multigrade differentiation strategies.

Ecological competence cannot be converted into expanded capability without territorial redistribution. Redistribution is not charity; it is the structural equalization of opportunity conditions.

8.9.3 Continuity and Inclusion for Forcibly Displaced Learners

The Lima art-based intervention illustrates that isolated enrichment cannot offset the chronic stressors of displacement. For Venezuelan students who were forcibly displaced, emotional outcomes remained stable despite participation in creative programs. This underscores the necessity of continuity architecture: flexible identification windows to accommodate interrupted schooling, documentation accommodations, trauma-informed school climates, translanguaging pedagogies, and enrichment models that engage families.

Salas-Wright et al. (2022) stress that migration-related stress poses significant mental health challenges. Hobfoll et al. (2021) note that in trauma-responsive settings, safety, connection, and empowerment constitute foundational elements.

Consequently, enrichment must be embedded within broader social, emotional, and structural supports for forcibly displaced gifted learners. Recognition by itself is not enough without stability and sustained developmental support.

8.10 Conclusion: Recognition as Educational Justice

Invisibility across Indigenous, rural, and migrant contexts is not incidental but structurally produced. Talent remains present yet institutionally unrecognized. The ecological–capability–decolonial framework reframes gifted education in Latin America as a matter of educational justice. Ecological fit enables lived competencies to become institutionally legible; capability expansion ensures conversion of potential into opportunity; decolonial epistemology affirms the legitimacy of plural knowledge systems.

The Lima intervention illustrates both promise and limitation. Enrichment can reduce affective stress for some learners, yet without sustained differentiation and structural support, it cannot overcome systemic discontinuities. The future of gifted education in Latin America depends on whether recognition systems become epistemically plural, territorially equitable, and developmentally continuous. Educational justice requires architectural redesign rather than incremental expansion.

References

Amnesty International. (2023). *Peru/Chile: Authorities must end border militarization and protect people in need of international protection*. https://www.amnesty.org

Blumen, S. (2000). *Identification of and attention for the highly able in Lima* (Doctoral dissertation). Radboud University Nijmegen.

Blumen, S. (2013). New trends in talent development in Peru. *Journal for the Education of the Gifted, 36*(3), 346–364. https://doi.org/10.1177/0162353213492925

Blumen, S. (2021). Talent development, cultural diversity, and equity: The challenge of the Andean countries. In R. J. Sternberg & D. Ambrose (Eds.), *Conceptions of giftedness and talent* (pp. 21–35). Palgrave Macmillan.

Bronfenbrenner, U. (1979). *The ecology of human development*. Harvard University Press.

Corbett, M. (2007). *Learning to leave: The irony of schooling in a coastal community*. Fernwood Publishing.

Economic Commission for Latin America and the Caribbean (ECLAC). (2020). *Panorama social de América Latina*. Naciones Unidas.

Fleith, D. S., & Alencar, E. M. L. S. (2016). Gifted education in Brazil: Historical perspectives and current issues. *Gifted Education International, 32*(3), 234–245.

Fricker, M. (2007). *Epistemic injustice: Power and the ethics of knowing*. Oxford University Press.

Hobfoll, S. E., et al. (2021). Five essential elements of immediate and mid-term mass trauma intervention. *Psychiatry, 84*(4), 311–346.

Inter-Agency Coordination Platform for Refugees and Migrants from Venezuela (R4V). (2024). *Refugees and migrants from Venezuela*. https://www.r4v.info

Kroesbergen, E. H., Hooijdonk, M., Van Viersen, S., Middel/Lalleman, M. M. N., & Reijnders, J. J. W. (2016). The psychological well-being of early identified gifted children. *Gifted Child Quarterly, 60*(1), 16–30. https://doi.org/10.1177/0016986215609113

López, L. E. (2009). Intercultural bilingual education in Latin America: Balancing unity and diversity in the quest for quality. *Prospects, 39*, 27–42.

Mignolo, W. D. (2011). *The darker side of Western modernity: Global futures, decolonial options*. Duke University Press.

Ministerio de Educación del Perú. (2021). *Guía de orientaciones para la conformación, organización y funcionamiento de los SAANEE*. Ministerio de Educación del Perú.

Ministerio de Educación del Perú. (2023). *Situación de los estudiantes venezolanos en Perú*. Repositorio Institucional MINEDU.

Nussbaum, M. (2011). *Creating capabilities*. Harvard University Press.

OECD. (2019). *PISA 2018 results* (Vol. I). OECD.

Organización Internacional para las Migraciones. (2025). *Portal de datos mundiales sobre la migración: Perú*.

Pérez, S. G., & Freitas, S. N. (2014). Políticas públicas para altas habilidades/superdotação no Brasil. *Revista Educação Especial, 27*(49), 251–266.

Portes, A., & Rumbaut, R. G. (2014). *Immigrant America: A portrait* (4th ed.). University of California Press.

Quijano, A. (2000). Coloniality of power and Eurocentrism in Latin America. *International Sociology, 15*(2), 215–232.

Renzulli, J. S., & Reis, S. M. (2014). *The Schoolwide enrichment model* (3rd ed.). Routledge.

Salas-Wright, C. P., Maldonado-Molina, M. M., Pérez-Gómez, A., Trujillo, J. M., & Schwartz, S. J. (2022). The Venezuelan diaspora: Migration-related experiences and mental health. *Current Opinion in Psychology, 47*, 101430. https://doi.org/10.1016/j.copsyc.2022.101430

Sen, A. (1999). *Development as freedom*. Oxford University Press.

Smith, L. T. (2012). *Decolonizing methodologies: Research and indigenous peoples* (2nd ed.). Zed Books.

Suárez-Orozco, C., Suárez-Orozco, M. M., & Todorova, I. (2010). *Learning a new land: Immigrant students in American society*. Harvard University Press.

Urban, K. K. (2004). Assessing creativity: The Test for Creative Thinking–Drawing Production (TCT-DP). *Psychology Science, 46*(3), 387–397.

Walsh, C. (2009). Interculturalidad crítica y pedagogía de-colonial. *Revista Educación y Pedagogía, 21*(55), 25–36.

Chapter 9
Teacher Training and Professional Development in High-Ability Education across Latin America

9.1 Introduction: From Recognition to Realization—Teacher Preparation as Conversion Infrastructure

Across Latin America, the legislative recognition of students with high intellectual ability has increased, often under the umbrella of inclusive education, special education, or "diversity" frameworks. Yet classroom realization remains inconsistent and, in many contexts, episodic. Policies may acknowledge *altas capacidades*, *altas habilidades/superdotação*, or related constructs, but the professional systems that would enable regular teachers to identify, plan for, and teach advanced learners have not evolved with equivalent speed or coherence.

This chapter builds directly on the ecological–capability–equity framework articulated in Chap. 3. In that model, high ability is not treated as a fixed internal property or a purely psychometric label. It is conceptualized as **developmental potential**—a set of emergent capacities that require conversion factors in order to become realized functioning. Conversion factors include institutional opportunity structures (curriculum flexibility, access to specialized support, enrichment pathways), cultural legitimacy (beliefs about who "deserves" challenge), and pedagogical mediation (teachers' diagnostic noticing, differentiation capacity, and socio-emotional scaffolding).

Teachers are the principal conversion agents in schooling. They interpret policy into classroom meaning and translate recognition into sectors. Where formal preparation is scarce, advanced learning opportunities concentrate in urban, elite, or privately resourced settings. Conversely, the advanced learner in a low-resourced public school may depend almost entirely on the regular classroom teacher's capacity and willingness to differentiate. In this sense, teacher training is not merely a quality improvement strategy; it is a **mechanism of equity**.

The chapter also integrates a twice-exceptionality lens developed in Chap. 7. Twice-exceptional learners experience a double bind: disability-related needs may

S. Blumen, *High Ability and Talent Development in Latin America*,
https://doi.org/10.1007/978-3-032-27468-7_9

obscure strengths, while high ability may obscure support needs. Without teacher preparation that integrates strength-based identification and accommodation-based scaffolding, 2e learners are systematically under-identified and misserved, which produces a distinctive form of structural marginalization.

From the ecological–capability–equity perspective, teacher preparation is therefore not ancillary reform. It is the structural hinge connecting recognition to realization.

9.2 Conceptual and Terminological Fragmentation as a Training Challenge

A defining feature of high-ability education across Latin America is its conceptual and terminological heterogeneity. Different jurisdictions—and sometimes subnational territories within the same country—use diverse labels shaped by Iberian intellectual traditions, global discourse diffusion, and local professional communities. Examples include: *altas capacidades* (Chile), *altas habilidades/superdotação* (Brazil), *altas capacidades intelectuales* (Argentina and Paraguay), and broader constructs such as talent development, exceptional potential, or endowment.

Pluralism may reflect conceptual nuance and sociocultural specificity, yet it also generates practical difficulties for teacher education. When a field lacks a stable shared vocabulary, teacher preparation becomes structurally vulnerable to fragmentation. This "lexicon balkanization" has at least four ramifications for training systems:

1. **Curricular Development**

   Pre-service curricula often treat gifted education as marginal because there is no stable national consensus on what "giftedness" entails, how it relates to inclusive education, and what instructional responsibilities follow from recognition. Gifted education may be treated as an elective topic, a brief inclusion module, or an enrichment "specialty," rather than as a core competence of teaching (García-Cepero & Proestakis, 2010).
2. **Assessment in Chaos**

   In the absence of coherent professional language, teachers rely disproportionately on grades, compliance behaviors, teacher nominations shaped by stereotypes, and narrow indicators of "brightness." Multi-criteria frameworks—combining performance evidence, learning rate, creativity indicators, problem-solving, and contextual information—are rarely internalized through formal training (CEPAL, 2022; García-Cepero, 2009).
3. **Legal Ambiguity**

   Terminological confusion intersects with regulatory uncertainty: teachers may not know whether high-ability supports are a right, an option, or a privilege. In ambiguous contexts, teachers may avoid differentiation and acceleration because uncertainty increases perceived risk (Ford, 2014; Freire, 1970).

4. **Professional Isolation**
   Teacher networks and communities of practice struggle to build shared expertise across divergent terms and local models. When language differs across systems, professional exchange becomes translation labor rather than pedagogical growth (Schön, 1983).

A cohesive regional agenda for teacher preparation must therefore begin with conceptual literacy: teachers need a map connecting local terminology to broader constructs of talent development and capability expansion, and from there to implications for identification, instruction, pacing, and socio-emotional support (Dweck, 2006; OECD, 2019).

9.3 Teachers as Capability Mediators in an Ecological System

Chapter 3 established that equitable talent development unfolds within interacting ecological systems. When this architecture is applied to teacher preparation, a clearer structural diagnosis emerges: professional learning is not an auxiliary reform but the mechanism through which ecological alignment becomes possible.

9.3.1 Macrosystem: Norms, Values, Cultural Scripts

At this layer (Bronfenbrenner, 1979), teachers inherit social narratives about merit, elitism, "normal" development, and chronological age placement. In many contexts, gifted education is culturally framed as either elitist privilege or as an exceptional "extra" that schools cannot afford. These beliefs shape whether teachers feel morally authorized to differentiate (Rosenthal & Jacobson, 1968).

9.3.2 Exosystem: Policy, Regulations, Certification Systems

Here, the issue is not only whether policies exist but whether teachers can interpret them into usable classroom decisions. Regulatory structures can also produce chilling effects: if teachers perceive acceleration as prohibited or bureaucratically burdensome, they will default to static pacing (Tourón & Santiago, 2015).

9.3.3 *Mesosystem: Institutional Coordination*

Teacher learning depends on the coordination among universities, schools, enrichment programs, families, and specialist services. Where coordination is weak—e.g., university enrichment exists but does not diffuse into schools—expertise becomes localized and stratified (UNESCO, 2021).

9.3.4 *Microsystem: Classroom Practice*

This is where capability conversion occurs day to day: identification practices, differentiated instruction, grouping, pacing, classroom climate, and socio-emotional scaffolding. Teachers' micro-decisions can either expand or contract the learner's capability set.

From a capability perspective (Nussbaum, 2011; Sen, 1999), talent development is the process through which potential is converted into functioning via access to challenge, feedback, pacing flexibility, recognition, and legitimate opportunity (Gagné, 2004; Renzulli & Reis, 2014; Winner, 1996). Without teacher training, capability deprivation is not unusual even for advanced learners: boredom, disengagement, and underachievement become predictable. Conversely, teachers equipped with compacting, inquiry-based enrichment, flexible grouping, and monitored acceleration can expand capability sets even under constraint.

Critically, the ecological–capability framing clarifies why teacher training is an equity issue rather than merely a "quality" issue. Without training, identification and enrichment tend to privilege students with higher cultural and educational capital—dominant language fluency, familiarity with school norms, families able to advocate, and access to private assessment. Training can expand recognition thresholds and legitimized forms of potential, including culturally embedded and community-defined excellence.

9.4 Regional Evidence: Recognition without Preparation

Across Latin America, regular education teachers commonly report little or no formal training in giftedness. The region exhibits a recurring pattern: policy recognition expands faster than professional capacity. Country cases illustrate shared dynamics in distinct forms.

9.4.1 Argentina: Policy Visibility, Minimal Systematic Preparation, and Low-Leverage Classroom Responses

Argentina illustrates a common regional pattern: recognition discourse exists, yet teacher preparation remains thin and uneven. Irueste (2017) documents gifted education in Argentina and, critically for the present chapter, highlights the limited institutionalization of teacher preparation pathways for high-ability education. Consistent with that structural condition, regional evidence summarized in this chapter indicates that when teachers encounter advanced learners, they most often rely on additive extensions (extra worksheets or additional tasks) rather than qualitative differentiation (depth, complexity, abstraction, or acceleration). The instructional implication is not merely inefficiency: "Extra work" preserves age-based pacing while leaving the learner's readiness differential structurally unresolved."

Claim supported by evidence: Where teacher preparation is not systematically developed, teachers default to low-leverage management strategies that preserve age-norm pacing and foreclose acceleration as a considered option (Irueste, 2017; chapter synthesis).

9.4.2 Brazil: Formal Policy Recognition, Persistent Teacher Ambivalence toward Acceleration, and the Centrality of Socio-Emotional Concerns

Brazil is distinct in the region in that high ability is explicitly framed within special education policy discourse, and a substantial scholarly community has developed around *altas habilidades/superdotação* (Pérez & Freitas, 2016; Wechsler & Fleith, 2017). Yet the training gap remains consequential: the empirical pattern is not a lack of policy awareness but implementation hesitation, especially around acceleration. Maia-Pinto and Fleith (2016) examined perceptions of acceleration among students, mothers, and teachers and found strongly positive orientations overall, while teacher ambivalence clustered around socio-emotional maturity and adjustment concerns. This finding is analytically significant: it locates teacher reluctance not in ideological resistance but in professional uncertainty regarding socio-emotional readiness assessment and transition monitoring. Brazilian literature on teacher formation in gifted education further underscores uneven diffusion of preparation opportunities across contexts, meaning that evidence-informed practices depend heavily on localized access to training (Delou, 2018; Virgolim, 2014).

Claim supported by evidence: In Brazil, policy recognition is necessary but insufficient; teacher ambivalence toward acceleration is empirically anchored in socio-emotional concern patterns, indicating that professional learning must explicitly train readiness assessment and monitoring rather than merely promote acceleration as a principle (Delou, 2018; Maia-Pinto & Fleith, 2016; Virgolim, 2014).

9.4.3 Paraguay: Receptive Teachers, Weak Specialized Preparation, and the Shifting of Instructional Burden to Families under Policy Volatility

Paraguay demonstrates how limited teacher preparation generates downstream equity effects through family substitution. Evidence integrated in this chapter indicates that teachers are often receptive to supporting learners with altas capacidades yet have not been provided sustained specialized preparation; in such conditions, families frequently supply enrichment materials and strategies, effectively transferring instructional design responsibilities from schools to households. This dynamic is empirically consistent with Paraguayan work on teacher conceptions and inclusive framing of high ability (Lobo & Vuyk, 2023) and with broader Paraguayan studies describing identification and program participation pathways (Vuyk et al., 2023; Barrios et al., 2020). The equity risk is structural: opportunity becomes contingent on parental advocacy capacity and resources. The chapter's synthesis further notes policy fragility—progressive regulatory moves followed by restrictive interpretations—which heightens the importance of teacher legal literacy and procedural competence.

Claim supported by evidence: In Paraguay, inadequate professional preparation contributes to a compensatory reliance on families and to inconsistent implementation under shifting policy conditions; training must therefore combine pedagogical tools (e.g., compacting) with legal/procedural literacy to reduce gatekeeping driven by uncertainty (Lobo & Vuyk, 2023; Vuyk et al., 2023; Barrios et al., 2020).

9.4.4 Chile: Concentrated Enrichment Ecosystems, Limited Mainstream Diffusion, and the Utility of a Learning-Resource (Actiotope) Lens

Chile is empirically distinctive: it hosts well-developed university-centered enrichment programs and a strong research base on barriers and facilitators within regular schooling. Gómez-Arízaga et al. (2020a) identify context-level facilitators and barriers for addressing high ability in Chilean schools, while Gómez-Arízaga et al. (2020b) document gifted students' lived experiences with teaching practices in regular classrooms—evidence that classroom-level differentiation often remains insufficient despite the existence of enrichment nodes. More recently, Gómez-Arizaga, Conejeros-Solar, and Cornejo-Araya (2024) analyze Chilean gifted education through a learning-resource perspective, highlighting how learning resources and opportunity structures are unevenly distributed and how teacher professional preparation in mainstream settings remains optional rather than guaranteed. This configuration exemplifies the ecological asymmetry foregrounded in this chapter:

concentrated mesosystem excellence coupled with inconsistent microsystem enactment.

Claim supported by evidence: In Chile, enrichment capacity is real but unevenly distributed; empirical studies show mainstream classrooms often fail to translate enrichment capital into daily instructional opportunity, supporting a reform focus on diffusion mechanisms—teacher preparation, partnerships, and practice-based PD framed through a learning-resource lens (Gómez-Arízaga et al., 2020a, 2020b, 2024).

9.4.5 Peru: Evidence that Teacher Retraining Improves Identification Accuracy, Plus an Institutional Model (COAR) that Embeds Professional Rigor

Peru provides one of the clearest regional demonstrations that sustained teacher learning can strengthen identification and service delivery. Blumen's (2004) meta-analytic synthesis of identification and attention to talent and giftedness in Peru emphasizes the value of multi-measure approaches and the effects of sustained professional engagement. Blumen (2016) further extends the discussion to serving Indigenous Peruvian learners, underscoring the need for culturally and linguistically responsive identification and programming. In institutional terms, the COAR model functions as a professionally structured environment: teachers operate within a high-demand curriculum culture, supported through specialized preparation and ongoing professional expectations. The significance of this chapter is not that COAR "solves" the national training gap but that it demonstrates a *design principle*: when professional learning is embedded in institutional structure, the conversion chain (recognition → opportunity → realized capability) becomes more reliable.

Claim supported by evidence: Peru offers both empirical and institutional support for the argument that teacher preparation is conversion infrastructure: research demonstrates gains in identification when teacher learning is sustained and multi-measure, and COAR exemplifies how embedded professional culture can sustain high-conversion schooling environments (Blumen, 2004, 2016; chapter synthesis).

9.5 Cultural Barriers: Myth, Elitism, and Age Norms

Teacher training does not expand simply by adding content; it must confront cultural narratives embedded in professional beliefs and institutional routines. Three barriers recur across the region.

9.5.1 *Socio-Emotional Myths about Acceleration*

A dominant argument against acceleration is fear of socio-emotional harm: stress, isolation, bullying, and developmental asynchrony. Yet longitudinal evidence outside the region indicates that academic acceleration is not associated with reduced psychological well-being over time. The training implication is not "ignore socio-emotion"—it is the opposite: teach structured socio-emotional readiness assessment, peer-climate planning, and post-implementation monitoring so that acceleration becomes a supported pathway rather than a leap into uncertainty.

9.5.2 *Elitism Narratives*

Gifted education is often framed as elitist, a narrative made potent by the region's histories of stratification. Yet the equity reality is inverted: when schools fail to differentiate, privileged students secure enrichment privately, while advanced learners in under-resourced public schools remain constrained. Teacher education must therefore reframe gifted support as inclusion: readiness-based instruction is a right, not a luxury.

9.5.3 *Rigid Age Norms*

Chronological age placement is deeply institutionalized. Teachers may treat advanced pacing as an administrative violation even when policy allows flexibility. Training must include (a) legal literacy—what is permitted, (b) curriculum compacting skills to align mastery evidence with pacing adjustments, and (c) institutional negotiation strategies for implementing flexibility within bureaucratic constraints.

9.6 Acceleration as a Professional Competency

Acceleration occupies a paradoxical position within Latin American high-ability discourse. It is simultaneously among the most empirically supported interventions and among the least professionally normalized. Understanding this paradox requires examining acceleration not as a policy option alone but as a competence-dependent practice.

Acceleration competence includes:

1. **Assessment literacy:** identifying readiness via multiple indicators rather than single tests or informal impressions

2. **Instructional design:** aligning compacting, enrichment, and pacing plans to curricular requirements
3. **Socio-emotional monitoring:** evaluating adjustment, peer integration, stress, and belonging
4. **Family and institutional coordination:** communicating goals, managing expectations, documenting outcomes

9.6.1 Whole-Grade Acceleration and Early Entrance

These options are often framed as rare, bureaucratic, and fear-laden. Even where technically allowed, teachers may refuse due to socio-emotional concerns and institutional reticence. Training must equip educators to distinguish myth-based fear from evidence-based risk management and to implement readiness and monitoring protocols.

9.6.2 Subject Acceleration and Systemic Suppression

Subject acceleration is especially neglected and, in some policies, discouraged. This is consequential for domains such as mathematics, where talent development depends on sustained progression and access to advanced content. When students are required to repeat mastered material, motivation and self-concept can deteriorate. Even when formal subject acceleration is constrained, training in compacting and advanced problem-solving enrichment can mitigate suppression.

9.6.3 Curriculum Compacting as Entry Point

Curriculum compacting is strategically important because it is often permissible even in rigid systems. It replaces "busywork extension" with mastery-based progression and can be delivered through short, scalable modules. In many contexts, compacting functions as the professional bridge that opens teacher willingness toward broader pacing flexibility.

9.7 Multicultural Contexts and Assessment Literacy

Latin America's linguistic and cultural diversity complicates identification and teacher judgment. In bilingual or multilingual contexts, assessment tools often align with dominant languages and cultural forms, creating bias. In linguistically stratified contexts, language-loaded indicators frequently become proxies for ability, distorting recognition pathways.

Teacher preparation must therefore include:

- Awareness of linguistic bias in assessment and classroom interaction
- Portfolio methods and performance-based evidence
- Community-informed notions of talent
- Culturally responsive pedagogy and legitimacy-building

From a capability perspective, culturally responsive training strengthens conversion factors for marginalized learners: it increases the likelihood that teachers recognize potential beyond dominant language performance and that enrichment decisions are not distorted by cultural mismatch.

The actiotope perspective offers a productive conceptual transition: from asking "Who is gifted?" to "What actions does this learner need opportunities to perform?" This shift reframes the teacher as an environmental designer and capability expander rather than a label gatekeeper. It also carries an equity advantage: focusing on observable learning needs and opportunity structures can reduce stereotype-driven judgments.

9.8 Twice-Exceptionality Integration

Twice-exceptional learners demonstrate advanced reasoning alongside disability-related limitations (attention, executive functioning, language, sensory differences, socio-emotional vulnerability). In systems where inclusion is structured primarily along disability lines and where gifted education is underdeveloped, 2e learners face a double bind:

- Disability masks ability, leading to lowered expectations
- Ability masks disability, leading to unaddressed support needs

Teacher training must integrate:

1. Multi-criteria, strength-based identification (avoiding single-test gatekeeping)
2. Strength-based pedagogy plus accommodations (challenge with scaffolding)
3. Belonging and socio-emotional supports (reducing misinterpretation of distress)
4. Thoughtful acceleration decision-making (monitored flexibility, not neglect)

Without twice-exceptionality integration, equitable talent development remains structurally incomplete. The absence of integrated preparation does not merely delay identification; it produces structural misalignment in which challenge and accommodation are incorrectly treated as mutually exclusive rather than co-constitutive.

9.9 Promising Models for Effective Training: From COAR to Practice-Based Modules

Despite systemic gaps, the region contains promising models that suggest feasible pathways.

9.9.1 The COAR Model (Peru): Institutionalized Professional Rigor

COAR demonstrates how excellence can be scaled through the integration of teacher preparation with institutional design. COAR teachers participate in specialized development aligned with high-demand curricular structures and professional expectations. From the ecological–capability perspective, COAR functions as a high-conversion context: teacher knowledge, assessment culture, and opportunity structures are aligned to sustain advanced capability development.

9.9.2 Peru: Historical Advocacy and Teacher Networks

Peru's history also suggests the diffusion potential of teacher networks. Workshops and professional communities can function as mesosystem bridges that spread expertise even when pre-service systems change slowly. Networks can reduce isolation and legitimize practice innovations in settings where gifted education is culturally contested.

9.9.3 Practice-Based Modules: Embed Rather than Overhaul

Regional analysis indicates that wholesale redesign of teacher certification may be unrealistic in the short term. A scalable approach is to embed short, practice-based modules in existing professional development structures. High-utility modules can target the following: curriculum compacting, readiness assessment, acceleration decision-making, differentiation planning, and socio-emotional scaffolding.

9.9.4 Specialist Presence and Coaching

Systems can increase implementation fidelity through specialist coaching, whether on-site or regionally distributed. Specialists can support identification, codesign interventions, provide risk management for acceleration, and reduce teacher anxiety.

9.10 Case Vignettes: Teachers as Capability Mediators in Regional Scenarios

The following vignettes synthesize documented regional dynamics into realistic cases aligned with the evidence and conceptual frame of this chapter. They are not fictional decorations; they function as analytic micro-cases showing how teacher preparation shifts capability conversion.

9.10.1 Vignette 1: Argentina—From Extra Tasks to Differentiation

A primary teacher in Buenos Aires notices a student finishing quickly and disrupting peers. With no training, she assigns extra worksheets. The student becomes more disengaged. After a short module on compacting and enrichment, she pre-assesses mastery, compacts repetitive content, and assigns a project-based inquiry task requiring higher-order reasoning and disciplinary depth. Engagement rises and behavior stabilizes.

Capability mechanism: mastery documentation + instructional redesign.

Equity implication: differentiation becomes available within a standard classroom rather than through private resources.

9.10.2 Vignette 2: Brazil—Acceleration Resistance Reframed through Evidence

A school team hesitates to accelerate a student due to immaturity concerns. After professional development that reviews evidence and introduces readiness assessment protocols, the team implements monitored subject acceleration with socio-emotional supports and check-ins. The student's well-being and engagement improve; teacher confidence increases because decisions are procedural rather than fear-driven.

Capability mechanism: evidence-informed risk management + structured monitoring.

Equity implication: acceleration becomes a supported option rather than an exceptional gamble.

9.10.3 *Vignette 3: Paraguay—Reducing Family Pressure through Specialist Support*

A family pushes for acceleration, but teachers lack training and rely on informal judgments. Parents begin supplying enrichment materials, unintentionally reproducing inequity by tying opportunity to family capacity. A regional specialist begins monthly coaching, supporting teachers to implement compacting and structured enrichment. Instructional responsibility recenters in the school, teacher anxiety decreases, and family pressure reduces.

Capability mechanism: mesosystem bridging + coached implementation.

Equity implication: schools, not families, become the primary providers of opportunity.

9.10.4 *Vignette 4: Chile—When Enrichment Knowledge Enters the Classroom*

A student attends a university enrichment program but experiences low challenge in regular class. Through a university–school partnership, the classroom teacher learns actiotope-informed strategies: she designs opportunities that expand the student's action repertoire rather than relying on trait labels. She increases depth, complexity, and autonomy in classroom tasks, aligning enrichment with everyday schooling.

Capability mechanism: diffusion of learning resources into mainstream practice.

Equity implication: enrichment is no longer trapped in specialized nodes.

9.10.5 *Vignette 5: Peru—COAR Professional Culture as a Template*

A COAR teacher draws on inquiry pedagogy, performance assessment, and structured socio-emotional supports. Through peer mentoring with teachers from nearby public schools, she models compacting and differentiation strategies that can be adapted in regular classrooms. This creates diffusion through teacher networks rather than policy directives alone.

Capability mechanism: professional culture transfer through networks.

Equity implication: COAR becomes a regional resource rather than an isolated elite pathway.

Policy Box
Building a Regional Teacher Preparation Framework for High-Ability and Twice-Exceptional Learners

Guiding Principle

Supporting high-ability learners is an equity obligation grounded in readiness-based instruction and capability expansion; it is not an optional enrichment privilege.

Core Components

1. **Pre-service integration:** Embed competencies for gifted education and twice-exceptionality (2e) within core teacher education curricula rather than as elective specialization.
2. **Practice-based in-service modules:** Deliver short, high-utility professional learning on curriculum compacting, differentiation design, acceleration decision-making, and socio-emotional scaffolding within existing PD systems.
3. **Evidence-informed myth reduction:** Train educators to evaluate socio-emotional concerns about acceleration using research evidence, readiness indicators, and monitoring procedures rather than fear narratives.
4. **Culturally responsive assessment literacy:** Prepare teachers to reduce linguistic and cultural bias through multi-criteria identification, portfolios, performance tasks, and community-informed conceptions of talent.
5. **Specialist coaching capacity:** Ensure access to gifted/2e expertise (on-site or regional) to coach teachers, support identification, codesign interventions, and improve implementation fidelity.
6. **Teacher networks for diffusion:** Build communities of practice that translate expertise across schools and regions, reducing professional isolation and sustaining innovation.
7. **Monitoring and equity audits:** Track identification and service representation by socioeconomic status, gender, language, ethnicity/Indigeneity, geography, disability/2e status, and school sector to detect underrepresentation and adjust practice.

Note: A regional framework need not require immediate overhaul of certification systems; scalable gains can be achieved by embedding modules, coaching, and equity monitoring within existing professional learning infrastructures

9.11 Comparative Ecological Synthesis: Teacher Preparation as Conversion System

The preceding country analyses reveal variation in policy histories, institutional design, and professional cultures across Latin America. Yet beneath these contextual differences lies a structurally consistent pattern: teacher preparation functions as the decisive conversion layer linking recognition to realization. When examined comparatively through the ecological–capability–equity framework, the regional evidence does not suggest isolated national shortcomings; it reveals a systemic misalignment across ecological layers.

At the **macrosystem level**, cultural narratives surrounding elitism, equality-as-sameness, and age-norm rigidity shape the moral legitimacy of differentiation and acceleration. Where these narratives remain unchallenged in teacher preparation, professional hesitation persists even in the presence of enabling policies.

At the **exosystem level**, policy recognition without procedural clarity produces ambiguity rather than empowerment. Teachers may be formally permitted to differentiate or accelerate yet lack the legal literacy and decision-making frameworks necessary to act with confidence. The result is regulatory underuse rather than prohibition.

At the **mesosystem level**, coordination gaps emerge. University enrichment programs, specialized initiatives, or high-performing institutional models (such as Peru's COAR network) can generate concentrated excellence; however, without diffusion mechanisms—teacher networks, specialist coaching, partnership infrastructures—these resources remain localized. Conversion capacity accumulates unevenly.

At the **microsystem level**, the consequences become visible in daily practice: additive assignments replace qualitative differentiation, acceleration remains rare, multicultural learners are under-identified, and twice-exceptional students oscillate between invisibility and misinterpretation. In capability terms, advanced potential is acknowledged rhetorically but not systematically expanded through opportunity structures.

Comparative insight is therefore structural rather than national: **teacher preparation operates as an ecological conversion system**. It mediates whether macro-level narratives become enabling or constraining, whether exosystem policies are implemented or avoided, whether mesosystem expertise diffuses or isolates, and whether microsystem practice expands or contracts learners' capability sets.

Table 9.1 synthesizes this conversion logic across ecological layers, identifying recurring regional patterns, enabling mechanisms, and associated equity risks. The purpose is not to homogenize national contexts but to clarify the structural leverage points through which teacher preparation can transform symbolic inclusion into sustained developmental opportunity.

Table 9.1 Teacher preparation as ecological conversion infrastructure in high-ability education across Latin America (selected cases)

Ecological layer	Illustrative regional pattern	Capability mechanism (enables conversion)	Equity risk (blocks conversion)
Macrosystem (values, norms, legitimacy)	"Elitism" narrative; fear of acceleration; equality interpreted as sameness	Equity reframing: Readiness-based instruction as inclusion; legitimacy-building narratives that normalize advanced learning needs	Giftedness treated as privilege; fear-based refusals; stigma attached to differentiation and pacing flexibility
Exosystem (policy, decrees, standards)	Acceleration regulated but restricted or underused; ambiguous procedures; uneven guidance	Clear, usable procedures; teacher legal literacy; documentation protocols for readiness and monitoring	Bureaucratic barriers; rigid age norms; prohibitions/constraints on subject acceleration; avoidance under uncertainty
Mesosystem (coordination among institutions)	Enrichment ecosystems concentrated in nodes (e.g., universities) without classroom diffusion; family substitution where schools lack expertise	University–school partnerships; specialist coaching; teacher networks and communities of practice that diffuse expertise	Enrichment isolated; diffusion slow; opportunity stratified by SES and geography; reliance on parental advocacy/resources
Microsystem (classroom practice)	Extra tasks instead of differentiation; reluctance to accelerate; narrow identification practices	Curriculum compacting; differentiated instruction; monitored acceleration; mentorship; strength-based 2e supports	Under-identification; boredom and disengagement; 2e invisibility; lowered expectations; misinterpretation of asynchrony

Note: The table synthesizes how teacher preparation functions as a conversion system linking policy recognition to classroom opportunity. Patterns vary across national contexts, but the conversion logic (and associated equity risks) is regionally recurrent

9.12 Scalable Reform Pathways

The region's evidence suggests reform need not wait for wholesale certification redesign. Incremental capacity-building can generate measurable change at mesosystem and microsystem levels while building advocacy for exosystem reforms.

Four scalable approaches emerge:

1. **Modules:** high-utility training on compacting, mastery evaluation, acceleration decision-making, and differentiation planning
2. **Evidence-based storytelling:** contextualized case examples that counter fear narratives and provide "how-to" legitimacy
3. **Specialist support:** coaching and codesign to improve fidelity and reduce anxiety
4. **Teacher networks:** communities of practice that sustain learning, normalize innovation, and support diffusion across schools

Crucially, all pathways must integrate **2e perspectives**. Systems that separate giftedness from disability will continue to misidentify and underserve dual-profile learners. Teachers must be trained to think in terms of strengths and needs: expand challenge while offering accommodations and belonging supports.

9.13 Conclusion: Investing in Teachers to Democratize Excellence

Latin America opened this volume as a region abundant in talent yet marked by structural fragmentation in opportunity. That tension converges in the domain of teacher preparation. The decisive question is no longer whether advanced potential exists, nor whether it merits recognition; it is whether the region will institutionalize the professional capacity required to sustain its development. Where teachers are systematically prepared—conceptually grounded, procedurally equipped, and ethically committed—advanced capability becomes visible, legitimate, and cultivable within ordinary classrooms. Where preparation remains peripheral, excellence drifts toward isolated or privatized spaces, and inequity deepens beneath inclusive rhetoric. If Chap. 2 asserted that Latin America does not lack talent, Chap. 9 affirms that the region must not lack the professional infrastructure to nurture it. Teacher learning is the hinge upon which that promise turns.

References

Barrios, L., Vega, R., & Vuyk, M. A. (2020). Historias de vida de estudiantes con altas capacidades en Paraguay: Participantes de un programa especializado en matemáticas. *Eureka Revista Científica de Psicología, 17*(1), 96–111.

Blumen, S. (2004). Meta-análisis sobre estudios de identificación y atención al talento y la superdotación en el Perú. *Revista de Psicología de la PUCP, 22*(2), 277–317.

Blumen, S. (2016). Gifted education programming: Serving the native Peruvian. In J. L. Davis & J. Moore (Eds.), *Gifted children of color around the world: Diverse needs, exemplary practices, and directions for the future* (pp. 1–15). Emerald Group.

Bronfenbrenner, U. (1979). *The ecology of human development: Experiments by nature and design*. Harvard University Press.

CEPAL. (2022). *La educación en tiempos de pandemia en América Latina y el Caribe*. Naciones Unidas.

Delou, C. M. C. (2018). Formação de professores e altas habilidades/superdotação. *Revista Educação Especial, 31*(60), 233–248.

Dweck, C. S. (2006). *Mindset: The new psychology of success*. Random House.

Ford, D. Y. (2014). *Culturally responsive gifted education*. Prufrock Press.

Freire, P. (1970). *Pedagogia do oprimido*. Paz e Terra.

Gagné, F. (2004). Transforming gifts into talents: The DMGT as a developmental theory. *High Ability Studies, 15*(2), 119–147.

García-Cepero, M. C. (2009). Identificación y educación de estudiantes con altas capacidades en América Latina. *Revista Latinoamericana de Psicología, 41*(2), 251–264.

García-Cepero, M. C., & Proestakis, A. (2010). Talent development in Chile. *Gifted and Talented International, 25*(2), 77–88.

Gómez-Arízaga, M. P., Conejeros-Solar, M. L., Sandoval-Rodríguez, K., Catalán Henríquez, S., & García-Cepero, M. C. (2020a). Atender las altas capacidades en Chile: Facilitadores y barreras del contexto escolar. *Revista de Psicología (PUCP), 38*(2), 667–703. https://doi.org/10.18800/psico.202002.012

Gómez-Arízaga, M. P., Valdivia-Lefort, M. C., Castillo-Hermosilla, H., Hébert, T. P., & Conejeros-Solar, M. L. (2020b). Tales from within: Gifted students' lived experiences with teaching practices in regular classrooms. *Education Sciences, 10*(5), 137. https://doi.org/10.3390/educsci10050137

Gómez-Arizaga, M. P., Conejeros-Solar, M. L., & Cornejo-Araya, C. (2024). Gifted education in Chile: Analyses from a learning-resource perspective. *Cogent Education, 11*(1), 2397217. https://doi.org/10.1080/2331186X.2024.2397217

Irueste, P. (2017). Gifted education in Argentina. *Cogent Education, 4*(1), 1364899. https://doi.org/10.1080/2331186X.2017.1364899

Lobo, M., & Vuyk, A. (2023). Concepciones de docentes del nivel medio de un colegio privado de Asunción-Paraguay sobre altas capacidades intelectuales en estudiantes desde una perspectiva de inclusión. *Revista Científica Estudios e Investigaciones, 12*(1), 23–37. https://doi.org/10.26885/rcei.12.1.23

Maia-Pinto, R. R., & Fleith, D. S. (2016). Percepção de alunos superdotados, mães e professores acerca da aceleração de ensino. *Interação em Psicologia, 19*(2). https://doi.org/10.5380/psi.v19i2.29744

Nussbaum, M. C. (2011). *Creating capabilities: The human development approach*. Harvard University Press.

OECD. (2019). *PISA 2018 results (Volume II): Where all students can succeed*. OECD Publishing.

Pérez, S. G. P., & Freitas, S. N. (2016). Políticas públicas para altas habilidades/superdotação no Brasil. *Revista Educação Especial, 29*(55), 223–238.

Renzulli, J. S., & Reis, S. M. (2014). *The schoolwide enrichment model: A comprehensive plan for the development of talents and giftedness* (3rd ed.). Prufrock Press.

Rosenthal, R., & Jacobson, L. (1968). *Pygmalion in the classroom: Teacher expectation and pupils' intellectual development*. Holt, Rinehart & Winston.

Schön, D. A. (1983). *The reflective practitioner: How professionals think in action*. Basic Books.

Sen, A. (1999). *Development as freedom*. Knopf.

Tourón, J., & Santiago, R. (2015). *Altas capacidades en la escuela inclusiva*. Narcea.

UNESCO. (2021). *Reimagining our futures together: A new social contract for education*. UNESCO.

Virgolim, A. M. R. (2014). *Altas habilidades/superdotação: Processos criativos e afetivos*. Papirus.

Vuyk, M. A., Barrios, L. A., Méndez, N. M., & Zalazar, P. (2023). Mapa de talentos: Un procedimiento piloto de detección universal del talento en estudiantes del Paraguay. *Revista Paraguaya de Educación, 12*(2), 13–31.

Wechsler, S. M., & Fleith, D. S. (2017). The scenario of gifted education in Brazil. *Cogent Education, 4*(1), 1332812. https://doi.org/10.1080/2331186X.2017.1332812

Winner, E. (1996). *Gifted children: Myths and realities*. Basic Books.

Chapter 10
Country Case Studies: Policy Enactment and Systemic Variation in Latin America

10.1 Introduction: From Regional Synthesis to National Enactment

Previous chapters sketched the conceptual debates, equity dilemmas, and policy trajectories influencing high-ability education in Latin America. Those conversations drew attention to tension between excellence and inclusion, selective and universal provision, and conceptual versus institutional approaches to giftedness. This chapter shifts from a macro-level analysis to a meso- and microlevel analysis of how policy is enacted in individual national systems.

The guiding question is straightforward yet analytically demanding: How does recognition become a pathway?

Legal recognition of high-ability learners is widespread across the region. Yet the existence of legal categories tells us little about how students are identified, what services they receive, or whether policy intentions translate into durable educational opportunities. To understand these processes, it is necessary to examine the institutional architectures through which policy is operationalized.

High-ability education provides a particularly revealing lens for comparative policy analysis because it lies at the intersection of multiple policy logics:

- Excellence and meritocracy
- Inclusion and equity
- Centralized standards and local autonomy
- Pedagogical differentiation and administrative routinization

As such, its institutionalization serves as a diagnostic of system coherence. Where high-ability education is stable, routinized, and visible, it signals the presence of aligned governance, capacity, and professional infrastructure. Where it remains fragmented, it reveals structural tensions within the broader education system.

S. Blumen, *High Ability and Talent Development in Latin America*,
https://doi.org/10.1007/978-3-032-27468-7_10

This chapter adopts a comparative policy-enactment perspective, drawing on the work of policy sociology and institutional analysis, which emphasizes that policy outcomes are shaped not only by formal legislation but also by organizational routines, professional practices, and resource configurations.

Six countries—Argentina, Brazil, Colombia, Chile, Mexico, and Peru—are examined because together they represent the principal governance configurations of the region:

- Federal systems with decentralized implementation (Argentina, Brazil, Mexico)
- Unitary systems with varying degrees of institutional consolidation (Chile, Peru, Colombia)

Each case is analyzed using a common template that allows cross-national comparison without flattening contextual differences.

By situating national variation within a shared analytical framework, this chapter shifts the discussion from descriptive comparison toward structural explanation. Rather than treating high-ability education as a set of isolated policy initiatives, it examines how governance arrangements, institutional capacity, and administrative positioning shape the translation of recognition into educational opportunity. In doing so, the chapter advances the central claim that the durability of provision depends less on formal acknowledgment than on the institutional conditions that sustain pathways over time.

10.2 Recognition and Pathway: Analytical Framework

A conceptual distinction between recognition and pathway runs through this chapter.

- **Recognition** refers to the formal inclusion of high-ability learners within legal or policy texts.
- **Pathway** refers to the institutional mechanisms through which recognition is translated into sustained educational response.

This distinction reflects the broader debates in policy studies between symbolic policy adoption and substantive implementation: Recognition can create legitimacy and visibility, but only pathways can create durable opportunity structures.

Across the six cases, three theoretical propositions guide the analysis:

1. Recognition is necessary but insufficient.
   Legal inclusion does not guarantee routinized provision.
2. Pathways are institutional, not merely pedagogical.
   They require stable funding, administrative anchoring, and professional routines.
3. Governance design shapes variability.
   Federal and unitary systems generate distinct patterns of territorial differentiation.

These propositions allow the chapter to move beyond descriptive comparison toward an explanatory account of policy variation.

Building on this conceptual framing, the following sections analyze the empirical impact of this enactment architecture in the region. Instead of analyzing the country cases as single examples, the analysis currently shifts to the ongoing comparative themes that outline variation in practice: the nature of pathways of institutionalization that evolve in regimes of governance, the territorial patterns generated by a federal versus unitary structure, the role of identification as an institutional process rather than a purely technical process, and the extent to which institutional capacity functions as the binding constraint for policy realization.

Taken together, these propositions establish the analytical lens through which the country cases are interpreted. The distinction between recognition and pathway solidity allows variation in policy enactment to be examined not simply as differences in legislative design but as differences in institutional translation. This framework therefore enables the subsequent analysis to move beyond description and to identify the structural mechanisms through which high-ability education is organized, stabilized, or diluted across national contexts.

10.2.1 Country Case Studies

Argentina: Mandate Without Centralized Delivery

Argentina provides a paradigmatic example of a **mandate-driven federal model**. The National Education Law (Ley 26.206) establishes the obligation to support students with special capacities or talents, including identification, follow-up, and curricular adaptation. However, responsibility for implementation lies with provinces and the Autonomous City of Buenos Aires (Argentina, 2006; Gobierno de la Ciudad Autónoma de Buenos Aires, Ministerio de Educación, 2025; Ministerio de Educación de la Nación Argentina, 2024).

This design reflects the broader structure of Argentine federalism, in which national legislation sets principles while subnational jurisdictions control operationalization. As a result, high-ability education emerges not as a unified subsystem but as a mosaic of jurisdictional initiatives. Provincial examples illustrate the range of enactment. The Buenos Aires Province guidance on "trayectorias escolares con altas capacidades" provides operational criteria for schools (Dirección General de Cultura y Educación, 2019), while CABA's regulatory framework establishes monitoring and pedagogical accompaniment mechanisms (Gobierno de la Ciudad Autónoma de Buenos Aires, 2025). Other provinces, such as Chubut, have issued their own dispositions, indicating a gradual diffusion of policy instruments.

Despite these developments, implementation remains uneven. The absence of a national delivery mechanism means that access to services depends heavily on local capacity, professional expertise, and policy prioritization. Argentina therefore illustrates how a strong legal mandate can coexist with heterogeneous institutionalization. In doing so, the chapter advances a structural explanation of policy variation that foregrounds institutional architecture as the key mediating factor between recognition and educational opportunity.

Brazil: Rights-Based Recognition in an Inclusion Framework

Brazil stands out for its explicit legal recognition of high abilities within national legislation. The Lei de Diretrizes e Bases da Educação (LDB) identifies students with altas habilidades/superdotação as part of the target population of special education (Brasil, 1996). The National Policy on Special Education from the Perspective of Inclusive Education further consolidates this recognition (Brasil, 2008).

In theory, the framework positions high-ability learners within a rights-based model of inclusive education. In practice, however, implementation depends on the Specialized Educational Assistance (AEE) system, delivered through multifunctional resource rooms (Pérez & Freitas, 2011).

Research by Alencar and Fleith (2001, 2007) and later analyses (Fleith, 2019) highlight persistent challenges: limited teacher training, reliance on local initiative, and uneven service distribution. Federal governance amplifies these disparities, with more developed regions exhibiting stronger provision than less resourced areas (Virgolim, 2014).

Brazil thus exemplifies a recurring regional pattern: strong normative visibility combined with uneven operationalization.

Colombia: Legal Visibility and Administrative Diffusion

Colombia's category of "capacidades o talentos excepcionales" is formally recognized in national law (Ley 115) and regulatory decrees (Ministerio de Educación Nacional, 2009). Yet high-ability education remains institutionally diffuse because implementation is embedded within inclusive education structures oriented primarily toward disability (Ministerio de Educación Nacional, 1994, 2017).

Guidance documents developed by the Ministry provide conceptual frameworks and identification criteria (Ministerio de Educación Nacional, 1994; Cedeño-Ángel & García-Cepero, 2015), but local education secretariats determine operationalization. Studies on teacher conceptions of high ability reveal persistent misconceptions that further hinder identification (Gutiérrez-Ruiz, 2022).

Colombia therefore illustrates institutional invisibility. Recognition exists, but pathways remain weakly consolidated.

Chile: Programmatic Coherence Through Institutional Partnerships

Chile represents a distinctive **program ecosystem model**. Rather than relying on a single legislative framework, high-ability education is structured through the interaction of special educational needs regulations (Ley 20.370; Decreto 170) and national talent-promotion initiatives (Biblioteca del Congreso Nacional de Chile, 2009, 2010).

A defining feature is the long-standing network of university-linked enrichment programs, such as PENTA UC, and BETA PUCV (Paz, 2024), which provide structured opportunities for academically talented students (Pontificia Universidad Católica de Chile, 2025). Research on Chilean practice highlights both facilitators and barriers to school-level differentiation (Gómez-Arízaga et al., 2020).

The Chilean case demonstrates how programmatic coherence can emerge from institutional partnerships even in the absence of a centralized gifted subsystem.

Mexico: Recognition Amid Reform Cycles
Mexico's education system combines federal governance with frequent reform cycles, creating a context of policy volatility. Students with outstanding abilities are recognized within special education guidelines issued by the Secretaría de Educación Pública (Mexico, 2019; SEP, 2024), and multidimensional identification frameworks have been developed (Valadez et al., 2016).

Implementation occurs primarily through USAER teams, which provide support to regular schools. However, these units are often overstretched, and high-ability services compete with disability priorities.

Mexico thus illustrates how policy recognition can coexist with programmatic discontinuity, particularly when governance reforms repeatedly reshape administrative priorities.

Peru: Selective Excellence as Institutional Strategy
Peru's model is defined by centralized programmatic innovation (World Bank, 2023). The COAR network of high-performance public schools represents the most institutionalized pathway for high-achieving students (Ministerio de Educación del Perú, 2003, 2021, 2025).

Research by Blumen (2010, 2021) highlights the broader challenges of identification within mainstream schools, including limited assessment infrastructure and uneven teacher preparation.

Peru exemplifies a strategy of selective depth concentrated investment in a flagship pathway rather than system-wide differentiation.

10.3 Cross-Case Comparative Analysis

10.3.1 From Comparative Description to Conceptual Mapping

The six country cases examined in this chapter clearly show that high-ability education in Latin America is more about a group of enactment architectures than a single regional approach. It is evident that, while each national system has its own specific historical path and institutional configuration, the comparative analysis always indicates that the difference lies in how legal recognition is translated into practices.

To synthesize these insights, it is useful to transition from descriptive comparison to conceptual abstraction. The variation across systems is interpreted through the interaction of two core dimensions: the level of policy recognition and the firmness of institutional pathways through which recognition is put into practice. The term "recognition" encapsulates the legal and normative visibility of high-ability learners, and "pathway solidity" refers to how stable mechanisms (such as programs, routinized services, or structured identification processes) convert recognition into sustained educational responses. These dimensions are mediated by institutional capacity, including professional expertise, assessment infrastructure, and fiscal stability, as well as the governance design, which organizes the allocation of responsibility and resources among territorial units.

A conceptual model incorporating these elements and plotting the major enactment architectures seen throughout the region is shown in Fig. 10.1. In doing so, the figure acts as a heuristic lens through which the following comparative themes may be analyzed.

The model clarifies that differences between national systems are due not mainly to ideological commitment or definitional variation; they are grounded in institutional alignment regarding recognition and pathways. Symbolic recognition systems, positioned at legal visibility without routinizing provision, rely mostly on local initiative to implement. Diffuse inclusion architectures have high abilities embedded within larger inclusive education structures that attenuate institutional focus despite formal recognition. Program ecosystem models show how coherent pathways can develop within partnerships and targeted initiatives without having a national, dedicated subsystem, whereas selective depth architectures can integrate resources into long-lasting, well-established excellence pathways that offer stability to a narrow population.

Importantly, these architectures are not static. Systems may shift position over time as capacity, governance arrangements, or policy priorities evolve. The model

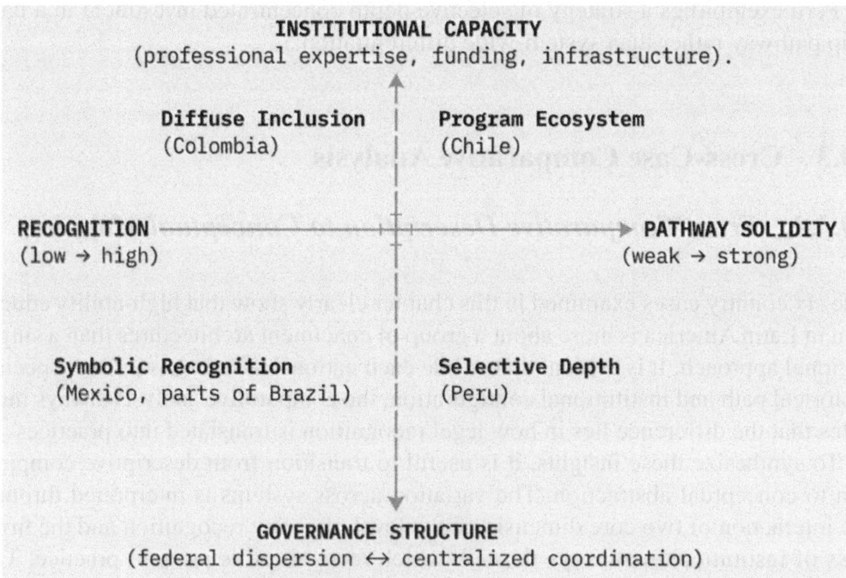

Fig. 10.1 Model of enactment architectures in high-ability education. The figure conceptualizes variation across Latin American systems along two primary dimensions: recognition (legal and policy visibility) and pathway solidity (degree of institutional routinization). Institutional capacity mediates movement toward sustained implementation, while governance structure shapes the territorial distribution of provision. The four quadrants represent ideal-type architectures: symbolic recognition, diffuse inclusion, program ecosystems, and selective depth

should therefore be understood as an analytical heuristic rather than a typology of fixed categories.

From a methodological standpoint, the model was developed based on an iterative cross-case comparison of the six national analyses conducted through the shared policy-enactment framework. Evidence from statutes, ministerial guidance, and academic works was coded on shared dimensions—recognition, governance, institutional anchoring, identification, programmatic pathways, and implementation constraints—to find recurrent configurations connecting legal visibility to institutional routinization. The next subsections explain how such structural relations appear over governance arrangements, identification processes, and capacities.

10.3.2 *Empirical Grounding: Institutional Features across Systems*

Table 10.1 represents the empirical landscape grounded in theory for the conceptual differences illustrated in Fig. 10.1. By summarizing governance structures, legal positioning, identification patterns, and primary pathways across the six countries, the table transforms the conceptual model into a descriptive mapping of institutional arrangements.

10.3.3 *Patterns of Enactment*

With this conceptual map established, the examination will now look at the actual configuration of these architecture configurations working in practice. The six cases reveal four recurrent patterns:

1. **Mandate-driven federal systems (Argentina)**, where legal obligations are strong but implementation depends on subnational capacity
2. **Inclusion-embedded recognition (Brazil, Colombia, and partly Mexico)**, where high ability is formally recognized but operationalization occurs within broader inclusive education frameworks
3. **Program ecosystem models (Chile)**, characterized by institutional partnerships and targeted initiatives that create coherent pathways without a centralized subsystem
4. **Selective excellence pathways (Peru)**, where institutional depth is achieved through highly structured programs serving a limited population

These patterns confirm that institutional design—not policy rhetoric—explains most variation in outcomes.

Table 10.1 Comparative overview of high ability policy architecture in Peru, Brazil, Mexico, Colombia, Chile, and Argentina

Dimension	Peru	Brazil	Mexico	Colombia	Chile	Argentina
Governance structure shaping enactment	Central policy design with regional implementation; flagship selective excellence pathway (COAR)	Federal; strong state/municipal autonomy under national framework	Federal; national guidance with substantial state variation	Unitary but territorially uneven enactment via Secretarías de Educación	Unitary; national regulatory and program layers, plus university-linked ecosystem	Federal; national law mandates jurisdictional program design/provinces/CABA are decisive in enactment
Explicit legal recognition/policy category	COAR targets high performance within public system; national education law provides general basis	Explicit recognition of high abilities/giftedness in LDB	Official category of *aptitudes sobresalientes* in SEP guidance	Explicit category high abilities or exceptional talents in law 115… regulatory decree	High ability/talent typically routed through NEE regulatory frameworks and national talent-promotion program layer	National law (LEN 26.206) art. 93 requires jurisdictions to design programs for students with high abilities or special talents
Dedicated national gifted/high ability unit	No standalone unit evident; excellence provision institutionalized via COAR network	No standalone national gifted agency; embedded in special/inclusive education architecture	No standalone national unit; housed within special/inclusive education channels	No stand-alone unit; recognition exists but is institutionally diffuse	No standalone ministry unit; program + regulatory ecosystem (often program-anchored)	No dedicated national gifted unit evidenced; national level issues norms/guidance, while jurisdictions implement programs
Primary national mechanism/pathway	COAR admissions and schooling pathway (selective, publicly funded)	Special education modality and AEE as intended service route (implementation uneven)	SEP guidance and operational lineaments; school-level implementation varies by state	Legal recognition + MEN guidance; pathways depend on territorial routines and capacity	National talent-promotion program layer + university-linked enrichment pathways (e.g., PENTA-type models)	Jurisdictional programs mandated by national law; evidence of subnational enactment via Buenos Aires Province guidance and CABA legal/regulatory framework

Dimension	Peru	Brazil	Mexico	Colombia	Chile	Argentina
Identification & access pattern	Formalized selection mainly via COAR; mainstream identification not systematized nationally	No unified national identification protocol; locality driven	Guidance and tools exist; operationalization varies by state capacity	Recognition + definition exist; operational identification varies by territory	Program-entry and NEE-related routinization; not universal national screening	National norms emphasize early identification and educational response; practical access depends on jurisdictional frameworks (e.g., BA, CABA) and local capacity
Coverage model produced by the system	Selective depth (high investment for admitted students) rather than universal mainstream gifted provision	Uneven/fragmented despite strong legal recognition	Uneven/reform-sensitive and state-variable	Low institutional consolidation: Recognition with highly variable enactment	Selective enrichment + program ecosystems, not universal	Provincial and CABA-dependent implementation pattern: National mandate exists, but enactment density depends on jurisdictional policy instruments and implementation capacity

10.3.4 Governance and Territorial Variability

Governance structure is a determinant of opportunities as they unfold. Federal systems produce variability through subnational autonomy, while unitary systems vary according to institutional consolidation and resource allocation. This finding aligns with comparative research indicating that decentralization amplifies disparities unless accompanied by strong coordination mechanisms.

10.3.5 Identification as Institutional Practice

Rather, it is frequently associated with program entry or driven by local initiative, thus reinforcing stratifying access patterns. That point again emphasizes that identification involves more than technical work and is institutional—a matter of routine and expertise of an organization.

10.3.6 Capacity as the Binding Constraint

The most consistent explanatory factor among countries is institutional capacity. Skilled personnel, assessment infrastructure, and stable funding determine whether recognition translates to sustained practice. So capacity is the structural condition that both facilitates and restricts pathways consolidation.

The comparative analysis shows that high-ability education across Latin America is structured by identifiable institutional logics rather than by isolated national trajectories. When interpreted through the interaction of recognition, pathway solidity, governance design, and capacity conditions, the diversity of national arrangements reveals patterned forms of enactment that cut across individual systems. The model presented in this section thus serves not as a classificatory scheme but as an explanatory tool that clarifies how structural configurations shape the opportunities available to high-ability learners across the region.

10.4 Final Analytical Reflection

High-ability education throughout Latin America highlights an overarching lesson of policy studies: institutional architecture acts as a mediator of policy. Recognition without a pathway gives rise to symbolic inclusion, a pathway without the capacity for uneven implementation. Sustained provision only arises when governance, funding, and professional infrastructure cohere.

The regional landscape is therefore best understood not as a continuum of policy commitment but as a structured spectrum of institutional configurations, each producing distinct patterns of opportunity. Seen in this light, high-ability education functions as a revealing case of how educational systems translate normative inclusion into sustained practice. This perspective underscores the importance of institutional design for explaining how recognition acquires practical meaning within diverse governance contexts.

References

Alencar, E. M. L. S., & Fleith, D. S. (2001). *Superdotação: Determinantes, educação e ajustamento*. EPU.

Alencar, E. M. L. S., & Fleith, D. S. (2007). *Desenvolvimento de talentos e altas habilidades: Orientação a pais e professores*. Artmed.

Argentina. (2006). *Ley de Educación Nacional N.° 26.206*. Infoleg, Ministerio de Justicia y Derechos Humanos.

Biblioteca del Congreso Nacional de Chile. (2009). *Ley 20.370: Establece la Ley General de Educación*.

Biblioteca del Congreso Nacional de Chile. (2010). *Decreto 170: Fija normas para determinar los alumnos con necesidades educativas especiales que serán beneficiarios de las subvenciones para educación especial*.

Blumen, S. (2010). High ability students in Peru: Policy and practice. *Revista de Psicología, 28*(2), 213–238.

Blumen, S. (2021). Innovative practices to support high-achieving deprived young scholars in an ethnic-linguistic diverse Latin American country. In S. R. Smith (Ed.), *Handbook of giftedness and talent development in the Asia-Pacific* (pp. 223–238). Springer.

Brasil. Ministério da Educação. (2008). *Política nacional de educação especial na perspectiva da educação inclusiva*.

Brasil. Presidência da República. (1996). *Lei n.° 9.394, de 20 de dezembro de 1996: Lei de Diretrizes e Bases da Educação Nacional*.

Cedeño-Ángel, F., & García-Cepero, M. C. (2015). *Orientaciones para la atención educativa a estudiantes con capacidades o talentos excepcionales*. Ministerio de Educación Nacional.

Dirección General de Cultura y Educación, Provincia de Buenos Aires. (2019). *Comunicación conjunta N.° 5: Trayectorias escolares con altas capacidades*.

Fleith, D. S. (2019). Gifted education in Brazil: Policy and practice. *Gifted Education International, 35*(3), 1–15.

Gobierno de la Ciudad Autónoma de Buenos Aires. (2025). *Instrumento normativo asociado a altas capacidades intelectuales (referencias administrativas y funciones)*.

Gobierno de la Ciudad Autónoma de Buenos Aires, Ministerio de Educación. (2025). *Resolución 1430-MEDGC/25: Aprueba el marco de acompañamiento pedagógico para estudiantes con altas capacidades intelectuales*.

Gómez-Arízaga, M. P., Conejeros-Solar, M. L., Sandoval-Rodríguez, K., Catalán Henríquez, S., & García-Cepero, M. C. (2020). Atender las altas capacidades en Chile: Facilitadores y barreras del contexto escolar. *Revista de Psicología, 38*(2), 667–703. https://doi.org/10.18800/psico.202002.012

Gutiérrez-Ruiz, K. (2022). Conocimientos y mitos de profesores colombianos sobre altas capacidades. *Revista Latinoamericana de Ciencias Sociales, Niñez y Juventud, 20*(2), 1–22. https://doi.org/10.11600/rlcsnj.20.2.4913

Mexico. (2019). *Constitución Política de los Estados Unidos Mexicanos (Artículo 3)*.

Ministerio de Educación de la Nación Argentina. (2024). *Resolución ministerial N.° 4648/2024: Altas capacidades.*

Ministerio de Educación del Perú. (2003). *Ley General de Educación N.° 28044.*

Ministerio de Educación del Perú. (2021). *Guía de orientaciones para la conformación, organización y funcionamiento de los SAANEE.*

Ministerio de Educación del Perú. (2025). *Lineamientos de los colegios de alto rendimiento.*

Ministerio de Educación Nacional. (1994). *Ley 115 de 1994 (Ley General de Educación).*

Ministerio de Educación Nacional. (2009). *Decreto 366 de 2009: Organización del servicio de apoyo pedagógico para estudiantes con discapacidad y con capacidades o talentos excepcionales.*

Ministerio de Educación Nacional. (2017). *Decreto 1421 de 2017: Atención educativa a la población con discapacidad en el marco de la educación inclusiva.*

Paz, V. (2024). *La alta capacidad en Chile: La experiencia del programa BETA de la PUCV en Chile.* Pontificia Universidad Católica de Valparaíso.

Pérez, S. G. P. B., & Freitas, S. N. (2011). Altas habilidades/superdotação e o atendimento educacional especializado. *Educação Especial, 24*(41), 451–464.

Pontificia Universidad Católica de Chile. (2025). *Academia de Desarrollo de Talentos PENTA UC.* https://academiadetalentos.uc.cl

Secretaría de Educación Pública. (2024). *Lineamientos para la atención educativa de alumnos con aptitudes sobresalientes: Preescolar, primaria y secundaria.* https://educacionespecial.sep.gob.mx/storage/2YFEsGdb8J-AS_Atencion-educativao-estudiantes-Version-Revisada.pdf

Valadez, M. D., Borges, A., & Zambrano, R. (2016). Students with high abilities in Mexico: Policy and educational responses. *Revista Mexicana de Investigación Educativa, 21*(71), 1199–1223.

Virgolim, A. M. R. (2014). Altas habilidades/superdotação: Encaminhamentos pedagógicos. *Revista Educação Especial, 27*(49), 423–438.

World Bank. (2023). *World development indicators: Peru education expenditure.* https://databank.worldbank.org/reports.aspx?source=2&country=PER

Part III
Toward Coherence: A Regional Model and Future Directions

Chapter 11
Toward a Latin American Model of Talent Development

11.1 Introduction: Why a Regional Model Is Theoretically and Practically Necessary

The preceding chapters of this volume have traced the historical evolution, policy recognition, institutional tensions, and pedagogical controversies (Alencar & Fleith, 2008; García-Cepero & Iglesias-Velasco, 2020) regarding high ability and talent development in Latin America.

A persistent paradox has surfaced. Legislation recognizes students with high abilities, exceptional talents, or outstanding performance in many countries. But recognition has not always been accompanied by coherent identification schemes, sustainable programming, or fair access (Alcázar & Balarín, 2016; Alencar & Fleith, 2001; Asensio et al., 2019; Gómez-Arízaga et al., 2024; OECD, 2023; Pérez & Rodríguez, 2013; Vuyk et al., 2026).

The region comprises symbolic inclusion and structural fragmentation (OECD, 2019, 2023; Programa Nacional de Becas y Crédito Educativo/ PRONABEC, 2023; UNESCO, 2017). Nonetheless, formal recognition comes with territorial inequalities, fiscal discontinuity, scarce teacher training, and uneven institutional capacity. High-ability students in elite urban schools may be provided with greater curricula and paths to acceleration, while their peers who are equivalent in a rural, Indigenous, or underprivileged community may go undiagnosed or without support (Economic Commission for Latin America and the Caribbean/ECLAC, 2022; Fleith & Vilarinho-Pereira, 2025; Guenther & Németh-Torres, 2015).

The disjunction between recognition and realization requires theoretical intervention. A regional model is then an imperative, not because Latin America lacks conceptual resources but because it confronts structural conditions in which those resources require their functional outcomes.

Consequently, the Latin American model of talent development (LAMTD) does not claim universality. Instead, it proffers a theoretically integrative and

S. Blumen, *High Ability and Talent Development in Latin America*,
https://doi.org/10.1007/978-3-032-27468-7_11

contextually calibrated strategy that can accommodate the unique intertwining of inequality, diversity, and institutional fragility of the region.

The necessity of a regional model rests on four interrelated arguments:

1. Structural inequality shapes developmental trajectories.
2. Cultural and linguistic plurality complicates standard identification paradigms.
3. Institutional fragmentation undermines continuity across educational levels.
4. Global North models cannot be transferred without contextual recalibration.

The LAMTD therefore emerges as an architectural synthesis—one that consolidates psychological theory, sociological insight, educational policy, and ethical philosophy into a coherent developmental ecology.

11.2 Structural Conditions Shaping Talent Development

11.2.1 Persistent Inequality as Developmental Constraint

Latin America remains one of the most unequal regions globally. Income disparities, territorial asymmetries, racialized exclusion, and intergenerational poverty shape access to schooling quality, enrichment, and mentorship. Data from international assessments repeatedly indicate that students' performance in the region is strongly associated with their socioeconomic circumstances (OECD, 2023; UNESCO, 2022).

This correlation does not indicate an unequal distribution of potential. Rather, it reveals unequal distribution of opportunity structures. The distinction is critical.

Talent development depends on developmental catalysts: advanced curricula, intellectual stimulation, supportive mentors, stable schooling, and psychological safety (Gagné, 2004; Nussbaum, 2011; Pfeiffer, 2015; Renzulli, 2005; Sternberg, 2003; Subotnik, et al., 2011; Ziegler, 2005). In contexts where these catalysts are unevenly distributed, identification mechanisms risk functioning as mirrors of privilege rather than detectors of aptitude.

The LAMTD therefore begins with a structural premise: talent development is inseparable from social policy. Redistribution, territorial equity, digital access, and institutional strengthening have become components of talent architecture—not peripheral concerns.

11.2.2 Cultural and Linguistic Plurality

The region's ethnolinguistic landscape includes hundreds of Indigenous languages and knowledge systems (World Bank Group, 2019). These epistemologies encode ecological knowledge, community governance models, artistic traditions, and cognitive flexibility, often unrecognized by Western psychometric measures.

Conventional IQ-based identification, when used in isolation, risks misidentifying culturally distinct cognitive expressions as deficits rather than differences. In this sense, the LAMTD highlights that excellence needs to be interpreted in ways that are rooted in specific cultural contexts.

This does not entail abandoning psychometric rigor. Rather, it requires integrating quantitative measures with qualitative, contextualized assessments capable of recognizing distributed and culturally mediated forms of competence.

11.2.3 Institutional Fragmentation

Many Latin American education systems display fragmentation across:

- Early childhood, primary, and secondary levels
- Urban and rural governance structures
- Public and private sectors
- General and specialized education services

Fragmentation interrupts developmental continuity (Gay, 2010; Ladson-Billing, 1995; Quijano, 2000; Sen 1999). A child identified in primary school may encounter no pathway in secondary education. Acceleration policies may exist in law but lack implementation guidelines (Steenbergen-Hu & Moon, 2011). University partnerships may operate independently of national identification systems.

The LAMTD addresses fragmentation through systemic alignment. Talent development must operate as a vertically coherent trajectory rather than a series of disconnected interventions.

11.3 Theoretical Foundations: Recalibrating Global Theory for Regional Context

The Latin American model of talent development draws on five major theoretical traditions, each adapted for regional realities.

11.3.1 Developmental Systems and Ecological Embeddedness

Developmental systems theory conceptualizes talent as emergent from interactions among individuals and environmental systems. Bronfenbrenner's bioecological model underscores the nested nature of these interactions—family, school, community, policy (Bronfenbrenner & Morris, 2006).

In Latin America, these systems are often shaped by volatility: economic instability, territorial isolation, community violence, or infrastructural scarcity. Yet they are also shaped by resilience: extended family networks, communal mentorship, and cultural solidarity (Guenther & Németh-Torres, 2015).

The LAMTD adopts an ecological lens that recognizes both vulnerability and strength within contextual systems. Talent is neither fully innate nor purely socially constructed; it is relationally actualized within ecological constraints and supports.

11.3.2 Differentiated Conceptions of Giftedness

The LAMTD synthesizes insights from Renzulli (1978, 2005), Gagné (2004), Sternberg (2003), and Ziegler (2005) while introducing contextual recalibration.

- **Potential (aptitude)** may exist independently of achievement.
- **Achievement (performance)** depends on access to developmental catalysts.
- **Catalysts (opportunity structures)** are unevenly distributed under conditions of inequality.

This tripartite differentiation becomes especially salient in unequal societies. High aptitude without opportunity remains unrealized; high opportunity without aptitude produces superficial achievement; alignment between aptitude and opportunity yields sustainable excellence.

Thus, the model reframes identification as detection of developmental readiness within constrained ecosystems—not mere measurement of static traits.

11.3.3 Capability Approach as Ethical Framework

The capability approach shifts evaluative focus from resources to freedoms. In the context of talent development, the question becomes as follows: do students possess the real freedom to convert potential into valued functionings?

Capability deprivation in Latin America may arise from:

- Geographic isolation
- Linguistic marginalization
- Gender norms
- Economic instability

- Institutional underinvestment

Talent development, within this framework, becomes a form of capability expansion. It is not elitist enrichment; it is structural justice.

11.3.4 Culturally Responsive Pedagogy

Culturally responsive pedagogy ensures that instruction, curriculum, and identification practices resonate with students' lived experiences and epistemic traditions.

Within the LAMTD, this includes:

- Multilingual screening tools
- Community consultation during identification
- Curriculum incorporating Indigenous science, literature, and art
- Collective excellence recognition

Cultural legitimacy strengthens psychological belonging and academic engagement—both critical for sustained talent development.

11.3.5 Twice Exceptionality and Socio-Emotional Integration

Twice-exceptional learners often remain invisible in systems lacking diagnostic sophistication. Underdiagnosis of disabilities and stigmatization of mental health concerns exacerbate invisibility (Reis, Baum, & Burke, 2014).

The LAMTD embeds socio-emotional development within talent architecture. Psychological well-being is not ancillary; it is foundational.

Acceleration, enrichment, and specialization must therefore include structured socio-emotional monitoring to prevent isolation, burnout, or misalignment.

11.4 Core Principles: Operationalizing the Model

11.4.1 Equity-Centered Identification

Identification must integrate:

- Standardized cognitive measures
- Performance assessments
- Dynamic assessment models
- Teacher and community nominations
- Portfolio reviews

- Re-evaluation opportunities

Static thresholds entrench inequity. Dynamic reassessment recognizes developmental fluidity.

11.4.2 Development over Labeling

Labels function as service gateways, not identity categories. Emphasis shifts from "who is gifted" to "how is development supported."

11.4.3 Multi-Tiered Pathways

A tiered framework ensures universal enrichment while preserving targeted specialization.

- **Tier 1:** Enriched curriculum for all students
- **Tier 2:** Targeted interventions for emerging high ability
- **Tier 3:** Intensive programming for advanced development

This architecture aligns with inclusive education while permitting differentiated pacing.

11.4.4 Acceleration as Evidence-Based Equity

Acceleration remains among the most empirically supported interventions globally. Within Latin America, its equitable implementation requires:

- Clear legal frameworks
- Cultural destigmatization
- Teacher training
- Socio-emotional oversight

Acceleration becomes an instrument of structural fairness when accessible beyond elite contexts.

11.4.5 Teacher Preparation as Systemic Lever

Teacher preparation remains the single most powerful implementation variable. The LAMTD proposes:

- Mandatory preservice modules.
- In-service certification pathways
- Integration with inclusive education training
- Regional micro-credentialing platforms

Professional capacity determines policy realization.

11.4.6 Rural and Indigenous Inclusion

Equitable talent architecture must include:

- Mobile identification teams
- Digital access infrastructure
- Indigenous-language assessments
- Culturally sensitive residential enrichment options
- Community mentorship networks

Territorial equity becomes a nonnegotiable design principle.

11.4.7 Regional Collaboration

Latin American countries share structural challenges. Collaborative research networks, shared teacher training curricula, and policy exchange forums reduce duplication and increase sustainability.

11.4.8 Policy Coherence and Sustainability

Coherence requires alignment across:

- Legislation
- Budget allocation
- Teacher certification
- Monitoring and evaluation
- University partnerships

Without coherence, innovation remains episodic.

11.5 Structural Architecture: Four Interacting Ecological Levels

11.5.1 Level 1: Individual Development

Talent development begins with:

- Cognitive complexity
- Creative production
- Intrinsic motivation
- Emotional regulation
- Identity integration

Resilience becomes especially critical under structural adversity.

11.5.2 Level 2: Educational Environment

Schools operationalize differentiation through:

- Curriculum compacting
- Enrichment clusters
- Flexible grouping
- Acceleration
- Arts and interdisciplinary programs

Institutional flexibility predicts developmental sustainability.

11.5.3 Level 3: Community and Family Context

Families and communities transmit cultural capital, expectations, and mentorship. Parent education programs enhance advocacy and continuity.

Community knowledge integration legitimizes diverse excellence forms.

11.5.4 Level 4: Policy and Structural Supports

Policy frameworks determine:

- Funding stability
- Teacher preparation mandates

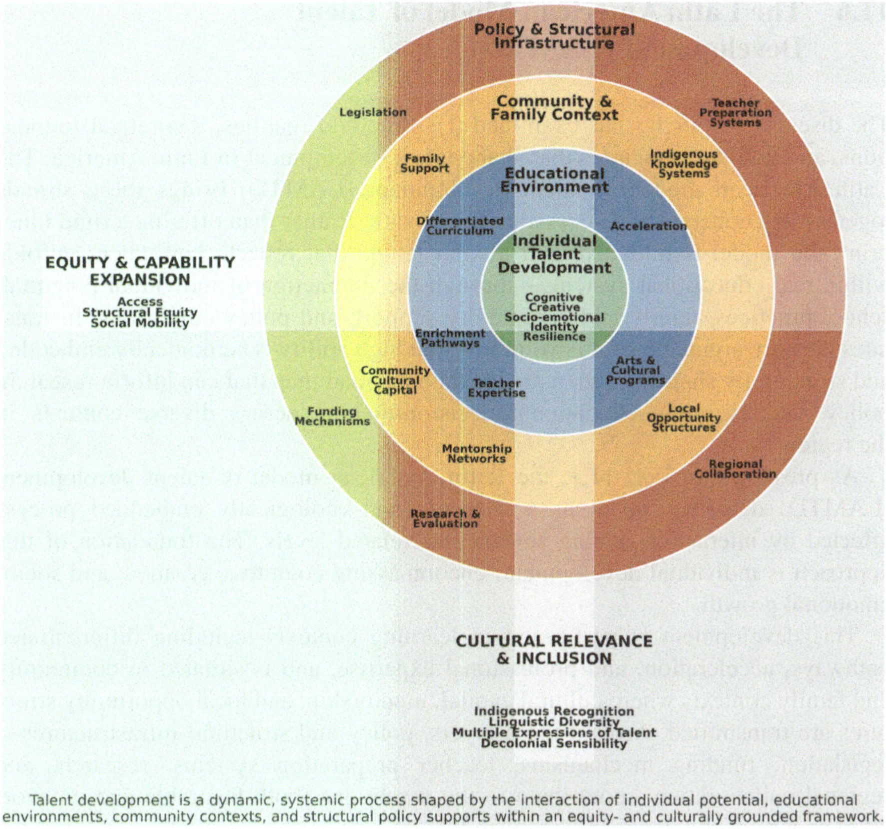

Fig. 11.1 The Latin American model of talent development (LAMTD)

- Data systems
- Research investment
- Regional cooperation

Policy coherence transforms isolated success into systemic transformation.

As illustrated in Fig. 11.1, the Latin American model of talent development conceptualizes talent as a dynamic process embedded within interacting ecological and structural systems.

11.6 The Latin American Model of Talent Development (LAMTD)

The discussion thus far has examined the structural realities, theoretical foundations, and guiding principles that shape talent development in Latin America. The Latin American model of talent development (LAMTD) brings these strands together in a coherent and accessible framework. Rather than offering a rigid blueprint, the model is intended as a flexible guide that reflects how talent unfolds within real educational systems—through the interaction of individual potential, school practices, family and community support, and policy conditions. It translates the core argument of this volume—that high ability is ecologically embedded and structurally shaped—into a practical conceptual map that can inform research, policy, and everyday educational decision-making across diverse contexts in the region.

As presented in Fig. 11.1, the Latin American model of talent development (LAMTD) describes talent as a dynamic and ecologically embedded process affected by interaction among several interrelated levels. The foundation of this approach is individual development, encompassing cognitive, creative, and socio-emotional growth.

This development is performed in learning contexts including differentiated pathways, acceleration, and professional expertise, and is situated in community and family contexts where cultural capital, mentorship, and local opportunity structures are transmitted. Around these layers, policy and structural infrastructures—legislation, funding mechanisms, teacher preparation systems, research, and regional collaboration—contribute to the conditions (both favorable and unfavorable) under which talent can be realized.

There are two cross-cutting dimensions that come alive across all levels of the model: equity and capability expansion, which emphasize access and structural justice; and cultural relevance and inclusion, which acknowledge linguistic diversity, Indigenous epistemologies, and multiple expressions of human potential. We therefore interpret talent development as a systemic, justice-oriented process, situated in a sociocultural context and institutional coherence.

11.7 Implementation Pathways across Contexts

11.7.1 Low-Resource Rural Systems

Strategies include:

- Universal enrichment integrated into regular classrooms
- Creativity-based pedagogy requiring minimal infrastructure

- Teacher micro-credentials delivered digitally
- Community-based mentorship initiatives

11.7.2 Urban Public Systems

Urban contexts can expand:

- Magnet schools with equity safeguards
- STEM academies linked to public universities
- Scholarship bridges for low-income students
- Monitoring systems preventing elitist capture

11.7.3 Higher Education Transition

University access remains unequal. Bridging programs, financial aid, mentorship networks, and socio-emotional support structures ensure continuity of high-ability trajectories.

11.8 Research Agenda for the Next Decade

The LAMTD requires empirical consolidation through:

- Longitudinal tracking studies
- Indigenous conceptualizations of excellence
- Acceleration outcome research
- Twice-exceptionality prevalence studies
- Gender and STEM participation analysis
- Regional research infrastructure development

Evidence generation must be regionally anchored and internationally dialogic.

11.9 Ethical Commitments and Democratic Imperatives

The LAMTD affirms:

- Human dignity
- Anti-elitism
- Opportunity expansion

- Cultural pluralism
- Democratic inclusion

Talent development becomes ethically legitimate only when it expands collective flourishing rather than reinforcing hierarchy.

11.10 Conclusion: From Visibility to Architecture

Chapter 2 positioned Latin America as an analytical lens through which excellence and inequality become inseparable. This chapter transforms that lens into architecture.

The Latin American model of talent development does not emerge from abstraction. It emerges from structural visibility.

Giftedness is not a trait awaiting detection; it is a systemic alignment requiring coordinated opportunity architecture.

Where developmental ecosystems, ethical commitment, cultural recognition, and institutional coherence converge, excellence becomes structurally enabled rather than contingently achieved.

Latin America stands not at the margins of talent theory but at its clarifying edge. The arc of this volume is complete: from diagnosis to design, from visibility to model, from regional condition to theoretical refinement.

The future of talent development depends not solely on identifying exceptional individuals but on constructing systems in which relational emergence becomes possible.

In that construction lies the transformation of inequality—from limiting condition to generative catalyst—so that distributed human potential becomes not structurally latent but developmentally realized.

The references that follow anchor this regional architecture within the broader intellectual traditions and empirical scholarship that continue to shape the evolving field of talent development.

References

Alcázar, L., & Balarín, M. (2016). Informe final: Evaluación del diseño e implementación de los colegios de Alto Rendimiento (COAR). *Grupo de Análisis para el Desarrollo (GRADE).*

Alencar, E. M. L. S., & Fleith, D. S. (2001). *Superdotados: Determinantes, educação e ajustamento*. EPU.

Alencar, E. M. L. S., & Fleith, D. S. (2008). Barreiras à promoção da criatividade no ensino fundamental. *Psicologia: Teoria e Pesquisa, 24*, 59–66.

Asensio, R., & Burneo de la Rocha, M. L. (Eds.). (2019). *Estudio cualitativo: Modelo de servicio educativo para estudiantes de alto desempeño implementado a través de los colegios de Alto Rendimiento (COAR).* Instituto de Estudios Peruanos.

Bronfenbrenner, U., & Morris, P. A. (2006). The bioecological model of human development. In R. M. Lerner & W. Damon (Eds.), *Handbook of child psychology: Theoretical models of human development* (6th ed., pp. 793–828). Wiley.

Economic Commission for Latin America and the Caribbean (ECLAC). (2022). *Social panorama of Latin America 2022*. United Nations.

Fleith, D., & Vilarinho-Pereira, D. R. (2025). Assessing creativity in the school environment: Evidence-based practices and future directions. In J. Katz-Buonincontro & T. Kettler (Eds.), *The Oxford handbook of creativity and education* (pp. 775–796). Oxford University Press.

Gagné, F. (2004). Transforming gifts into talents: The DMGT. *High Ability Studies, 15*(2), 119–147.

García-Cepero, M. C., & Iglesias-Velasco, J. (2020). Hacia una comprensión de las aproximaciones institucionales a los estudiantes con capacidades y talentos excepcionales. *Revista Colombiana de Educación, 79*, 423–444. https://doi.org/10.17227/rce.num79-10040

Gay, G. (2010). *Culturally responsive teaching* (2nd ed.). Teachers College Press.

Gómez-Arízaga, M. P., Conejeros-Solar, M. L., & Cornejo-Araya, C. (2024). Gifted education in Chile: Analyses from a learning-resource perspective. *Cogent Education, 11*(1). https://doi.org/10.1080/2331186X.2024.2397217

Guenther, Z., & Németh-Torres, G. (2015). In spirituality: A pers Quijano pective from a traditionally Latin culture. *Gifted Education International, 32*(3), 216–223.

Ladson-Billings, G. (1995). Toward a theory of culturally relevant pedagogy. *American Educational Research Journal, 32*(3), 465–491.

Nussbaum, M. (2011). *Creating capabilities*. Harvard University Press.

OECD. (2019). *PISA 2018 Results (Vol. II): Where all students can succeed*. OECD Publishing.

OECD. (2023). *PISA 2022 Results* (Vol. I). OECD.

Pérez, L., & Rodríguez, A. (2013). Altas capacidades intelectuales en América Latina. *Revista Iberoamericana de Educación, 63*, 85–104.

Pfeiffer, S. I. (2015). *Essentials of gifted assessment*. Wiley.

Programa Nacional de Becas y Crédito Educativo (PRONABEC). (2023). *Memoria anual: Beca 18*. Ministerio de Educación del Perú.

Quijano, A. (2000). Coloniality of power, Eurocentrism, and Latin America. *Nepantla: Views from South, 1*(3), 533–580.

Reis, S. M., Baum, S. M., & Burke, E. (2014). An operational definition of twice-exceptional learners. *Gifted Child Quarterly, 58*(3), 217–230.

Renzulli, J. S. (1978). What makes giftedness? *Phi Delta Kappan, 60*, 180–184.

Renzulli, J. S. (2005). The three-ring conception of giftedness: A developmental model for promoting creative productivity. In R. J. Sternberg & J. E. Davidson (Eds.), *Conceptions of giftedness* (2nd ed., pp. 246–279). Cambridge University Press.

Sen, A. (1999). *Development as freedom*. Knopf.

Steenbergen-Hu, S., & Moon, S. (2011). The effects of acceleration. *Review of Educational Research, 81*(2), 220–252.

Sternberg, R. J. (2003). *Wisdom, intelligence, and creativity synthesized*. Cambridge University Press. https://doi.org/10.1017/CBO9780511509612

Subotnik, R. F., Olszewski-Kubilius, P., & Worrell, F. (2011). Rethinking giftedness and gifted education. *Psychological Science in the Public Interest, 12*(1), 3–54.

UNESCO. (2017). *A guide for ensuring inclusion and equity in education*. UNESCO.

UNESCO. (2022). *Global education monitoring report 2022*. UNESCO.

Vuyk, A., Gómez-Arízaga, M. P., & Barrios, L. A. (2026). Acceleration in South America. In J. L. Roberts & T. Clark (Eds.), *International perspectives on acceleration in gifted education* (pp. 22–37). Routledge.

World Bank Group. (2019). *Languages at risk in Latin America and the Caribbean*. https://www.worldbank.org/en/news/infographic/2019/02/22/lenguas-indigenas-legado-en-extincion

Ziegler, A. (2005). The actiotope model of giftedness. In R. J. Sternberg & J. E. Davidson (Eds.), Conceptions of giftedness (2nd ed., pp. 411–436). Cambridge University Press.

Chapter 12
Conclusions and Future Directions

12.1 Closing the Arc: From Fragmentation to Coherence

This volume opened with a foundational question: *What would it mean to conceptualize high ability from Latin America rather than merely in Latin America?* That distinction—seemingly semantic—proved structurally consequential. To conceptualize *in* a region is to apply imported categories within local boundaries. To conceptualize *from* a region is to allow its historical conditions, cultural traditions, and structural realities to reshape the very architecture of theory.

Across the preceding chapters, we have argued that Latin America requires more than policy transplantation or isolated programmatic innovation. It needs epistemic repositioning, structural awareness, and developmental coherence. High capacity in the area cannot be disentangled from inequality, diversity on an intercultural level, migrations, marginalization in rural areas, or institutional failure. Nor can it be boiled down to psychometric categorization separated from opportunity structures.

The core contribution of this book is a rethinking of talent development as an ecological, relational, and structurally mediated process. Building on psychological theory, education research, analyses of region and regional policy, and empirical case studies, the chapters together illustrate that high-ability development happens within systems of stratified access and recognition. Socioeconomic inequality, geographic isolation, linguistic diversity, forced displacement, and neurodiversity: these are not abstract or peripheral variables; they are developmental conditions.

Spanning the conceptual underpinning to national policy lessons learned, from teacher training to twice-exceptionality, from Indigenous invisibility to migration-related discontinuity, to the Latin American model of talent development (LAMTD), the volume has promoted a consistent argument: talented Latin Americans abound, but development pathways are weak in structure.

The purpose of this concluding chapter is therefore not recapitulation but consolidation and projection. It synthesizes the book's contributions to psychology and

S. Blumen, *High Ability and Talent Development in Latin America*,
https://doi.org/10.1007/978-3-032-27468-7_12

education, articulates a forward-looking research agenda, and identifies policy commitments capable of transforming recognition into sustainability.

12.2 Contributions to Psychology: Expanding the Developmental Lens

12.2.1 From Individual Cognition to Ecological Development

One of the volume's principal contributions to psychology lies in broadening the analytic category of giftedness. Although cognitive assessment is not irrelevant, the book is clear that ability is not developed in a vacuum. This ecological–developmental lens presented throughout the volume makes high ability the product of interplay amongst family capital, school quality, teacher knowledge, peer culture, mental health access, and policy continuity. Cognitive potential is not enough for developmental outcomes. Recognition depends upon alignment between individual characteristics and institutional scaffolding.

This reframing challenges reductionist interpretations of underachievement. In contexts of poverty, territorial isolation, migration instability, or other systemic discrimination, interrupted development often reflects systemic discontinuity rather than individual deficit. High-ability learners disengage not with potential but with the collapse of opportunity structures. By integrating ecological systems theory and contemporary talent development research, this book extends the scope of psychological inquiry beyond trait identification to systemic analysis. High ability becomes not a fixed category but a developmental trajectory embedded within stratified environments.

12.2.2 Neurodiversity and Twice-Exceptionality in Stratified Systems

Chapter 7 presented a more contextualized account of twice-exceptionality in Latin American educational systems. Instead of silencing 2e learners as diagnostic anomalies, the volume conceptualizes twice-exceptionality as a dynamic between cognitive strength and structural constraint.

In educational systems with uneven access to psychological services and limited teacher preparation, high-ability learners with ADHD, autism spectrum conditions, dyslexia, anxiety disorders, or emotional regulation challenges often experience dual invisibility. Their cognitive competencies disguise their weaknesses; their weaknesses conceal their gifts. The result is misrecognition and interrupted developmental continuity.

Situating twice-exceptionality within Latin American structural conditions contributes to global psychological debates on neurodiversity and equity. It underscores the necessity of multidimensional identification processes and the integration of socio-emotional support within talent development frameworks.

12.2.3 Talent as Contextually Expressed Potential

The Latin American model of talent development presented in Chap. 11 integrates the psychological contributions of the volume. The LAMTD combines cognitive aptitude, socio-emotional functioning, contextual opportunity structures, and institutional alignment. It affirms that talent is neither purely innate nor purely socially constructed; it is contextually expressed as potential requiring sustained cultivation.

This integrative perspective expands the ontology of giftedness itself. It recognizes intercultural competence, resilience, collective leadership, and creative adaptability as forms of excellence alongside traditional academic achievement. In doing so, the volume positions Latin America not as a peripheral case study but as a site of theoretical refinement and innovation.

12.3 Contributions to Education: Policy, Practice, and Preparation

12.3.1 From Legislative Recognition to Institutional Coherence

Across national case analyses, a recurring pattern emerged: legislative acknowledgment of high-ability learners often outpaces implementation capacity. Ministries of education may recognize giftedness formally, yet classroom-level differentiation remains inconsistent.

The gap between policy declaration and pedagogical reality reflects systemic misalignment. Sustainable gifted education requires coordination among legislation, funding allocation, teacher preparation, assessment protocols, and accountability systems. Without coherence, recognition remains symbolic.

By documenting regional patterns rather than isolated national cases, this volume advances the conversation from episodic reform to structural design. It emphasizes that policy durability, not pilot innovation alone, determines developmental continuity.

12.3.2 Acceleration, Enrichment, and Differentiated Instruction

The analysis of acceleration reframed regional debates that frequently equated academic advancement with elitism. When implemented responsibly—with socio-emotional monitoring, teacher training, and legal clarity—acceleration represents one of the most empirically supported interventions for high-ability learners.

The broader argument advanced throughout the book is that equality of treatment does not guarantee equality of opportunity. High-ability students are not entitled to differentiated instruction, enriched curricula, flexible pacing, or advanced engagement; these are developmental necessities.

The sustainability of gifted education in Latin America requires embedding the principles of differentiation within mainstream classrooms rather than confining them to isolated centers of excellence.

12.4 Reframing Urgency: Inequality, Diversity, and Moral Responsibility

Latin America is still characterized by profound inequality. Income hierarchy collides with racialized exclusion, geographic marginalization, and language hierarchy. In these settings, high-ability learners from Indigenous, rural, migrant, and low-income communities are disproportionately under-identified.

The invisibility of these students represents not merely pedagogical oversight but moral contradiction. Talent is widely distributed; opportunity is not.

The urgency emphasized throughout this volume is therefore dual:

- **Developmental urgency**: Early recognition and sustained support are necessary for the full realization of potential.
- **Societal urgency**: Nations confronting economic instability, environmental challenges, technological transformation, and democratic fragility cannot afford to neglect human capital.

When conceptualized ecologically, gifted education becomes integral to inclusive excellence rather than antithetical to equity.

12.5 A Forward-Looking Research Agenda

To streamline local research and make a positive global contribution, there are several research priorities for the future.

12.5.1 Longitudinal Developmental Inquiry

The need for longitudinal studies tracing high-ability learners through learning transitions is immediate. This type of research must study not only the stability of identification but also other socio-emotional trajectories, mobility patterns, rural–urban migration, access to higher education, and job choices. Longitudinal data enable predictive modeling and policy evaluation, moving the field beyond cross-sectional description.

12.5.2 Culturally Responsive Identification

Future research needs to adjust these approaches of assessment frameworks that are based on culturally relevant approaches, with the addition of both standardized measures and dynamic assessment, performance-based assessment, teacher nomination systems with bias mitigation, and community-based competence indicators.

Cultural anchoring in assessment is vital in multilingual and Indigenous contexts for equitable recognition.

12.5.3 Mental Health Integration

High-ability learners in stratified systems are often dealing with perfectionism, identity challenges, economic stress, and belonging uncertainty. There is an urgent need for more research examining protective factors (e.g., mentorship, culturally relevant pedagogy, and inclusive school climate).

Sustainable talent development requires integration of psychological well-being within educational frameworks.

12.5.4 Implementation Science and Teacher Preparation

Few regional studies systematically assess the impact of teacher training in gifted education. Research needs to explore fidelity to implementation, the translation of principles of differentiation in classrooms, and institutional barriers toward delivering policy. Bridging theory and practice demands rigorous implementation methodologies.

12.5.5 Comparative and Cross-National Scholarship

Latin America must start a comparative dialogue with regions where similar structural problems prevail. Cross-linking works for methodological sophistication and to locate regional innovation in global discussions. The LAMTD offers a framework for such comparative testing and refinement.

12.6 Policy Priorities for the Next Decade

Converting scholarship into structural durability involves collective action:

- **Institutional continuity** through protected funding and stable legal frameworks
- **Universal screening with equity safeguards** to mitigate referral bias
- **Mandatory teacher preparation** in differentiated instruction and high-ability education
- **Integrated mental health services** within school systems
- **Targeted support for marginalized high-ability populations**

Policy coherence, not episodic reform, ensures sustainability.

12.7 Toward an Internationally Informed and Regionally Grounded Field

Latin America occupies a generative position in the global gifted education debate. Its structural heterogeneity requires flexible models that can consider such dimensions of inequality, cultural diversity, and resilience. An internationally literate field does not correspond to concept-based reliance. It requires reciprocal exchange.

Latin American researchers contribute empirical studies, theoretical refinements, and policy models in the context of international discussions. The LAMTD represents one such contribution. It invites empirical testing, critique, and contextual adaptation. Its purpose is not closure but dialogue.

12.8 A Call to Psychologists, Educators, and Decision-Makers

To psychologists: expand assessment paradigms toward ecological sensitivity and structural awareness.

To educators: practice courageous differentiation grounded in intellectual respect.

To policymakers: translate legislative recognition into durable systems.

To researchers: pursue cumulative, transparent, regionally grounded inquiry.

Above all, commit collectively to the visibility, voice, and value of Latin America's high-potential youth.

12.9 Final Reflection: Visibility as Justice

The book closes where it began—with visibility.

Across Latin America, countless children demonstrate analytical precision, creative fluency, leadership capacity, and extraordinary resilience. Yet many move through educational systems that neither recognize nor sustain their potential. The decisive variable is rarely aptitude itself; it is the continuity—or rupture—of opportunity.

Excellence without inclusion reproduces privilege. Inclusion without intellectual challenge dilutes potential. When talent development is embedded within culturally responsive and structurally coherent systems, excellence and equity cease to compete: they converge.

Chapter 2 asked what it would mean to conceptualize high ability *from* Latin America rather than merely *in* Latin America. The chapters that followed offered one sustained response: it means confronting structural inequality without normalizing it; valuing cultural plurality without romanticizing marginalization; and designing institutional architectures capable of transforming distributed potential into enduring contribution.

The future of the region depends on its capacity to cultivate human potential in all its diversity. Such cultivation demands rigorous research, coherent policy, courageous pedagogy, institutional stability, and sustained political will.

The work, therefore, does not conclude here.

Latin America does not lack talent. It lacks durable structures for its recognition and development. To construct those structures—thoughtfully, inclusively, and sustainably—is the task ahead.

And so, we return, deliberately and without abstraction, to the question that opened this book: what would it mean to conceptualize—and to develop—high ability from Latin America rather than merely in Latin America?

Index

A
Acceleration, 3, 5, 7, 9, 14, 15, 17, 41, 47–50, 53, 54, 57–59, 85, 88–89, 92, 95–98, 116, 122, 123, 135, 140–143, 145–154, 171, 173, 175, 176, 178, 179, 181, 188
Actiotope model, 13, 22–24, 36
Assessment validity, 78

B
Beca 18, 5, 94, 97, 98

C
Capability approach, 9, 13, 21, 37, 128, 174
Colegios de Alto Rendimiento (COAR), 5, 7, 16, 37, 38, 52–53, 57, 59, 68, 71–73, 76, 90–94, 97, 98, 135, 144–145, 148–149, 151–152, 161, 164, 165
Cultural bias, 151
Cultural responsiveness, 81
Curriculum compacting, 7, 146, 147, 149, 151, 153, 178
Curriculum innovation, 85–99

D
Decolonial education, 136
Decoloniality, 134
Decolonial perspectives, 35, 89, 98
Developmental systems, 9, 173–174
Differentiated instruction, 16, 53, 57, 86, 142, 153, 188, 190

E
Ecological-developmental framework, 5, 104, 123
Ecological systems, 21, 77, 128, 134, 141–142, 186
Educational decentralization, 70
Educational equity, 40
Educational inequality, 75
Educational justice, 6, 9, 15, 86, 127, 136
Education/educational policies, 47, 70, 82, 106, 117, 120, 122, 143, 172
Enrichment, 4–7, 15, 17, 24, 27, 28, 30, 37, 38, 52–54, 56–58, 63, 65, 67, 68, 71, 77, 79, 82, 85, 87–89, 92, 96, 97, 99, 103, 104, 106, 107, 110, 111, 114–116, 118, 120–122, 124, 125, 128–134, 136, 139–147, 149–153, 160, 164, 165, 172, 174–178, 180, 188
Equity, 5, 15, 21, 49, 87, 111, 139, 157, 187
Equity and excellence, 5

G
Gifted education, 2, 3, 9, 13, 22, 25, 26, 29, 30, 32–34, 36–39, 41, 55, 56, 71, 82, 85, 88, 103, 107, 110, 116, 122, 124, 127–129, 136, 140–145, 148, 149, 151, 187–190
Giftedness, 1, 13, 21, 47, 85, 104, 140, 157, 181, 186

H
High ability, 3, 22, 47, 94, 103, 128, 139, 160, 171, 186

S. Blumen, *High Ability and Talent Development in Latin America*, https://doi.org/10.1007/978-3-032-27468-7

High-ability education, 3, 4, 7, 8, 47, 59, 129, 139–154, 157–162, 166, 167, 190
High-ability learners, 8, 47, 49, 53, 56, 58, 85–99, 107, 108, 132, 133, 151, 157, 158, 160, 161, 166, 186–189
Human potential, 22, 34, 180, 182, 191

I
Identification, 1, 13, 23, 47, 85, 103, 127, 140, 159, 171, 186
Inclusion, 3–7, 9, 16, 32, 33, 35, 38, 40, 47, 49, 50, 58, 66, 69, 73, 76, 81, 88, 95, 104, 121–124, 129, 133–136, 140, 146, 148, 153, 154, 157, 158, 160, 162, 166, 167, 171, 176–177, 180, 181, 191
Inclusive education, 3, 31, 40, 48–51, 53, 56, 70–72, 81, 103, 116, 120, 122, 124, 139, 140, 160, 162–164, 176
Inclusive excellence, 9, 188
Indigenous education, 28
Indigenous students, 14, 66, 134
Inequalities, 1–9, 14–17, 21, 24, 27–29, 32, 34, 39, 40, 51, 56, 63, 65–69, 71, 72, 74, 75, 79, 80, 82, 86, 91, 92, 103, 108–109, 118, 119, 121–122, 124, 130, 171, 172, 174, 181, 182, 185, 188, 190, 191
International Baccalaureate (IB), 5, 91, 92, 97, 98

L
Latin America, 1, 14, 21, 47, 86, 103, 127, 139, 157, 171, 185

M
Mental health, 3, 5, 9, 17, 95, 103–125, 136, 175, 186, 189, 190
Migrant students, 69, 134
Multicultural assessment, 7

N
Neurodevelopmental diversity, 5, 103, 118, 121, 123, 124

O
Opportunity structures, 6, 13, 14, 23, 24, 33, 37, 56–59, 64, 67, 75, 79, 80, 86, 89, 93, 127, 135, 139, 144, 147, 148, 153, 158, 172, 174, 179–180, 185–187

P
Policy coherence, 17, 177, 178, 190
Policy implementation, 97
Professional development, 73, 93, 139–154

R
Rural education, 135, 136, 189

S
Socioeconomic inequality, 67, 185
Socioemotional development, 108–109, 124

T
Talent development, 1, 13, 21, 49, 85, 117, 141, 171, 185
Talent identification, 5, 63, 70, 71, 80, 85, 141, 144, 159
Teacher beliefs, 141, 145
Teacher training, 15, 22, 30, 76, 85, 87, 90, 96, 139–154, 160, 171, 176, 177, 185, 188, 189
Twice-exceptionality, 5, 7, 9, 15, 17, 94, 103–104, 106–109, 113, 118–121, 123–125, 127, 139, 148, 151, 175, 181, 185–187
Twice-exceptional learners, 5, 103–125, 139, 148, 151, 175

U
Underrepresentation, 66–69, 74, 81, 127, 129, 134, 152
Universal screening, 70–72, 76, 78–80, 190

The manufacturer's authorised representative in the EU is Springer Nature Customer Service Centre GmbH, Europaplatz 3, 69115 Heidelberg, Germany. If you have any concerns regarding our products, please contact ProductSafety@springernature.com

Printed and bound by CPI Group (UK) Ltd, Croydon, CR0 4YY
16/09/2026
02217815-0002